NE능률 영어교과서

대한민국 고등학생 **10**명 중 **4.7** 명이 보는 교과서

영어 고등 교과서 점유율 1위
〔7차, 2007 개정, 2009 개정, 2015 개정〕

READING TUTOR

그동안 판매된
리딩튜터 1,900만 부
차곡차곡 쌓으면 19만 미터

에베레스트 21 배 높이

190,000m

에베레스트 8,848m

능률보카

그동안 판매된
능률VOCA 1,100만 부

대한민국 박스오피스
천만명을 넘은 영화 단 28개

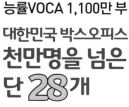

VO CA

그래머존

그동안 판매된 450만 부의 그래머존을 바닥에 쭉 ~ 깔면

1000km 서울-부산 왕복가능

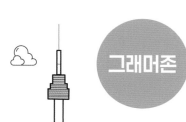

서울

부산

교재 검토에 도움을 주신 선생님들

1316
GRAMMAR LEVEL 3

지은이	NE능률 영어교육연구소
선임연구원	김지현
연구원	장경아, 가민아, 오보은
영문교열	Angela Lan
디자인	닷츠
내지 일러스트	김기환
맥편집	한서기획

Let's grow together

NE능률이
미래를
창조합니다.

건강한 배움의 고객가치를 제공하겠다는 꿈을 실현하기 위해
40년이 넘는 시간 동안 열심히 달려왔습니다.

앞으로도 끊임없는 연구와 노력을 통해
당연한 것을 멈추지 않고

고객, 기업, 직원 모두가 함께 성장하는 NE능률이 되겠습니다.

NE 능률

기초부터 내신까지 중학 영문법 완성

1316 GRAMMAR

LEVEL 3

STRUCTURE & FEATURES

Grammar Points

최신 개정 교육과정을 분석하여 필수
문법 사항을 쉽고 명확하게 설명하였
습니다.

Tip 주의! : 예외 또는 주의가 필요한 문법 사항

Tip 비교! : 비교해서 알아 두면 도움이 되는 문법 사항

✓ Grammar UP : 심화 문법 사항

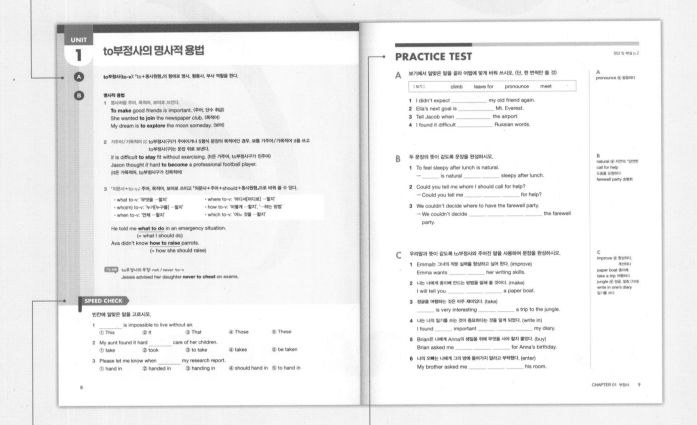

Speed Check

간단한 문제를 통해 Grammar Points에서
배운 내용을 이해했는지 확인할 수 있습니다.

Practice Test

Grammar Points에서 배운 내용을
다양한 유형의 주관식 문제를 통해
익힐 수 있습니다.

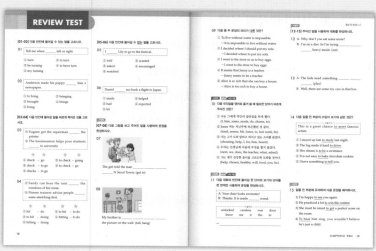

Review Test

학교 내신 시험과 가장 유사한 유형의 문제로 구성하여 실전에 대비할 수 있게 하였습니다.

NEW **내신 기출** : 최근 학교 내신에서 출제되고 있는 최신 유형

서술형 및 **고난도** : 서술형 주관식 문제 및 고난도 문제를 골고루 수록

실전 모의고사

출제 확률이 높은 내신형 문제로 구성된 실전 모의고사 2회를 수록하여 실제 내신 시험을 치르는 것처럼 연습할 수 있게 하였습니다.

Workbook

서술형 주관식 문제로 구성된 Unit별 연습 문제로, 모든 문법 사항을 충분히 연습할 수 있게 하였습니다.

CONTENTS

CHAPTER

01

부정사

UNIT 1

to부정사의 명사적 용법

A **to부정사(to-v):** 「to＋동사원형」의 형태로 명사, 형용사, 부사 역할을 한다.

B **명사적 용법**

1 명사처럼 주어, 목적어, 보어로 쓰인다.

To make good friends *is* important. (주어, 단수 취급)

She wanted **to join** the newspaper club. (목적어)

My dream is **to explore** the moon someday. (보어)

2 가주어／가목적어 it: to부정사(구)가 주어이거나 5형식 문장의 목적어인 경우, 보통 가주어／가목적어 it을 쓰고 to부정사(구)는 문장 뒤로 보낸다.

It is difficult **to stay** fit without exercising. (It은 가주어, to부정사구가 진주어)

Jason thought *it* hard **to become** a professional football player.

(it은 가목적어, to부정사구가 진목적어)

3 「의문사＋to-v」: 주어, 목적어, 보어로 쓰이고 「의문사＋주어＋should＋동사원형」으로 바꿔 쓸 수 있다.

• what to-v: '무엇을 …할지'	• where to-v: '어디서[어디로] …할지'
• who(m) to-v: '누가[누구를] …할지'	• how to-v: '어떻게 …할지', '…하는 방법'
• when to-v: '언제 …할지'	• which to-v: '어느 것을 …할지'

He told me **what to do** in an emergency situation.

(= what I should do)

Ava didn't know **how to raise** parrots.

(= how she should raise)

 to부정사의 부정: not / never to-v

Jessie advised her daughter **never to cheat** on exams.

SPEED CHECK

빈칸에 알맞은 말을 고르시오.

1 _____ is impossible to live without air.

① This ② It ③ That ④ Those ⑤ These

2 My aunt found it hard _____ care of her children.

① take ② took ③ to take ④ takes ⑤ be taken

3 Please let me know when _____ my research report.

① hand in ② handed in ③ handing in ④ should hand in ⑤ to hand in

PRACTICE TEST

정답 및 해설 p.2

A 보기에서 알맞은 말을 골라 어법에 맞게 바꿔 쓰시오. (단, 한 번씩만 쓸 것)

| 보기 | climb leave for pronounce meet

1 I didn't expect ______________ my old friend again.
2 Ella's next goal is ______________ Mt. Everest.
3 Tell Jacob when ______________ the airport.
4 I found it difficult ______________ Russian words.

A
pronounce [동] 발음하다

B 두 문장의 뜻이 같도록 문장을 완성하시오.

1 To feel sleepy after lunch is natural.
→ _______ is natural _______ _______ sleepy after lunch.

2 Could you tell me whom I should call for help?
→ Could you tell me _______ _______ _______ for help?

3 We couldn't decide where to have the farewell party.
→ We couldn't decide _______ _______ _______ _______ the farewell party.

B
natural [형] 자연의; *당연한
call for help
도움을 요청하다
farewell party 송별회

C 우리말과 뜻이 같도록 to부정사와 주어진 말을 사용하여 문장을 완성하시오.

1 Emma는 그녀의 작문 실력을 향상하고 싶어 한다. (improve)
Emma wants _______ _______ her writing skills.

2 나는 너에게 종이배 만드는 방법을 말해 줄 것이다. (make)
I will tell you _______ _______ _______ a paper boat.

3 정글을 여행하는 것은 아주 재미있다. (take)
_______ is very interesting _______ _______ a trip to the jungle.

4 나는 나의 일기를 쓰는 것이 중요하다는 것을 알게 되었다. (write in)
I found _______ important _______ _______ _______ my diary.

5 Brian은 나에게 Anna의 생일을 위해 무엇을 사야 할지 물었다. (buy)
Brian asked me _______ _______ _______ for Anna's birthday.

6 나의 오빠는 나에게 그의 방에 들어가지 말라고 부탁했다. (enter)
My brother asked me _______ _______ _______ his room.

C
improve [동] 향상하다, 개선하다
paper boat 종이배
take a trip 여행하다
jungle [명] 정글, 밀림 (지대)
write in one's diary
일기를 쓰다

to부정사의 형용사적 용법, 부사적 용법

A

형용사적 용법: 형용사처럼 (대)명사를 수식하거나, be to-v의 형태로 주어를 설명한다.

1 (대)명사 수식: 『(대)명사+to-v』 '…할', '…하는'

Do you know <u>*the best way*</u> **to get** there?

> **Tip 주의!** 수식 받는 (대)명사가 『to-v + 전치사』의 의미상 목적어일 때 전치사를 반드시 같이 쓴다.
> Do you need <u>*a pencil*</u> **to write with**? (→ … write with a pencil)

2 be to-v: 의무, 예정, 의도, 운명, 가능을 나타낸다.

You **are to complete** the task by eight o'clock. (의무: '…해야 한다')

The vice-president **is to visit** China next month. (예정: '…할 예정이다')

If we **are to get** there on time, we must hurry. (의도: '…하려고 하다')

They **were to meet** again someday. (운명: '…할 운명이다')

Nothing **was to be seen** in the darkness. (가능: '…할 수 있다')

B

부사적 용법: 목적, 감정의 원인, 판단의 근거·이유, 결과, 조건 등을 나타내는 부사 역할을 한다.

A lot of people are waiting **to enter** the stadium. (목적: '…하기 위해')

Tom was very happy **to see** his family again. (감정의 원인: '…해서')

He must be foolish **to believe** such a silly thing. (판단의 근거·이유: '…하다니')

Ann grew up **to be** a famous figure skater. (결과: '(…해서) ~하다')

She opened the box **only to find** it empty. (부정적 결과 only to-v : '결국 …하고 말다')

To hear him talk, you would think he was a foreigner. (조건: '…한다면')

This question was <u>*easy*</u> **to answer**. (형용사 수식: '…하기에')

> **Grammar UP** **in order to-v**와 **so as to-v**: 목적의 의미를 강조한다.
> She closed the window (**in order** / **so as**) **to keep** out the noise.

SPEED CHECK

빈칸에 알맞은 말을 고르시오.

1 Patrick is not a good person _____.

① work ② to work ③ to work with ④ working ⑤ working with

2 Andy turned the music down _____ the phone.

① answer ② to answer ③ to be answering ④ to be answered ⑤ to have answered

PRACTICE TEST

정답 및 해설 p.2

A 다음 문장에서 틀린 부분을 찾아 바르게 고치시오.

1 I have some good news tell you.
2 Jack worked hard in order achieve his goal.
3 The child has many toys to play.
4 We are pleased have you as our guest.
5 Jamie needs a piece of paper to write.

A
achieve [동] 달성하다, 성취하다
pleased [형] 기쁜
as [전] …로서

B 두 문장의 뜻이 같도록 문장을 완성하시오.

1 Evan went back to America. He wanted to visit his grandmother.
→ Evan went back to America _______ _______ his grandmother.

2 I saw the terrible car crash. I was shocked.
→ I was _______ _______ _______ the terrible car crash.

3 Students in our school must wear school uniforms.
→ Students in our school _______ _______ _______ school uniforms.

4 If you want to pass the exam, you should study hard.
→ If you _______ _______ _______ the exam, you should study hard.

B
car crash 교통사고
shocked [형] 충격을 받은
school uniform 교복

C 다음 문장을 해석하시오.

1 I was happy to come home early.
→ ______________________________

2 The school principal is to give a speech this afternoon.
→ ______________________________

3 Olivia was careless to shout in front of so many people.
→ ______________________________

4 Gavin was looking for a house to buy.
→ ______________________________

5 We will go to the park to enjoy the warm weather.
→ ______________________________

6 This shirt is very comfortable to wear.
→ ______________________________

C
principal [명] (단체의) 장, 학장, 교장
give a speech 연설하다
careless [형] 부주의한; *경솔한
comfortable [형] 편한

to부정사의 의미상 주어, 시제, 수동태

A

to부정사의 의미상 주어: to부정사가 나타내는 행위의 주체를 말한다.

1 의미상 주어를 따로 표시하지 않는 경우

She loves *to see* her friends. (의미상 주어 = 문장의 주어)

My parents expect **me** *to become* a doctor. (의미상 주어 = 문장의 목적어)

It's good (**for us**) *to work out* every day. (의미상 주어 = 일반인)

2 의미상 주어를 따로 표시하는 경우

1) 『**for+목적격**』: 대부분의 경우 의미상 주어는 『for+목적격』을 쓴다.

Here are the problems **for you** to solve.

It is important **for us** *to do* our best.

2) 『**of+목적격**』: 사람의 성품·성격을 나타내는 형용사(kind, foolish, wise, polite, cruel, careless, nice, silly, generous, clever 등)가 보어로 쓰이면 의미상 주어로 『of+목적격』을 쓴다.

It was *nice* **of him** *to take* me home.

B

to부정사의 시제

1 단순부정사(to-v): to부정사의 시제가 문장의 시제와 같거나 그 이후를 나타낼 때 쓴다.

He **seems to love** you. (→ It *seems* that he *loves* you.)

2 완료부정사(to have v-ed): to부정사의 시제가 문장의 시제보다 앞설 때 쓴다.

He **seems to have loved** you. (→ It *seems* that he *loved* you.)

C

to부정사의 수동태

1 단순수동태(to be v-ed): 수동의 뜻을 가지며 to부정사의 시제가 문장의 시제와 같거나 그 이후를 나타낼 때 쓴다.

We respect others and hope **to be respected** as well.

2 완료수동태(to have been v-ed): 수동의 뜻을 가지며 to부정사의 시제가 문장의 시제보다 앞설 때 쓴다.

Mark was happy **to have been elected** student president.

SPEED CHECK

빈칸에 알맞은 말을 고르시오.

1 It was wise _____ to apologize to you.

① him ② his ③ for him ④ of him ⑤ with him

2 He seems _____ poor when he was young.

① to be ② be ③ to have been ④ to had been ⑤ have to been

3 The payment needs _____ by this Friday.

① to make ② to have make ③ to be made

④ to have been made ⑤ to made

PRACTICE TEST

정답 및 해설 p.3

A

(　　) 안에서 알맞은 말을 고르시오.

1 It was difficult (of them / for them) to find a nice hotel.
2 He wanted (for me / me) to read my sister a storybook before bedtime.
3 It was very clever (of you / for you) to think of calling the police.
4 My mother seems (to be / to have been) popular in her teenage years.
5 The elevator was expected (to have repaired / to have been repaired) last weekend.

A
bedtime [명] 취침 시간
teenage [형] 십 대의
repair [동] 고치다, 수리하다

B

두 문장의 뜻이 같도록 문장을 완성하시오.

1 It seems that water pollution gets worse.
→ Water pollution seems _______ _______ _______.

2 It seems that they fought yesterday.
→ They seem _______ _______ _______ yesterday.

3 I am sorry that I broke my promise again.
→ I am sorry _______ _______ _______ my promise again.

4 I was pleased that I was invited to the ceremony.
→ I was pleased _______ _______ _______ to the ceremony.

B
water pollution
수질 오염
fight [동] 싸우다
(fought-fought)
break one's promise
약속을 어기다
ceremony [명] 의식, 식

C

우리말과 뜻이 같도록 to부정사와 주어진 말을 사용하여 문장을 완성하시오.

1 나의 아버지는 화나셨던 것 같다. (seem, be)
My father _______ _______ _______ _______ upset.

2 모든 아이들은 보호되어야 할 필요가 있다. (protect)
All children need _______ _______ _______.

3 그녀가 그 이야기를 믿는 것은 어리석다. (foolish, believe)
It is _______ _______ _______ _______ _______ the story.

4 그들이 그 프로젝트를 내일까지 끝내는 것은 불가능하다. (impossible, finish)
It is _______ _______ _______ _______ _______ the project by tomorrow.

5 그녀는 내 이메일 계정의 비밀번호를 알고 있는 것 같다. (seem, know)
She _______ _______ _______ the password of my email account.

C
protect [동] 보호하다
impossible [형] 불가능한
password [명] 비밀번호
email account
이메일 계정

목적격 보어로 쓰이는 to부정사와 원형부정사

A **to부정사를 목적격 보어로 쓰는 동사:** 「want, expect, tell, ask, order, advise, allow 등+목적어+to-v」

I *expected* him **to teach** me how to dance.

I *asked* Martha **to forgive** him.

> **Tip 주의!** help는 to부정사와 원형부정사 모두 목적격 보어로 쓸 수 있다.
> I *helped* my mom **(to) prepare** dinner.

B **원형부정사를 목적격 보어로 쓰는 동사**

1 **지각동사:** 「see, watch, hear, listen to, feel, notice 등+목적어+원형부정사」

I *saw* something bright **move** in the sky.

He *felt* someone **touch** his shoulder.

2 **사역동사:** 「make/have/let+목적어+원형부정사」

He *made* his son **go** to law school.

My dad *had* me **plan** my sister's birthday party.

I *let* my dog **run** free in the yard.

> **Tip 비교!** get은 사역('…하게 하다')의 뜻을 갖지만 목적격 보어로 to부정사를 쓴다.
> Jenny *got* her boyfriend **to carry** her backpack.

✓ Grammar UP **목적격 보어로 쓰일 수 있는 현재분사와 과거분사**

1 **지각동사:** 목적어와 목적격 보어의 관계가 능동일 때 진행의 뜻을 강조하고자 목적격 보어로 현재분사(v-ing)를 쓸 수 있고, 수동일 때 과거분사(v-ed)를 쓸 수 있다.

I saw *him* **crossing** the street. (능동·진행)

I heard *my name* **called**. (수동)

2 **사역동사:** 목적어와 목적격 보어의 관계가 수동일 때 목적격 보어로 과거분사(v-ed)를 쓸 수 있다.

Lily had *her car* **fixed**. (수동)

SPEED CHECK

빈칸에 알맞은 말을 고르시오.

1 The doctor advised me _____ eating spicy food.

① stop   ② stopped   ③ to stop   ④ to stopping   ⑤ to be stopped

2 Mr. Brown made the students _____ in line.

① wait   ② waits   ③ waited   ④ to wait   ⑤ waiting

3 I felt someone _____ at me.

① stares   ② stared   ③ to stare   ④ staring   ⑤ to staring

PRACTICE TEST

A (   ) 안에서 알맞은 말을 고르시오.

1 I saw someone (take / to take) the wallet from her bag.
2 I want you (listen / to listen) to me very carefully.
3 Please, Dad, let me (get / getting) a puppy.
4 My parents ordered me (coming / to come) home early today.
5 Would you help me (studying / study) Japanese?

A
wallet 몡 지갑
carefully 뵈 주의하여

B 보기에서 알맞은 말을 골라 필요시 어법에 맞게 바꿔 쓰시오. (단, 한 번씩만 쓸 것)

| 보기 | paint   cry   study   turn up   play |

1 The teacher had her students _____ by themselves.
2 Did you tell me _____ the volume of the TV?
3 Alex listened to his older sister _____ the flute.
4 The sad ending of the movie made me _____.
5 My uncle had the old fence _____.

B
paint 통 페인트칠하다
turn up (소리를) 높이다
by oneself 혼자서;
            혼자 힘으로
volume 몡 용량; *음량
flute 몡 플루트
fence 몡 울타리

C 우리말과 뜻이 같도록 주어진 말을 사용하여 문장을 완성하시오.

1 나의 상사는 내가 그 회의를 위한 자료들을 준비하게 했다. (have, prepare)
    My boss _____ _____ _____ materials for the meeting.

2 나의 아버지는 그 차가 세차되는 것을 지켜봤다. (watch, wash)
    My father _____ _____ _____ _____.

3 나는 그가 성공한 작가가 될 것이라고 예상하지 못했다. (expect, be)
    I didn't _____ _____ _____ _____ a successful writer.

4 이 책은 내가 나의 미래에 대해 생각해 보게 했다. (get, think about)
    This book _____ _____ _____ _____ _____ my future.

5 그녀는 그 남자가 통화하는 것을 들었다. (hear, talk)
    She _____ _____ _____ _____ on the phone.

C
boss 몡 상사
material 몡 자료
successful 혱 성공한
talk on the phone
통화하다

to부정사를 이용한 주요 구문, 독립부정사

A

to부정사를 이용한 주요 구문

1 「too+형용사/부사+to-v」: '너무 …해서 ~할 수 없다', '~하기에 너무 …하다' (→「so+형용사/부사+that+주어+can't」)

He was **too young to get** a job.

(→ He was **so young that he could not get** a job.)

This coat is **too big for me to wear**.

(→ This coat is **so big that I can't wear** it.)

2 「형용사/부사+enough to-v」: '…할 만큼 충분히 ~하다' (→「so+형용사/부사+that+주어+can」)

Kevin is **strong enough to carry** these bricks.

(→ Kevin is **so strong that he can carry** these bricks.)

The room is **large enough for me to put** the double bed in it.

(→ The room is **so large that I can put** the double bed in it.)

3 「it takes+목적격+시간+to-v」: '…가 ~하는 데 (시간)이 걸리다'

It takes me 10 minutes **to walk** to school.

It took him two years **to apologize** to me.

B

독립부정사: 문장의 다른 부분으로부터 독립하여 단독으로 문장 전체를 수식하는 to부정사구이다.

- to begin with: '우선', '먼저'
- strange to say: '이상한 이야기지만'
- to be brief: '간단히 말하면'
- to be frank (with you): '솔직히 말하면'
- to make matters worse: '설상가상으로'
- to tell (you) the truth: '사실대로 말하면'

Strange to say, I have the same dream every night.

To make matters worse, the best player on our team twisted his ankle.

To tell you the truth, I was surprised and embarrassed.

SPEED CHECK

빈칸에 알맞은 말을 고르시오.

1 Jeff is _____ tall to wear those jeans.

① so   ② too   ③ very   ④ such   ⑤ enough

2 She sings well _____ to be a great singer.

① so   ② too   ③ very   ④ such   ⑤ enough

3 It took _____ three hours to pack for the trip.

① she   ② her   ③ hers   ④ for her   ⑤ of her

PRACTICE TEST

정답 및 해설 p.4

A ( ) 안에서 알맞은 말을 고르시오.

1 My daughter was (enough tall / tall enough) to ride the roller coaster.
2 Fiona was (too / enough) shocked to say anything.
3 It takes (him / for him) a half hour to get to work.
4 (To frank / To be frank), rock music makes me sleepy.
5 (To make / Make) matters worse, he dropped his lunch on the floor.

A
a half hour 30분
(= half an hour)
get to work 일하러 가다

B 두 문장의 뜻이 같도록 문장을 완성하시오.

1 I'm too sleepy to finish my homework.
→ I'm _______ _______ _______ _______ _______ _______ my homework.

2 Ivy is smart enough to solve the problem by herself.
→ Ivy is _______ _______ _______ _______ _______ _______ the problem by herself.

3 My backpack is so big that it can carry 10 books.
→ My backpack _______ _______ _______ _______ _______ 10 books.

4 My father was so busy that he couldn't go on vacation last summer.
→ My father _______ _______ _______ _______ _______ on vacation last summer.

B
go on vacation
휴가를 가다

C 우리말과 뜻이 같도록 주어진 말을 사용하여 문장을 완성하시오.

1 그 환자는 퇴원할 만큼 충분히 건강하지는 않았다. (healthy, leave)
The patient wasn't _______ _______ _______ _______ the hospital.

2 그 쇼핑몰은 걸어가기에 너무 멀었다. (far, walk to)
The shopping mall was _______ _______ _______ _______ _______.

3 우선, 나는 그 색상이 마음에 들지 않는다. (begin)
_______ _______ _______, I don't like the color.

4 내가 그 텐트를 설치하는 데 한 시간이 걸렸다. (take, set up)
_______ _______ _______ an hour _______ _______ _______ the tent.

5 이 포도주스는 그녀가 마시기에 너무 달다. (sweet, drink)
This grape juice is _______ _______ _______ _______ _______ _______.

C
leave the hospital
퇴원하다
patient [명] 환자
set up …을 세우다;
*설치하다

REVIEW TEST

[01-02] 다음 빈칸에 들어갈 수 있는 말을 고르시오.

01

> Tell me when _____ left or right.

① turn
② to turn
③ be turning
④ to have turn
⑤ my turning

02

> Anderson made his puppy _____ him a newspaper.

① to bring
② bringing
③ brought
④ brings
⑤ bring

[03-04] 다음 빈칸에 들어갈 말을 바르게 짝지은 것을 고르시오.

03

> ⓐ Eugene got the repairman _____ the printer.
> ⓑ The businessman helps poor students _____ to university.

　　　ⓐ　　　ⓑ　　　　　ⓐ　　　ⓑ
① check – go 　② to check – going
③ check – to go 　④ to check – go
⑤ checks – to go

04

> ⓐ Sandy can hear the rain _____ the windows of her room.
> ⓑ Fitness trainers advise people _____ some stretching first.

　　　ⓐ　　　ⓑ　　　　　ⓐ　　　ⓑ
① hit – do 　② to hit – to do
③ to hit – doing 　④ hitting – to do
⑤ hitting – doing

[05-06] 다음 빈칸에 들어갈 수 <u>없는</u> 말을 고르시오.

05

> I _____ Lily to go to the festival.

① told
② wanted
③ asked
④ encouraged
⑤ watched

06

> Daniel _____ me book a flight to Japan.

① made
② helped
③ had
④ expected
⑤ let

[07-08] 다음 그림을 보고 주어진 말을 사용하여 문장을 완성하시오.

07

The girl told the man _____ _____ _____ _____ N Seoul Tower. (get to)

08

My brother is _____ _____ _____ _____ the picture on the wall. (tall, hang)

18

09 다음 중 두 문장의 의미가 <u>다른</u> 것은?

① To live without water is impossible.
  → It is impossible to live without water.
② I decided where I should put my sofa.
  → I decided where to put my sofa.
③ I went to the store so as to buy eggs.
  → I went to the store to buy eggs.
④ It seems that Jenny is a teacher.
  → Jenny seems to be a teacher.
⑤ Alice is so rich that she can buy a house.
  → Alice is too rich to buy a house.

고난도 NEW 내신 기출

10 다음 우리말을 영어로 옮겨 쓸 때 필요한 단어가 바르게 주어진 것은?

① 나는 그에게 약간의 집안일을 하게 했다.
  (I, him, some, made, do, chores, to).
② Jones 씨는 지난주에 피곤했던 것 같다.
  (tired, seems, Mr. Jones, to, last week, be).
③ 나는 그가 도와 달라고 외치고 있는 소리를 들었다.
  (shouting, help, I, for, him, heard).
④ 우리는 선생님께 다음에 무엇을 할지 물었다.
  (next, we, does, the teacher, what, asked).
⑤ 그는 네가 건강한 음식을 고르도록 도와줄 것이다.
  (help, chosen, healthy, will, food, you, he).

서술형 NEW 내신 기출

11 다음 대화의 빈칸에 들어갈 한 단어와 보기의 단어를 한 번씩만 사용하여 문장을 완성하시오.

> A: Your chair looks awesome!
> B: Thanks. It is made _____ wood.

| 보기 |
| unlocked | careless | was | door |
| leave | me | it | the | to |

→ _____

서술형

[12-13] 주어진 말을 사용하여 대화를 완성하시오.

12 A: Why don't you eat some more?
  B: I'm on a diet. So I'm trying _____ _____
    _____ heavy meals. (eat)

13 A: The kids need something _____ _____
    _____. (play)
  B: Well, there are some toy cars in that box.

14 다음 밑줄 친 부분의 쓰임이 보기와 같은 것은?

| 보기 |
This is a great chance <u>to meet</u> famous artists.

① I stayed up late <u>to study</u> last night.
② The fog made it hard <u>to drive</u>.
③ Her dream is <u>to be</u> a swimmer.
④ It is not easy <u>to bake</u> chocolate cookies.
⑤ I have something <u>to tell</u> you.

서술형

15 밑줄 친 부분에 유의하여 다음 문장을 해석하시오.

1) I'm happy <u>to see</u> you again.
2) He practiced a lot <u>to win</u> the contest.
3) She must be smart <u>to get</u> a perfect score on the exam.
4) <u>To hear</u> him sing, you wouldn't believe he's just a child.

16 다음 중 밑줄 친 부분의 뜻풀이가 <u>어색한</u> 것은?

① Passengers <u>are to follow</u> the safety rules.
(= must follow)

② The movie <u>is to be released</u> only in Asia.
(= will be released)

③ He <u>was</u> never <u>to walk</u> again after the accident.　(= was ready to walk)

④ If you <u>are to succeed</u>, you must work creatively.　(= want to succeed)

⑤ No water <u>is to be found</u> in this desert.
(= can be found)

서술형

17 두 문장의 뜻이 같도록 to부정사를 사용하여 문장을 완성하시오.

It seems that Glenn was in trouble with his teammates.

→ Glenn _____ _____ _____ _____ in trouble with his teammates.

고난도

18 다음 중 어법상 옳은 것은 모두 몇 개인가?

ⓐ Dan is smart enough to solve the puzzle.
ⓑ Susan didn't tell me when calling her.
ⓒ To make matters worse, it began to snow.
ⓓ He found that hard to master a second language.
ⓔ Sam was sad to have been scolded by his teacher.

① 1개　　② 2개　　③ 3개
④ 4개　　⑤ 5개

서술형　고난도

19 다음 중 어법상 <u>틀린</u> 것을 모두 골라 바르게 고치시오.

① Could you give me something to sit?
② My mom told me to take out the garbage.
③ I had my hair cut at a hair salon.
④ It was painful for him to give up his dream.
⑤ It is generous for him to donate his money to charity.

서술형

[20-23] 우리말과 뜻이 같도록 to부정사와 주어진 말을 사용하여 문장을 완성하시오.

20 그가 그 기사를 쓰는 데 3일이 걸렸다. (take, write)

→ It _____ _____ _____ _____ _____ _____ the article.

21 Daryl은 그의 행동에 대한 보상을 받아서 행복했다. (happy, reward)

→ Daryl was _____ _____ _____ for his act.

22 이 액션 영화는 십 대들이 보기에 너무 폭력적이다. (violent, teenagers, watch)

→ This action movie is _____ _____ _____ _____ _____ _____.

23 나는 그녀에게 몇 번 전화했지만 결국 녹음된 음악만 듣고 말았다. (hear)

→ I called her several times, _____ _____ _____ the recorded music.

CHAPTER

02

동명사

동명사의 역할

A 동명사(v-ing): 『동사원형＋-ing』의 형태로 동사의 뜻을 유지하며, 명사처럼 주어, 목적어, 보어로 쓰인다.

B **동명사의 역할과 의미상 주어**

1 주어: 주어로 쓰인 동명사(구)는 단수 취급한다.

Running a marathon *is* not easy.

Shopping online *has* become hugely popular.

2 보어: The best part of my day is **having** dinner with my family.

3 목적어

1) 동사의 목적어: He *started* **composing** music when he was a teenager.

2) 전치사의 목적어: Don't be afraid *of* **making** mistakes.

4 동명사의 의미상 주어: 동명사가 나타내는 행위의 주체를 말하며, 의미상 주어가 문장의 주어 또는 목적어와 다르거나 일반인이 아닐 때 동명사 앞에 소유격이나 목적격으로 나타낸다.

I don't like **his[him]** staying up late.

Mr. Smith is worried about **her** being late for school.

> **Tip 주의** 동명사의 부정: not / never v-ing
> He apologized for **not telling** the truth.

C **동명사의 시제**

1 단순동명사(v-ing): 동명사의 시제와 문장의 시제가 같거나 그 이후를 나타낼 때 쓴다.

She *is* good at **making** friends with strangers.

2 완료동명사(having v-ed): 동명사의 시제가 문장의 시제보다 앞설 때 쓴다.

I *am* ashamed of **having cried** in class.

D **동명사의 수동태**

1 단순수동태(being v-ed): 수동의 뜻을 가지며 동명사의 시제가 문장의 시제와 같거나 그 이후를 나타낼 때 쓴다.

She *hates* **being treated** like a child.

2 완료수동태(having been v-ed): 수동의 뜻을 가지며 동명사의 시제가 문장의 시제보다 앞설 때 쓴다.

He *is* upset about **having been ignored**.

SPEED CHECK

빈칸에 알맞은 말을 고르시오.

1 I stayed home instead of _____ shopping.

① go　　　　② to go　　　　③ going　　　　④ being went　　　⑤ having gone

2 I'm angry about _____ keeping me waiting for so long.

① he　　　　② his　　　　③ being him　　　④ for him　　　⑤ of him

PRACTICE TEST

정답 및 해설 p.6

A

(　　) 안에서 알맞은 말을 고르시오.

1 I'm tired of the bus (not being / being not) on time.
2 Can you imagine (he / him) dancing on the stage?
3 My first task was (being developed / developing) a new app.
4 He regrets (eating / having eaten) so much at the buffet yesterday.

A
be tired of 넌더리 나다
imagine [동] 상상하다
task [명] 일, 과제
develop [동] 성장하다; *개발하다
regret [동] 후회하다
buffet [명] 뷔페

B

다음 문장에서 <u>틀린</u> 부분을 찾아 바르게 고치시오.

1 I was surprised at she calling me.
2 My boss hates being not told important news immediately.
3 I'm excited about visit my uncle in Canada this summer.
4 Playing smartphone games too often are not good for you.

B
immediately [부] 즉시, 곧

C

두 문장의 뜻이 같도록 문장을 완성하시오.

1 I'm sorry that I wasted your time.
→ I'm sorry for _______ _______ your time.

2 I'm sure that he is polite and considerate.
→ I'm sure of _______ _______ polite and considerate.

C
polite [형] 예의 바른
considerate [형] 사려 깊은

D

우리말과 뜻이 같도록 동명사와 주어진 말을 사용하여 문장을 완성하시오.

1 나의 가장 큰 관심사는 환경을 보호하는 것이다. (protect, the environment)
My biggest concern is _______ _______ _______.

2 그녀는 그가 금연하지 않는 것에 대해 불평했다. (quit)
She complained about _______ _______ _______ smoking.

3 그는 비웃음당하는 것을 개의치 않았다. (laugh at)
He didn't mind _______ _______ _______.

4 Tom은 지난해에 파티에서 그녀를 만났던 것을 회상했다. (meet)
Tom recalled _______ _______ _______ at the party last year.

5 우리는 그녀가 그 경기에서 불공평하게 대우받았던 것에 대해 화가 난다. (treat)
We're upset about _______ _______ _______ _______ unfairly at the game.

D
protect [동] 보호하다
environment [명] 환경
concern [명] 걱정; *관심사
quit [동] (하던 일을) 그만두다
complain [동] 불평하다
laugh at …을 비웃다[놀리다]
mind [동] 언짢아하다, 꺼리다
recall [동] 회상하다
treat [동] 대하다, 다루다
unfairly [부] 불공평하게

목적어로 쓰이는 동명사와 to부정사

1 동명사만을 목적어로 쓰는 동사: finish, enjoy, mind, keep, avoid, give up, stop, quit, consider, deny 등

Robin **enjoys riding** a skateboard every day.

She **avoided eating** fast food for a month.

2 to부정사만을 목적어로 쓰는 동사: want, need, wish, decide, hope, ask, expect, refuse, plan, promise 등

I **hope to see** you again soon.

His son **refused to go** to kindergarten.

3 동명사와 to부정사 모두 목적어로 쓰는 동사

1) 의미 차이가 거의 없는 경우: like, love, hate, begin, start, continue 등

I **like walking[to walk]** on the grass.

She **loves going[to go]** camping with her friends.

2) 의미 차이가 있는 경우: remember, forget, try 등

- remember v-ing: '(과거에) …한 것을 기억하다' / remember to-v: '(미래에) …할 것을 기억하다'

He **remembers seeing** the Alps last year.

She always **remembers to lock** the door.

- forget v-ing: '(과거에) …한 것을 잊다' / forget to-v: '(미래에) …할 것을 잊다'

I **forgot calling** him, so I called again.

Don't **forget to call** him about our party plans.

- try v-ing: '(시험 삼아) …해 보다' / try to-v: '…하려고 노력하다'

If your computer isn't working, **try rebooting** it.

I **tried to eat** more vegetables.

 stop v-ing와 stop to-v

- stop v-ing: '…하는 것을 멈추다' (동명사: stop의 목적어)

He **stopped talking** to me.

- stop to-v: '…하기 위해 멈추다' (to부정사: 목적을 나타내는 부사적 용법)

He **stopped to talk** to me.

SPEED CHECK

빈칸에 알맞은 말을 고르시오.

1 The city considered _____ bike lanes on the street.

① build　　　② to build　　　③ building　　　④ to building　　　⑤ builds

2 They didn't want to wake up the sleeping baby, so they tried _____ quiet.

① were　　　② to be　　　③ not to be　　　④ not being　　　⑤ having been

PRACTICE TEST

정답 및 해설 p.7

A (   ) 안에서 알맞은 말을 고르시오.

1 I really wish (going / to go) abroad for school.
2 Hailey gave up (eating / to eat) sweets late at night.
3 My sister promised (buying / to buy) me a bike.
4 I finished (writing / to write) a thank-you letter to my parents.
5 I tried (doing / to do) my best to pass the exam, but I failed.
6 Don't forget (turning off / to turn off) the iron after using it.
7 Jason remembers (watching / to watch) the movie last week.

A
go abroad 외국에 가다
sweet 명 단것, 사탕류
thank-you letter
감사 편지
iron 명 다리미

B 보기에서 알맞은 말을 골라 어법에 맞게 바꿔 쓰시오. (단, 한 번씩만 쓸 것)

| 보기 |　　　take　　　work　　　move　　　become　　　meet |

1 Jamie is considering _____ to a big city.
2 I forgot _____ her at the conference last year.
3 I hope _____ a professor in the future.
4 He wanted _____ a break more than three times a day.
5 You look exhausted! You'd better stop _____.

B
conference 명 회의, 회담
professor 명 교수
break 명 휴식
exhausted 형 기진맥진한,
　　　　　　　 진이 다 빠진

C 우리말과 뜻이 같도록 주어진 말을 사용하여 문장을 완성하시오.

1 그는 지도를 보기 위해 멈췄다. (stop, read)
   He _____ _____ _____ a map.

2 Kelly는 그녀의 남자친구와 헤어지기로 결심했다. (decide, break up with)
   Kelly _____ _____ _____ _____ _____ her boyfriend.

3 그는 내 말을 듣기를 거부한다. (refuse, listen to)
   He _____ _____ _____ _____ me.

4 그는 계속 많은 소설과 시를 썼다. (continue, write)
   He _____ _____ _____ many novels and poems.

5 나는 오늘 오후에 그 회의에 참석할 것을 기억하고 있다. (remember, attend)
   I _____ _____ _____ the meeting this afternoon.

C
break up with
…와 결별하다
poem 명 (한 편의) 시
attend 통 참석하다

동명사를 이용한 주요 구문

1 go v-ing: '…하러 가다'

She **goes swimming** three days a week.

I **went fishing** for the first time last Saturday.

2 feel like v-ing: '…하고 싶다'

Jenny **felt like crying** after watching the musical.

I don't **feel like doing** anything.

3 look forward to v-ing: '…하기를 고대하다'

I'm **looking forward to taking** a trip.

Owen is really **looking forward to seeing** his nephew.

4 be worth v-ing: '…할 가치가 있다'

This movie **is worth seeing** again.

Life **is worth enjoying**.

5 cannot help v-ing: '…하지 않을 수 없다' (= 『cannot (help) but+동사원형』)

I **cannot help worrying about** his replies on my blog.

(→ I **cannot (help) but worry about** his replies on my blog.)

 기타 주요 동명사 구문

- be busy v-ing: '…하느라 바쁘다'
- keep (on) v-ing: '계속 …하다'
- there is no v-ing: '…할 수 없다', '…하는 것은 불가능하다'
- on[upon] v-ing: '…하자마자' (→ 『as soon as+주어+동사』)
- have trouble[difficulty] (in) v-ing: '…하는 데 어려움을 겪다'
- 『spend+시간[돈]+(on) v-ing』: '…하는 데 시간[돈]을 쓰다'
- 『keep[prevent]+목적어+from v-ing』: '…가 ~하는 것을 막다'
- How[What] about v-ing?: '…하는 게 어때?' (→ What do you say to v-ing?)

- it's no use v-ing: '…해 봐야 소용없다'
- be used to v-ing: '…하는 것에 익숙하다'

SPEED CHECK

빈칸에 알맞은 말을 고르시오.

1 Lisa went _____ with her family last weekend.

① camping ② camp ③ to camping ④ by camping ⑤ having camped

2 I'm looking forward _____ to the theater tonight.

① go ② goes ③ going ④ to go ⑤ to going

PRACTICE TEST

정답 및 해설 p.8

A 다음 문장에서 <u>틀린</u> 부분을 찾아 바르게 고치시오.

1 I spend a lot of time surf the Internet.
2 They went hike on Mt. Halla last Sunday.
3 The subway strike kept him in arriving on time.
4 Henry looks forward to listen to his new album.
5 I can't help but forgiving her when I see her smile.

A
surf the Internet
인터넷을 검색하다
strike 뎽 파업
forgive 뙤 용서하다

B 보기에서 알맞은 말을 골라 어법에 맞게 바꿔 쓰시오. (단, 한 번씩만 쓸 것)

| 보기 | enter   eat   make   buy   read   watch

1 How about _____ a new smartphone?
2 Jason is not used _____ Korean food.
3 I don't feel like _____ a baseball game right now.
4 I was busy _____ Jake's birthday cake.
5 Classic novels are worth _____ many times.
6 On _____ the house, she smelled something burning.

B
classic 혱 일류의
burning 혱 불타는

C 우리말과 뜻이 같도록 주어진 말을 사용하여 문장을 완성하시오.

1 일주일 동안 비가 계속 내렸다. (rain)
   It _____ _____ _____ for a week.

2 그는 항상 그의 차를 주차하는 데 어려움을 겪는다. (park)
   He always _____ _____ _____ his car.

3 지금 시험 결과에 대해 걱정해 봐야 소용없다. (worry about)
   _____ _____ _____ _____ the test results now.

4 우리는 당신과 함께 일하기를 고대한다. (work)
   We _____ _____ _____ _____ with you.

5 이 호수에서는 수영할 수 없다. (swim)
   _____ _____ _____ _____ in this lake.

6 그때 나는 그에게 거짓말하지 않을 수 없었다. (tell a lie)
   I _____ _____ _____ _____ to him at that moment.

C
park 뙤 주차하다
lake 뎽 호수

CHAPTER 02 동명사 27

REVIEW TEST

[01-02] 다음 빈칸에 들어갈 수 있는 말을 고르시오.

01

| Would you like to go _____ next Monday? |

① bowl   ② bowled

③ bowling   ④ to bowl

⑤ to bowling

02

| Kevin decided to quit _____ part-time. |

① work   ② worked

③ working   ④ to work

⑤ to working

NEW 내신 기출

03 다음 빈칸에 들어갈 ride의 형태가 나머지와 <u>다른</u> 것은?

① My son and I plan _____ bikes.

② Kevin likes _____ on large horses.

③ Do you enjoy _____ zip lines?

④ My uncle avoids _____ motorcycles.

⑤ I love _____ my skateboard every morning.

서술형

[04-05] 다음 문장에서 <u>틀린</u> 부분을 찾아 바르게 고치시오.

04 I'm busy pack for the business trip.

(   ) → (   )

05 Anna hates comparing to her sister.

(   ) → (   )

[06-08] 다음 밑줄 친 부분을 바르게 고친 것을 고르시오.

06

| Richard has given up <u>to learn</u> French. |

① learns   ② learned

③ learning   ④ to learning

⑤ being learning

07

| Andrew promised <u>helping</u> me with my homework. |

① helped   ② to help

③ to helping   ④ to be helped

⑤ having helped

08

| I am sorry about <u>he be</u> sick. |

① him to be   ② him be

③ he being   ④ his being

⑤ to his being

09 (A)와 (B)에서 알맞은 말을 골라 어법에 맞게 바꿔 문장을 완성하시오.

(A)	is looking forward to am not afraid of wants to be alone without

(B)	say "No" be disturbed go to her new home

1) Lucy _____ .

2) I _____ .

3) Mike _____ .

[10-11] 다음 중 어법상 틀린 것을 모두 골라 바르게 고치시오.

10 ① The dog continued barking at me.

② One of my habits is tapping my pen.

③ I'm considering drinking not coffee.

④ Taking pictures of animals are difficult.

⑤ He is proud of being elected as the team leader.

11 ① Matt wishes being a cook.

② She kept making the same mistake.

③ Jina likes reading all kinds of books.

④ My father stopped to smoke last year.

⑤ I tried to avoid making noise at night.

12 다음 두 문장을 한 문장으로 만든 것 중 옳은 것은?

> Emma met her favorite actor. She's still excited about it.

① Emma is still excited about being met her favorite actor.

② Emma is still excited about to have met her favorite actor.

③ Emma was still excited about meeting her favorite actor.

④ Emma is still excited about having met her favorite actor.

⑤ Emma was still excited about having met her favorite actor.

[13-14] 두 문장의 뜻이 같도록 문장을 완성하시오.

13 Do you mind if I turn off the radio?

→ Do you mind _____ ?

14 As soon as he arrived at the hotel, he knew something was wrong.

→ _____ , he knew something was wrong.

15 우리말과 뜻이 같도록 조건에 맞게 문장을 완성하시오.

> 우리는 그의 의견에 동의하지 않을 수 없었다.
>
> → _____
>
> → _____

| 조건 |
- help, agree with, opinion을 활용할 것
- 어법과 시제에 맞게 쓸 것
- 각각 8단어, 9단어의 완전한 문장으로 쓸 것

16 다음 밑줄 친 부분을 바르게 고친 것 중 어색한 것은?

① His music album is worth <u>to buy</u>.
　　　　　　　　　　　　　　→ buying

② Designing cartoon characters <u>were</u> my job.
　　　　　　　　　　　　　　　　→ was

③ Don't forget <u>bringing</u> your book to the next class!　　　　→ to bring

④ I was worried about <u>she</u> being weak.
　　　　　　　　　　　　→ her

⑤ My grandmother is not used to <u>having</u> a smartphone.　　　　　　　→ have

17 다음 우리말을 영어로 바르게 옮긴 것은?

> 나는 그가 너무 심하게 비판받았던 것에 대해 화가 난다.

① I am angry about him criticizing too much.
② I am angry about him being criticized too much.
③ I was angry about him being criticized too much.
④ I am angry about having been criticized too much.
⑤ I am angry about him having been criticized too much.

서술형

[18-20] 우리말과 뜻이 같도록 주어진 말을 사용하여 문장을 완성하시오.

18 그 도둑은 나의 지갑을 훔친 것을 부인한다.

(deny, steal)

→ The thief _____ _____ _____ my wallet.

19 나의 음악 선생님은 내가 나의 교과서를 가져오지 않은 것에 대해 실망했다. (bring, textbook)

→ My music teacher was disappointed with

_____ _____ _____ _____.

20 그 근로자들은 한 달 동안 혹사당했던 것에 대해 불평한다. (overwork)

→ The workers complain of _____ _____ _____ for a month.

21 다음 밑줄 친 부분의 쓰임이 나머지와 다른 것은?

① His job is <u>writing</u> novels for children.
② She has left without <u>letting</u> people know.
③ Ava likes <u>eating</u> Spanish food.
④ How about <u>drinking</u> something hot?
⑤ I thanked my friend for <u>buying</u> me lunch.

고난도

22 다음 중 어법상 옳은 것을 바르게 짝지은 것은?

> ⓐ Ella forgot sending an invitation, so nobody came.
> ⓑ I had difficulty learning math.
> ⓒ I think playing card games are exciting.
> ⓓ Some noisy people kept me from enjoying my dinner.
> ⓔ I avoid to meet Kevin because I lied to him.

① ⓐ, ⓑ　　　② ⓑ, ⓓ　　　③ ⓐ, ⓑ, ⓔ
④ ⓐ, ⓓ, ⓔ　　⑤ ⓒ, ⓓ, ⓔ

CHAPTER

03

분사

분사의 역할

A

분사: 『동사원형＋-ing』 형태의 현재분사와 『동사원형＋-ed』 형태의 과거분사가 있다.

1 현재분사(v-ing): 능동('…하는')이나 능동·진행('…하고 있는')의 뜻을 나타낸다.

This new novel is **thrilling**. (능동)

Sam heard someone **knocking** on the window. (능동·진행)

2 과거분사(v-ed): 수동('…되어[된]', '…해진')이나 완료('…한')의 뜻을 나타낸다.

Mr. Green had the roof **repaired** two weeks ago. (수동)

She is looking for the **escaped** snake. (완료)

B

분사의 역할: 형용사처럼 (대)명사를 수식하거나 보어로 쓰인다.

1 명사 수식: 단독으로는 앞에서, 수식어구와 함께 쓰여 길어질 때는 뒤에서 명사를 수식한다.

crying *baby* / **broken** *heart*

The guy **sitting** over there is Kelly's boyfriend.

2 보어: 주격 보어나 목적격 보어로 쓰인다.

The children sat **playing** with robots. (주격 보어)

I saw *her* **nodding** off during class. (목적격 보어)

> **Tip 주의!** 현재분사는 진행형(be v-ing)에, 과거분사는 완료형(have v-ed)과 수동태(be v-ed)에 쓰이기도 한다.

✔ Grammar UP 감정을 나타내는 분사

주어나 목적어, 수식을 받는 (대)명사가 감정을 일으킬 때는 현재분사를, 감정을 느낄 때는 과거분사를 쓴다.

- boring (지루하게 하는) – bored (지루해하는)
- exciting (신나게 하는) – excited (신난)
- shocking (충격적인) – shocked (충격을 받은)
- amazing (놀랄 만한) – amazed (놀란)
- interesting (흥미로운) – interested (흥미 있어 하는)
- surprising (놀라게 하는, 놀라운) – surprised (놀란)
- satisfying (만족스러운) – satisfied (만족한)
- disappointing (실망스러운) – disappointed (실망한)

My science test score was **disappointing**.

I was **disappointed** with my science test score.

SPEED CHECK

빈칸에 알맞은 말을 고르시오.

1 He reads a lot of books _____ in English.

① write ② writing ③ written ④ writes ⑤ wrote

2 The food at the restaurant is _____.

① satisfy ② satisfying ③ satisfied ④ satisfies ⑤ being satisfied

PRACTICE TEST

정답 및 해설 p.9

A ( ) 안에서 알맞은 말을 고르시오.

1 We eventually found the (hiding / hidden) treasure.
2 Who is that man (waving / waved) to the crowd?
3 The picture of a (smiling / smiled) baby makes me happy.
4 He heard his name (calling / called) from behind him.
5 Mary was (moving / moved) by her brother's thoughtful words.

A
eventually (분) 결국, 마침내
hide (동) 숨기다
        (hid-hidden)
treasure (명) 보물
crowd (명) 군중, 무리
move (동) 움직이다;
        *감동시키다
thoughtful (형) 생각에 잠긴;
        *사려 깊은

B 주어진 말을 문맥에 맞게 바꿔 빈칸에 쓰시오.

1 (surprise) I was _____ by his sudden visit.
            The results of the experiment were _____.
2 (interest) It's _____ to learn about different cultures.
            She is _____ in drawing cartoons.
3 (excite)   John found the film _____.
            I'm _____ about seeing my favorite soccer players.

B
sudden (형) 갑작스러운
experiment (명) 실험
culture (명) 문화
cartoon (명) 만화
film (명) 영화

C 우리말과 뜻이 같도록 보기에서 알맞은 말을 골라 어법에 맞게 바꿔 쓰시오.

| 보기 | test   send   bore   stand   make |

1 나는 중국에서 만들어진 새 모니터를 한 대 구입했다.
  I bought a new monitor _____ in China.
2 차 앞에 서 있는 그 소녀는 Linda이다.
  The girl _____ in front of the car is Linda.
3 내게 보내진 그 편지는 믿기 어려웠다.
  The letter _____ to me was hard to believe.
4 그녀는 수술 전에 그녀의 눈을 검사받았다.
  She had her eyes _____ before the surgery.
5 그들은 그 긴 소설을 읽는 것이 지겨워졌다.
  They got _____ with reading the long novel.

C
test (동) 검사하다
surgery (명) 수술

분사구문

A 분사구문
- 『접속사＋주어＋동사』의 부사절을 현재분사(v-ing)를 사용해 부사구로 줄여 쓴 구문이다.
- 부사절과 주절의 주어가 같을 때, 접속사와 주어를 생략하고 동사를 현재분사(v-ing)로 바꾼다.

Winning first prize, he felt happy. (← **When *he* won** first prize, *he* felt happy.)

B 분사구문의 의미

1 때: '…할 때(when / as)', '…하는 동안(while)', '…한 후에(after)', '…하자마자(as soon as)'
   Entering the house, we heard the kids running upstairs.
   (← **When we entered** the house, ...)

2 동시동작, 연속상황: '…하면서(as)', '…하고 나서(and)'
   Ken walked away, **waving** his hand. (동시동작)
   (← ... **as he waved** his hand.)
   The train left Seoul at 6, **reaching** Busan at 9. (연속상황)
   (← ... **and reached** Busan at 9.)

3 이유, 원인: '…하기 때문에(because / as / since)'
   Being a boy, he couldn't understand the girl's feelings. (← **Because he was** a boy, ...)

4 조건: '…하면(if)'
   Going to Hollywood, you'll be able to see many famous people.
   (← **If you go** to Hollywood, ...)

5 양보: '…일지라도', '…에도 불구하고' (although / though)
   Though living near a movie star's house, I have never seen her.
   (← **Though I live** near a movie star's house, ...)

   Tip 주의! 양보를 나타내는 분사구문은 일반적으로 접속사를 남겨 둔다.

 Grammar UP 주절의 주어가 부사절의 주어를 받는 대명사일 때

부사절의 주어를 생략한 후 주절의 주어가 대명사이면, 대명사를 부사절의 주어로 고친다.

As **the singer** danced, **she** turned toward the audience.
→ Dancing, **the singer** turned toward the audience.

SPEED CHECK

빈칸에 알맞은 말을 고르시오.

1 _____ no money, I had to walk home.
   ① Have   ② Had   ③ Being had   ④ Having   ⑤ To having

2 My mother cooked dinner in the kitchen, _____ to music.
   ① listen   ② listening   ③ is listening   ④ listened   ⑤ listens

PRACTICE TEST

정답 및 해설 p.10

A 보기에서 알맞은 말을 골라 어법에 맞게 바꿔 쓰시오.

| 보기 | join be sit jog

1 _______ on the sofa, I looked out the window.
2 _______ slow, the animal cannot escape from predators.
3 _______ along the street, Jake thought about what to do.
4 _______ this club, you can listen to various genres of music.

A
jog [동] 조깅하다, 천천히 뛰다
escape from …에서 달아나다
predator [명] 포식자
genre [명] 장르

B 다음 밑줄 친 부분을 분사구문으로 바꿔 쓰시오.

1 Because I forgot the password, I couldn't log on to the website.
→ _______ _______ _______, I couldn't log on to the website.

2 Although she looks weak, Emily is strong and healthy.
→ _______ _______ _______, Emily is strong and healthy.

3 He talked on the phone, as he took a memo.
→ He talked on the phone, _______ _______ _______.

B
password [명] 비밀번호
log on 로그인[로그온]하다
take a memo 메모하다

C 우리말과 뜻이 같도록 주어진 말을 사용하여 분사구문을 완성하시오.

1 Juliet을 보자마자 나는 내 심장이 뛰고 있는 것을 느꼈다. (see)
_______ _______, I felt my heart pounding.

2 그 가게에 도착했을 때 나는 내 지갑을 갖고 있지 않다는 것을 깨달았다. (arrive at)
_______ _______ _______ _______, I realized I didn't have my wallet.

3 인터넷을 검색하면 너는 그 주소를 찾을 수 있다. (search, the Internet)
_______ _______ _______, you can find the address.

4 그 가수의 팬이었기 때문에 Olivia는 그 콘서트에 신났었다. (be)
_______ a fan of the singer, Olivia was excited about the concert.

5 여러 번 설명했음에도 불구하고 나는 그를 이해시킬 수 없었다. (explain)
_______ _______ several times, I couldn't make him understand.

C
pound [동] (가슴이) 쿵쿵 뛰다
realize [동] 깨닫다
search [동] 찾아보다, 검색하다
address [명] 주소
explain [동] 설명하다

분사구문의 부정, 시제, 수동태

A 분사구문의 부정: 분사 앞에 not이나 never를 쓴다.

Not having enough time to sleep, he nodded off in class.

(← Because he did**n't** have enough time to sleep, he nodded off in class.)

B 분사구문의 시제

1 단순 분사구문(v-ing): 부사절의 시제가 주절의 시제와 같을 때 쓴다.

Looking into her eyes, I can see that she loves me.

(← When I **look** into her eyes, I **can see** that she loves me.)

2 완료 분사구문(having v-ed): 부사절의 시제가 주절의 시제보다 앞설 때 쓴다.

Having eaten a lot, she doesn't feel like eating more.

(← Because she **ate** a lot, she **doesn't feel** like eating more.)

Having finished my work, I can help you at any time.

(← Because I **finished** my work, I **can help** you at any time.)

C 분사구문의 수동태: being과 having been은 생략할 수 있어서 과거분사만 남는 경우가 많다.

1 단순수동태(being v-ed): 부사절이 수동태이고, 부사절의 시제가 주절의 시제와 같을 때 쓴다.

(Being) Asked to answer the question, he didn't know what to do.

(← When he **was asked** to answer the question, he **didn't know** what to do.)

2 완료수동태(having been v-ed): 부사절이 수동태이고, 부사절의 시제가 주절의 시제보다 앞설 때 쓴다.

(Having been) Brought up in Canada, he speaks English well.

(← Because he **was brought up** in Canada, he **speaks** English well.)

> **Grammar UP** 「being / having been＋형용사」: being이나 having been이 생략되어 형용사만 남는 경우도 있다.
>
> **Hungry**, I want to eat something.
>
> (← Being hungry, I want to eat something.)
>
> (← As I am hungry, I want to eat something.)

SPEED CHECK

빈칸에 알맞은 말을 고르시오.

1 _____ too much yesterday, I'm very tired.

① Talk   ② Talking   ③ Talked   ④ Not talking   ⑤ Having talked

2 _____ in history, Bob buys a lot of historical novels.

① Interesting   ② Interested   ③ Interest   ④ Interests   ⑤ To interest

PRACTICE TEST

정답 및 해설 p.10

A ( ) 안에서 알맞은 말을 고르시오.

1 (Writing / Written) in simple English, the book is easy to read.
2 (Not having / Having not) an umbrella, I didn't want to go out in the rain.
3 (Exciting / Excited) about the game, Mark forgot to call me.
4 (Seeing / Having seen) the show before, Emily knows the way it ends.
5 (Firing / Fired) by the company, he started looking for a new job.

A
fire 동 해고하다

B 다음 문장을 분사구문으로 바꿔 쓰시오.

1 If the new technique is used well, it can be very useful.
   → _____

2 As she lived in a big city, she knows little about country life.
   → _____

3 Because I was robbed before, I always lock the door.
   → _____

4 As I lost my cell phone, I can't call her now.
   → _____

B
technique 명 기술
rob 동 도둑질하다
lock 동 잠그다

C 우리말과 뜻이 같도록 주어진 말을 사용하여 분사구문을 완성하시오.

1 그 좋은 소식에 놀라서 그녀는 펄쩍펄쩍 뛰었다. (surprise at)
   _____ _____ the good news, she jumped up and down.

2 주의를 기울이지 않아서 Brad는 그의 버스 정류장을 놓쳤다. (pay attention)
   _____ _____ _____, Brad missed his bus stop.

3 그 기사를 읽었기 때문에 나는 그 문제를 이해한다. (read)
   _____ _____ the article, I understand the problem.

4 파티에 초대받았음에도 불구하고 나는 일 때문에 갈 수 없다. (invite)
   Though _____ _____ _____ to the party, I can't go because of work.

C
jump up and down
펄쩍펄쩍 뛰다
pay attention
주의를 기울이다
article 명 (신문·잡지의) 글, 기사

주의해야 할 분사구문

1 접속사를 생략하지 않는 분사구문: 분사구문의 뜻을 명확히 하기 위해 접속사를 남겨 두기도 한다.

After reading the reports, the team leader called a meeting.

(← **After** the team leader read the reports, he / she called a meeting.)

2 주어가 있는 분사구문: 부사절의 주어와 주절의 주어가 다를 때 부사절의 주어를 분사구문의 주어로 남겨 둔다.

The rain **having begun** to fall, *we* hurried to get back home.

(← Because **the rain** had begun to fall, **we** hurried to get back home.)

3 『with+(대)명사+분사』: 동시동작을 나타내는 분사구문의 하나이다.

　1) 『**with+(대)명사+현재분사**』: '…이 ~한 채'라는 뜻으로, (대)명사와 분사의 관계가 능동일 때 쓴다.

　　I can't focus on my work **with you standing** in front of me.

　2) 『**with+(대)명사+과거분사**』: '…이 ~된 채'라는 뜻으로, (대)명사와 분사의 관계가 수동일 때 쓴다.

　　Jessica sat **with her legs crossed**.

> **✓ Grammar UP**
> being은 보통 생략되어 『with+(대)명사+형용사 / 부사 / 전치사구』의 형태가 된다.
> Don't talk **with your mouth full**.
> The actress came on stage **with a beautiful dress on**.
> She waited for her husband **with her baby in her arms**.

4 관용적으로 쓰는 분사구문: 분사구문의 주어가 막연한 일반인일 경우 주절의 주어와 달라도 이를 생략한다.

• strictly speaking: '엄밀히 말해서'	• generally speaking: '일반적으로 말해서'
• frankly speaking: '솔직히 말해서'	• judging from: '…로 판단하건대'
• considering: '…을 고려하면', '…을 감안하면'	• roughly speaking: '대강 말하자면'
• speaking of: '… 이야기가 나왔으니 말인데'	

Strictly speaking, your answer is wrong.

Generally speaking, Korean is not easy to learn.

SPEED CHECK ▶

빈칸에 알맞은 말을 고르시오.

1 _____ a beautiful spring day, we went on a picnic at Riverside Park.

　① Being　　　　② To be　　　　③ It being　　　　④ That being　　　　⑤ Having been

2 She is walking with her music _____.

　① play　　　　② playing　　　　③ to play　　　　④ played　　　　⑤ having played

PRACTICE TEST

정답 및 해설 p.11

A ( ) 안에서 알맞은 말을 고르시오.

1 (Considering / Generally speaking) his age, he is very open-minded.

2 My cousin was listening to music with his eyes (closing / closed).

3 (The lesson being / Being) over, we ran out of the room.

4 I sang a song with my friends (dancing / danced) behind me.

5 (While / With) making pasta for dinner, I cut my finger.

A
open-minded
(형) 열린 사고의, 넓은 마음의
cut one's finger
손가락을 베다

B 다음 밑줄 친 부분을 분사구문으로 바꿔 쓰시오.

1 <u>As the sun set</u>, we played hide-and-seek.

→ _____, we played hide-and-seek.

2 <u>When the traffic light turned green</u>, Dan turned left.

→ _____, Dan turned left.

3 <u>Because it rained heavily</u>, the playground is muddy now.

→ _____, the playground is muddy now.

4 <u>Since there is a strong wind</u>, the fire will spread quickly.

→ _____, the fire will spread quickly.

B
set (동) (해가) 지다
(set-set)
hide-and-seek
(명) 숨바꼭질
muddy (형) 진흙투성이의,
진흙의
spread (동) 번지다, 퍼지다

C 두 문장의 뜻이 같도록 문장을 완성하시오.

1 He sat comfortably, and the cat was sleeping at his feet.
→ He sat comfortably _____ _____ _____ _____ at his feet.

2 It was a foggy morning, and the sun was hidden behind the clouds.
→ It was a foggy morning _____ _____ _____ _____ behind
the clouds.

3 He sat on the floor, and his head was buried in his hands.
→ He sat on the floor _____ _____ _____ _____ in his hands.

C
comfortably (부) 편안하게
foggy (형) 안개 낀
bury (동) 묻다;
*…을 덮어 감추다

REVIEW TEST

[01-03] 다음 빈칸에 들어갈 수 있는 말을 고르시오.

01

> I want to buy fresh vegetables _____ by local farmers.

① grow   ② grows

③ grown   ④ to grow

⑤ be grown

02

> _____ the room, she took off her jacket.

① Enters   ② Entered

③ Entering   ④ To entering

⑤ Be entering

03

> _____ in traffic, he was late for his friend's wedding.

① To stuck   ② To be stuck

③ Be stuck   ④ With being stuck

⑤ Having been stuck

04 주어진 말을 어법에 맞게 배열할 때 첫 번째 오는 말은?

> (do, to, knowing, not, what), he started to bite his finger-nails.

① do   ② to

③ knowing   ④ not

⑤ what

05 주어진 말을 어법에 맞게 바꿔 쓰시오.

She found her new job _____. (satisfy)

06 다음 문장에서 어법상 틀린 부분을 찾아 바르게 고쳐 문장을 다시 쓰시오.

> We felt exciting when the player hit a home run.

→ _____

[07-09] 다음 밑줄 친 부분을 분사구문으로 바꿔 쓰시오.

07 Because he read the same book several times, he wants to buy a new one.

→ _____,

he wants to buy a new one.

08 As I hadn't heard anything about the new teacher, I was very curious.

→ _____,

I was very curious.

09 When the elevator's doors were nearly closed, a man suddenly got on.

→ _____,

a man suddenly got on.

10 다음 밑줄 친 우리말을 영어로 옮긴 것 중 **틀린** 것은?

① 일반적으로 말해서, women live longer.
(→ Generally speaking)

② 엄밀히 말해서, you broke the law.
(→ Strictly speaking)

③ 그녀의 성격으로 판단하건대, she will reject it.
(→ Judging from her personality)

④ 네 기술을 고려하면, you should be promoted.
(→ Considering your skills)

⑤ 솔직히 말해서, I don't like Tom.
(→ Roughly speaking)

11 다음 밑줄 친 분사구문을 부사절로 바꿀 때 **어색한** 것은?

① Falling asleep, she missed the TV show.
→ Since she fell asleep

② Finishing your homework, you must clean your room.
→ After you finish your homework

③ Feeling cold, Susan put on her coat.
→ When she felt cold

④ Not having enough money, I can't afford a plane ticket.
→ Because I didn't have enough money

⑤ Calling Mark's name, Bob entered the classroom.
→ As he called Mark's name

[12-13] 다음 그림을 보고 주어진 말을 사용하여 문장을 완성하시오.

12

It was a sunny morning _____ _____ _____ in the sky. (with, birds, fly)

13

Nick is sleeping on the sofa _____ _____ _____ _____ _____.

(with, the TV, turn on)

[14-15] 다음 중 어법상 **틀린** 것을 고르시오.

14 ① My father had his hair cut.
② I've got some shocking news to tell you.
③ There's smoke coming out of the kitchen.
④ The baby doesn't look interested in the toys.
⑤ Accidents causing by sleepy drivers increase in the spring.

15 ① Be angry, she shouted at him.

② I saw her using my comb.

③ The mountain scenery is really amazing.

④ She stayed at home, doing nothing.

⑤ Look at the photos taken on sports day.

서술형

[16-19] 우리말과 뜻이 같도록 다음 밑줄 친 분사구문을 접속사를 포함한 부사절로 바꿔 쓰시오.

16 책의 마지막 페이지를 읽으면서 그는 울었다.

Reading the last page of the book, he cried.

→ _____

17 그 상자를 열면 너는 네 생일 선물을 보게 될 것이다.

Opening the box, you will see your birthday present.

→ _____

18 나는 Amy를 반갑게 맞이하고 나서 그녀에게 차를 대접했다.

I welcomed Amy, serving her some tea.

→ _____

19 피카소에 의해 영감을 받았었기 때문에 나는 그림을 그리기 시작했다.

Having been inspired by Picasso, I started painting.

→ _____

고난도

20 다음 중 어법상 옳은 것은 모두 몇 개인가?

ⓐ I had my office painting by Jacob.

ⓑ Using this coupon, you can get a free coffee.

ⓒ Surprised by the noise, Bob shouted.

ⓓ Hearing not the doorbell, she didn't get the delivery.

ⓔ Chloe spoke nervously with her legs shaking.

① 1개   ② 2개   ③ 3개

④ 4개   ⑤ 5개

서술형

[21-23] 우리말과 뜻이 같도록 주어진 말을 사용하여 문장을 완성하시오. (단, 분사 및 분사구문을 사용할 것)

21 쉬지 못했었기 때문에 Christy는 피곤함을 느꼈다. (take a break)

→ _____ _____ _____ _____ _____,

Christy felt tired.

22 어르신들께 말씀 드릴 때는 공손하라. (when, talk to)

→ Be polite _____ _____ _____ elderly people.

23 그 개가 내게 짖어서 나는 그 자리에 얼어붙었다. (the dog, bark)

→ _____ _____ _____ at me, I stood frozen.

CHAPTER

04

시제

현재완료

A

현재완료(have v-ed): 과거에 일어난 일이 현재까지 영향을 미칠 때 쓴다.

1 경험: '(지금까지) …한 적이 있다' (주로 함께 쓰는 어구: ever, never, before, once, often 등)

I **have** *never* **seen** such an amazing sight.

2 계속: '(지금까지 계속) …해 왔다' (주로 함께 쓰는 어구: since, for, how long 등)

They **have been married** *for* over 50 years.

> **Tip 비교!** since와 for
> since는 '… 이래로'의 뜻으로 기준 시점과 함께 쓰며, for는 '… 동안'의 뜻으로 기간과 함께 쓴다.
> We've been friends **since** *2006*.
> We've been friends **for** *eight years*.

3 완료: '막 …했다' (주로 함께 쓰는 어구: just, already, yet, recently 등)

He **has** *just* **returned** from his vacation.

4 결과: '…해버렸다 (그래서 지금은 ～이다)'

I **have lost** the pair to this glove. (I don't have it now.)

> **Tip 주의!** 명백하게 과거를 나타내는 말(yesterday, ago, last, when 등)은 현재완료와 함께 쓰지 않는다.
> The hair salon **was closed** *yesterday*. (← ~~The hair salon **has been closed** *yesterday*.~~)

> **✓ Grammar UP** have been to와 have gone to
> • have been to: '…에 가 본 적이 있다'
>   I **have been to** America twice.
> • have gone to: '…에 가고 (지금 여기에) 없다'
>   He **has gone to** America.

B

현재완료 진행(have been v-ing): '…해 오고 있다'의 뜻으로, 과거에 시작된 일이 현재에도 진행 중일 때 쓴다.

I**'ve been taking** driving lessons for three weeks.

(→ I started to take driving lessons three weeks ago. I am still taking driving lessons.)

SPEED CHECK

빈칸에 알맞은 말을 고르시오.

1 John _____ in the hospital since last weekend.

① is ② was ③ were ④ has been ⑤ is being

2 I miss Jenny. She _____ to Hong Kong.

① goes ② is going ③ has been ④ has gone ⑤ has been going

PRACTICE TEST

정답 및 해설 p.13

A ( ) 안에서 알맞은 말을 고르시오.

1 My family (went / has been) to the aquarium a week ago.
2 We've donated money to charity (for / since) more than 10 years.
3 Brian (visited / has visited) the modern art exhibition last weekend.
4 Mindy (is doing / has been doing) her homework for two hours.
5 Max (was / has been) on a diet since last month.

A
aquarium 명 수족관
donate 동 기부하다
charity 명 자선 단체
modern 형 현대의
art exhibition
미술 전시회
be on a diet
다이어트를 하다

B 두 문장의 뜻이 같도록 문장을 완성하시오.

1 He went to Spain four years ago, and then he came back.
  → He _____ Spain.

2 Ava forgot her uncle's phone number, and she still can't remember it.
  → Ava _____ her uncle's phone number.

3 I started to watch the movie an hour ago, and I'm still watching it.
  → I _____ the movie for an hour.

C 다음 문장을 해석하시오.

1 How long have you known James?
  → _____

2 The company has already released a variety of products.
  → _____

3 I have never eaten Mexican food in my life.
  → _____

4 He has broken his leg, so he can't go skiing.
  → _____

5 Emma has been waiting for Kevin for hours.
  → _____

C
release 동 풀어 주다;
       *출시하다
a variety of 다양한
product 명 상품, 제품

과거완료, 미래완료

A

과거완료(had v-ed): 과거 이전에 일어난 일이 과거까지 영향을 미칠 때 쓴다.
He **had** *never* **been** to a big city before he came to Toronto. (경험)
Noah **had been** a golfer before he became a coach. (계속)
The exam **had** *already* **begun** when I arrived at the school. (완료)
He **had hurt** his arm, so he couldn't play basketball. (결과)

 **대과거**

had v-ed는 과거에 일어난 두 가지 일 중 먼저 일어난 일을 나타낼 때 쓰기도 하는데, 이를 대과거라 한다.
I *lost* the wallet that my mom **had bought** for me.
(→ '내가 지갑을 잃어버린 것'보다 '어머니가 나에게 지갑을 사 준 것'이 시간상 먼저 일어남)

B

과거완료 진행(had been v-ing): 과거 이전에 시작된 일이 과거에도 진행 중이었을 때 쓴다.
I **had been studying** for two hours when the phone rang.
The police **had been looking** for the thief for three years before they caught him.

C

미래완료(will have v-ed): '…하는 / 한 게 될 것이다'의 뜻으로, 미래의 특정 시점에 완료되거나 계속될 일을 나타낸다.
By tomorrow we **will have been** here for a week.
I **will have mastered** English before I leave for the USA.

D

미래완료 진행(will have been v-ing): '…하고 있는 게 될 것이다'의 뜻으로, 미래의 특정 시점에도 진행 중일 일을
나타낸다.
Ava **will have been driving** for more than six hours when she arrives in Busan.
I **will have been cooking** for two hours by the time you come home.

SPEED CHECK

빈칸에 알맞은 말을 고르시오.

1 I _____ such cold weather before I went to Russia.
① has never experienced　　② don't experience　　③ wasn't experienced
④ had never experienced　　⑤ will never have experienced

2 When I watch the movie once more, I _____ it five times.
① have watched　　② will watch　　③ will have watched
④ had watched　　⑤ am watching

PRACTICE TEST

정답 및 해설 p.13

A ( ) 안에서 알맞은 말을 고르시오.

1 I (had gotten / will have gotten) a job by the time I graduate.
2 Ben felt better after he (has taken / had taken) a short break.
3 He (has been sleeping / had been sleeping) when he heard a loud noise.
4 Lisa remembered that she (has met / had met) her client before.
5 It (had been / will have been) raining for a week by tomorrow.

A
graduate [동] 졸업하다
client [명] 고객

B 다음 밑줄 친 부분을 어법에 맞게 고치시오.

1 She went home, so I didn't see her at the party.
2 Have you ever visited our school's website before yesterday?
3 She has been posting messages online when I came back home.
4 The workers say that they have finished the construction by next week.
5 I thought that he has slept until then.

B
post [동] 게시하다
worker [명] 노동자
construction [명] 건설, 공사

C 우리말과 뜻이 같도록 주어진 말을 사용하여 문장을 완성하시오.

1 그가 밖으로 나갔을 때 나는 TV를 보고 있던 중이었다. (watch)
I ______ ______ ______ TV when he went outside.

2 Angela는 내년이면 10년째 일본에서 살아 온 게 될 것이다. (live)
Angela ______ ______ ______ in Japan for 10 years next year.

3 나는 내가 나의 노트북을 집에 두고 왔다는 것을 깨달았다. (leave)
I realized that I ______ ______ my laptop at home.

4 그 아기는 정오 무렵이면 두 시간 동안 울고 있는 게 될 것이다. (cry)
The baby ______ ______ ______ ______ for two hours by noon.

5 Sophie는 그녀의 휴대 전화를 잃어버려서 그것을 사용할 수 없었다. (lose)
Sophie ______ ______ her cell phone, so she couldn't use it.

C
realize [동] 깨닫다
laptop [명] 휴대용 컴퓨터, 노트북

REVIEW TEST

[01-02] 다음 빈칸에 들어갈 수 있는 말을 고르시오.

01

> Since Thomas Edison first made motion pictures, movies _____ very popular.

① are   ② is

③ had been   ④ have been

⑤ will be

02

> If Jonathan visits the zoo this weekend, he _____ it three times.

① visits   ② will visit

③ had visited   ④ has visited

⑤ will have visited

03 다음 우리말을 영어로 바르게 옮긴 것은?

> 내가 그곳에 도착했을 때 나는 이미 300 마일을 이동했었다.

① By the time I get there, I have already traveled 300 miles.

② By the time I get there, I had already traveled 300 miles.

③ By the time I got there, I have already traveled 300 miles.

④ By the time I got there, I had already traveled 300 miles.

⑤ By the time I get there, I will have already traveled 300 miles.

서술형

[04-05] 주어진 말을 사용하여 대화를 완성하시오.

04 A: How long have you known Emily?

B: Almost 10 years. I _____ _____ her since we were little kids. (know)

05 A: When did you start playing the violin?

B: Three months ago. I _____ _____ _____ the violin until then. (never, play)

NEW 내신기출

06 다음 문장의 빈칸에 공통으로 들어갈 수 있는 것을 모두 고르면?

> • His uncle has driven the truck _____.
> • The rain has been pouring _____.

① yesterday   ② last weekend

③ for five days   ④ since Monday

⑤ three days ago

[07-08] 두 문장의 뜻이 같도록 할 때 빈칸에 들어갈 수 있는 말을 고르시오.

07

> It began snowing two hours ago, and it is still snowing.
> → It _____ for two hours.

① is snowing   ② was snowing

③ has been snowed   ④ had snowed

⑤ has been snowing

08

> Alex wrote more than 100 poems in his life. He died in 1990.
> → Alex _____ more than 100 poems before he died in 1990.

① writes   ② has written

③ will have written   ④ has been writing

⑤ had written

[09-10] 다음 대화의 빈칸에 들어갈 수 있는 말을 고르시오.

09

> A: When was your first trip to another country?
> B: Last summer. _____

① I have never been abroad.
② I have been abroad before.
③ I will have never been abroad.
④ I had been abroad before that time.
⑤ I had never been abroad before then.

10

> A: _____
> B: That's why you look tired these days.

① I don't sleep well for a few days.
② I hadn't slept well for a few days.
③ I'll have slept well for a few days.
④ I haven't slept well for a few days.
⑤ I have been sleeping well for a few days.

서술형

[11-12] 다음 문장에서 틀린 부분을 찾아 바르게 고치시오.

11 The annual flower festival has ended last week. So we can't go there.

(   ) → (   )

12 If Kelly tries again, she has taken her driving test three times.

(   ) → (   )

서술형

[13-14] 다음 그림을 보고 주어진 말을 사용하여 문장을 완성하시오.

13

two hours ago   15 minutes ago

→ The boy _____ _____ basketball before he took a shower. (play)

14

10 years ago   now

→ Julie _____ _____ _____ as a hobby for 10 years. (paint)

15 다음 중 보기의 밑줄 친 부분과 쓰임이 같은 것은?

> ┤ 보기 ├
> Amber has never lived outside of Sydney.

① I have taken an airplane before.
② Have they found the missing child?
③ He has worked at this company since 2011.
④ Mia has gone to the USA to live with her parents.
⑤ My sister has used the same microwave oven for seven years.

16 주어진 문장과 뜻이 같도록 조건에 맞게 문장을 완성하시오.

> My coworker left for Rome. She is still there.
>
> → _____

| 조건 |
- 현재완료를 사용할 것
- go를 활용할 것
- 6단어의 완전한 문장으로 쓸 것

17 다음 중 어법상 틀린 것은?

① Had you been waiting long before the bus came?

② I will have been practicing for the dance contest for two hours by 11.

③ Darren has been busy for a week when I met him.

④ By noon, the plane to Paris will have taken off.

⑤ Leah has been talking on the phone for an hour.

18 ( ) 안에서 알맞은 말을 골라 바르게 짝지은 것은?

> ⓐ Tom (has / will have) returned from Thailand by next Saturday.
> ⓑ Jane has studied art (since / for) 2000.
> ⓒ My father (has been / had been) a police officer before he retired.

	ⓐ	ⓑ	ⓒ
①	has	– since	– had been
②	has	– for	– has been
③	will have	– since	– had been
④	will have	– for	– had been
⑤	will have	– since	– has been

19 다음 중 어법상 옳은 것을 바르게 짝지은 것은?

> ⓐ When I arrived, he had been cleaning his house.
> ⓑ She didn't admit that she had made a mistake.
> ⓒ By next year, Anna has been in Chile for 30 years.
> ⓓ Luke had hurt his leg, so he decided not to run in the race.
> ⓔ She has been standing in line for an hour when she got her ticket.

① ⓐ, ⓒ   ② ⓑ, ⓔ   ③ ⓐ, ⓑ, ⓒ

④ ⓐ, ⓑ, ⓓ   ⑤ ⓑ, ⓓ, ⓔ

[20-21] 우리말과 뜻이 같도록 주어진 말을 사용하여 문장을 완성하시오. (단, 시제에 유의할 것)

20 나는 다음 주 월요일이면 한 달간 유럽을 여행하고 있는 게 될 것이다. (travel around, Europe)

→ _____

for a month by next Monday.

21 Amy가 학생 회관에 도착했을 때 그 마술 쇼는 이미 끝났었다. (the magic show, already, finish)

→ _____

when Amy arrived at the student hall.

CHAPTER

05

조동사

can, must, should / ought to, may, need

○ **조동사**: 본동사의 뜻에 능력, 추측, 의무, 충고, 허가 등의 뜻을 더한다. 조동사 뒤에는 항상 동사원형을 쓴다.

1 can: 능력·가능, 허가, 부정 추측의 뜻을 더한다.

We **can[are able to] translate** French into Korean. (능력·가능: '…할 수 있다' / = be able to)

Can I take your order now? (허가: '…해도 좋다')

That **can't[cannot] be** Tom; he's gone to Canada. (부정 추측: '…일 리가 없다')

> **Tip 주의!** 두 개의 조동사를 함께 쓸 수 없으므로 다른 조동사와 함께 쓸 때는 be able to를 쓴다.
> She **will be able to** drive next year.

2 must: 의무, 강한 추측의 뜻을 더한다.

Soldiers **must[have to] wear** a uniform. (의무: '…해야 한다' /= have to)

He **must be** tired after volunteering at the hospital. (강한 추측: '…임이 틀림없다')

> **Tip 주의!** must not과 don't have to
> You **must not use** your phone during the play. (강한 금지: '…해서는 안 된다')
> You **don't have to buy** this lotion. (불필요: '…할 필요가 없다' / = don't need to / need not)

3 should / ought to: 의무, 충고의 뜻을 더한다. ('…해야 한다', '…하는 것이 좋다')

You **should[ought to] eat** a balanced diet.

You **should not[ought not to] miss** this chance.

> **Tip 비교!** must / have to와 should / ought to
> • **must / have to**: 법적이거나 상황·규칙에 의해 어쩔 수 없이 해야 하는 강한 의무를 나타낼 때 주로 사용
> • **should / ought to**: 사회적 관습이나 윤리에 따른 충고나 권유를 나타낼 때 주로 사용

4 may: 허가, 약한 추측의 뜻을 더한다.

You **may come** here anytime after seven. (허가: '…해도 좋다')

It **may** or **may not be** true. (약한 추측: '…일지도 모른다')

5 need: 의무의 뜻을 더하며, 긍정문에서는 일반동사로만 쓴다.

Need he **work** on Saturday? (의무: '…할 필요가 있다')

She *needs to take* a walk every day. (일반동사 need to-v: '…할 필요가 있다')

> **Tip 비교!** need not과 don't need to: '…할 필요가 없다'
> • 조동사일 때 부정: You **needn't[need not]** apologize to me.
> • 일반동사일 때 부정: You **don't need to** apologize to me.

SPEED CHECK

빈칸에 알맞은 말을 고르시오.

You can't _____ photos in this museum.

① take   ② to take   ③ taking   ④ takes   ⑤ taken

PRACTICE TEST

정답 및 해설 p.15

A ( ) 안에서 알맞은 말을 고르시오.

1 They will (can / be able to) learn German easily with native teachers.
2 You (ought to not / ought not to) throw food at the monkeys in the cage.
3 We will eat out, so I (must not / don't have to) cook tonight.
4 The drought is severe, but it (should / may) rain soon.
5 Liam (must / should) be tired of staying up all night studying.

B 두 문장의 뜻이 같도록 문장을 완성하시오.

1 My father must go to work this Sunday.
  → My father _____ _____ go to work this Sunday.

2 Can I park my car in your spot for a while?
  → _____ I park my car in your spot for a while?

C 우리말과 뜻이 같도록 조동사와 주어진 말을 사용하여 문장을 완성하시오.

1 저 남자는 그녀의 오빠일 리가 없다. (be)
  That man _____ _____ her brother.

2 Allison은 내일 집에 오지 않을지도 모른다. (come)
  Allison _____ _____ _____ home tomorrow.

3 너는 약을 복용할 때 조심해야 한다. (be careful)
  You _____ _____ _____ when you take medicine.

4 너는 그의 외모로 그를 판단해서는 안 된다. (judge)
  You _____ _____ _____ him by his appearance.

5 너는 나를 위해 음량을 낮출 필요는 없다. (turn down)
  You _____ _____ _____ _____ _____ the volume for me.

6 Eric은 아침을 걸렀다. 그는 배가 고픈 것이 틀림없다. (be)
  Eric skipped breakfast. He _____ _____ hungry.

7 너는 충분한 시간이 있다. 너는 서두를 필요가 없다. (hurry)
  You have enough time. You _____ _____ _____.

A
German 몡 독일어
native 몡 (사람이) 모국어를
  하는
cage 몡 (짐승의) 우리
eat out 외식하다
drought 몡 가뭄
severe 몡 심한
stay up all night
밤을 새다

B
spot 몡 (특정한) 장소, 자리
for a while 잠시 (동안)

C
take medicine
약을 복용하다
judge 통 판단하다
appearance 몡 (겉)모습,
  외모
turn down
(소리를) 낮추다
volume 몡 볼륨, 음량
skip 통 거르다

had better, would rather, would, used to

1 had better: '…하는 게 좋겠다' (강한 충고나 권고)

You **had better listen** carefully and **take** notes during class.

You'**d better hurry up** if you want to get home before dark.

We **had better not be** late for work again.

2 would rather: '(차라리) …하는 편이 낫다' (선호)

It's beginning to rain. I **would rather stay** home.

I'**d rather not take** Mr. Kim's class.

> **Tip 비교!** would rather A than B: 'B하느니 차라리 A하겠다'
>
> I'**d rather** *play* sports **than** *play* games.
>
> I'**d rather spend** my money on *food* **than** *clothes*.

3 would: '…하곤 했다' (과거의 습관)

I **would** sometimes **go** bike riding with Jacob.

My family **would play** baseball on weekends.

4 used to: 과거의 습관이나 상태를 나타낸다.

I **used to go** mountain climbing every weekend. (과거의 습관: '…하곤 했다')

Bella **used to believe in** Santa Claus when she was a kid. (과거의 상태: '…이었다')

I **used not to exercise** regularly. (= I **didn't use to exercise** regularly.)

> **Tip 주의!** 과거의 습관을 나타낼 때는 would와 used to를 둘 다 쓸 수 있지만, 과거의 상태를 나타낼 때는 used to만 쓴다.
>
> I **would[used to] talk** about my dream with my friends.
>
> There **used to be** a café near my house.
>
> (← There **would be** a café near my house.)

SPEED CHECK ▶

빈칸에 알맞은 말을 고르시오.

1 You had better _____ their decision.

① accept   ② to accept   ③ accepting   ④ accepts   ⑤ accepted

2 My dog _____ hide my shoes. But he doesn't anymore.

① must   ② should   ③ used to   ④ had better   ⑤ would rather

PRACTICE TEST

정답 및 해설 p.15

A ( ) 안에서 알맞은 말을 고르시오.

1 You (used to / had better) start eating more vegetables for your health.

2 The bus is too crowded. I would (rather / better) take a taxi.

3 I (used to / would) be very shy when I was young.

4 I would rather go jogging (than / to) read a book.

5 I want to lose weight. So I (had not better / had better not) eat so much meat.

A
shy ⓥ 수줍음을 타는
meat ⓝ 고기, 육류

B 보기에서 알맞은 말을 골라 빈칸에 쓰시오. (단, 한 번씩만 쓸 것)

| 보기 | would rather   had better   would   used to |

1 너는 너무 많은 귀걸이를 사지 않는 게 좋겠다.

→ You _____ not buy too many earrings.

2 Daniel은 여자친구가 있었지만 지금 그는 혼자이다.

→ Daniel _____ have a girlfriend, but now he is single.

3 나는 변명하느니 차라리 진실을 말하겠다.

→ I _____ tell the truth than make excuses.

4 Ethan은 시간이 있을 때 그의 친구와 낚시하러 가곤 했다.

→ Ethan _____ go fishing with his friend when he had time.

B
single ⓥ 단 하나의;
*혼자의, 독신의
excuse ⓝ 변명

C 우리말과 뜻이 같도록 주어진 말을 사용하여 문장을 완성하시오.

1 그녀는 빗소리를 좋아했었다. (like)

She _____ _____ _____ the sound of rain.

2 늦었으니 나는 차라리 거기에 가지 않는 편이 낫겠다. (go)

As it's late, I would _____ _____ _____ there.

3 나는 나의 형들과 보드게임을 하곤 했다. (play board games)

I _____ _____ _____ _____ with my brothers.

4 나는 그의 명령을 따르느니 차라리 그만두겠다. (quit)

I _____ _____ _____ _____ follow his orders.

5 너는 네 친구들에게 그 소문에 대해 말하지 않는 게 좋겠다. (tell)

You _____ _____ _____ _____ your friends about the rumor.

C
quit ⓥ 그만두다
order ⓝ 순서; *명령
rumor ⓝ 소문

조동사＋have v-ed

○ **조동사＋have v-ed:** 과거의 일에 대한 추측, 유감, 가정 등을 나타낸다.

1 must have v-ed: '…했음이 틀림없다' (과거의 일에 대한 강한 추측)

Marie missed her flight. She **must have been** upset.

He **must have lied** to me. He kept avoiding my eyes.

2 can't have v-ed: '…했을 리 없다' (과거의 일에 대한 강한 의심)

My little brother **can't have read** such a difficult book.

David **can't have recognized** me. I was wearing a mask.

3 should have v-ed: '…했어야 했는데 (하지 않았다)' (과거의 일에 대한 후회나 유감)

The concert was great. You **should have come**.

I **should** not **have made** such a silly mistake.

4 may[might] have v-ed: '…했을지도 모른다' (과거의 일에 대한 약한 추측)

Eric **may have had** a stomachache from eating cold food.

I can't find my keys. I **might have left** them in my car.

5 could have v-ed: '…할 수도 있었다' (과거의 일에 대한 가능성이나 후회)

I **could have slept** longer, but I got up early.

You need to be more careful. You **could have hurt** someone in that accident.

SPEED CHECK

우리말과 뜻이 같도록 할 때 빈칸에 알맞은 말을 고르시오.

1 Sarah는 어제 우리 언니의 충고를 받아들였어야 했다.

→ Sarah _____ my sister's advice yesterday.

① should take   ② may have taken   ③ could have taken

④ should have taken   ⑤ must have taken

2 그는 그 당시에 Kate의 남자친구였을지도 모른다.

→ He _____ Kate's boyfriend at that time.

① may be   ② can't have been   ③ must have been

④ should have been   ⑤ may have been

PRACTICE TEST

정답 및 해설 p.16

A

(   ) 안에서 알맞은 말을 고르시오.

1 I ate all the food. I (must / should) have left some for my sister.
2 I didn't hear the bell. I (may / should) have been asleep.
3 She (can't / must) have failed the test. She studied hard.
4 He (can't / must) have lived in Seoul. He knows a lot about it.

B

우리말과 뜻이 같도록 다음 문장을 바르게 고치시오.

1 나는 오늘 아침에 늦잠을 잤다. 나는 내 자명종을 맞췄어야 했다.
I overslept this morning. I must have set my alarm clock.

2 Susan은 피곤해 보인다. 그녀는 어젯밤에 늦게 잤을지도 모른다.
Susan looks tired. She could have gone to bed late last night.

3 Fred가 이 훌륭한 파스타를 만들었을 리 없다. 그는 요리 솜씨가 좋지 않다.
Fred should have made this great pasta. He's not a good cook.

4 Leah의 눈이 빨갛다. 그녀는 울었음이 틀림없다.
Leah's eyes are red. She may have cried.

C

우리말과 뜻이 같도록 주어진 말을 사용하여 문장을 완성하시오.
(단, 부정문은 줄임말을 쓸 것)

1 그녀는 알약을 하루에 세 번 복용했어야 했다. (take)
She _______ _______ _______ a pill three times a day.

2 나는 그의 나이에 대해 묻지 말았어야 했다. (ask)
I _______ _______ _______ about his age.

3 그는 나의 생일을 잊었을 리 없다. (forget)
He _______ _______ _______ my birthday.

4 Jimmy가 네 컴퓨터를 고장 냈을지도 모른다. (break)
Jimmy _______ _______ _______ your computer.

5 Tim은 그의 카디건을 찾을 수 없었다. 그의 남동생이 그것을 가져갔음이 틀림없다. (take)
Tim couldn't find his cardigan. His brother _______ _______ _______ it.

6 그녀는 그의 전화를 받을 수도 있었지만 받지 않았다. (answer)
She _______ _______ _______ his call, but she didn't.

A
leave [동] 떠나다; *남기다 (left-left)

B
oversleep [동] 늦잠을 자다 (overslept-overslept)
set [동] 놓다; *(시계를) 맞추다 (set-set)
alarm clock 자명종

C
pill [명] 알약
break [동] 깨다; *고장 내다 (broke-broken)
cardigan [명] 카디건

REVIEW TEST

[01-02] 다음 빈칸에 들어갈 수 있는 말을 고르시오.

01
> Our car broke down, so we _____ go to the air show.

① might   ② couldn't

③ would   ④ must not

⑤ ought not to

02
> This fruit _____ smell weird, but it tastes amazing.

① may   ② can't

③ had to   ④ ought to

⑤ would rather

NEW **내신 기출**

03 다음 대화의 빈칸에 알맞은 말을 쓸 때 필요한 단어로만 이루어진 것은?

> A: Did your aunt pass the driving test?
> B: _____. She bought a new car recently.

① she, must, passed, it

② she, should, have, pass, it

③ she, can't, have, passed, it

④ she, must, have, passed, it

⑤ she, don't, have to, pass, it

서술형

04 조동사를 사용하여 대화를 완성하시오.

> A: I will buy a new tent for my family's camping trip!
> B: Oh, you _____ _____ _____. You can borrow mine!

[05-06] 다음 밑줄 친 부분과 바꿔 쓸 수 있는 말을 고르시오.

05
> You <u>should</u> listen carefully when others speak.

① can   ② may

③ used to   ④ ought to

⑤ would rather

06
> Bees <u>can</u> communicate with other bees by dancing.

① may   ② should

③ have to   ④ had better

⑤ are able to

서술형

[07-09] 두 문장의 뜻이 같도록 문장을 완성하시오.

07 I am sure that Erica is not satisfied with her current job.
> → Erica _____ _____ satisfied with her current job.

08 I'm sorry that I didn't check the weather before going out. Now our plans are ruined.
> → I _____ _____ _____ the weather before going out. Now our plans are ruined.

09 My father played golf, but he doesn't play it anymore.
> → My father _____ _____ play golf.

[10-11] 다음 중 어법상 **틀린** 것을 고르시오.

10 ① You had better not dive into the lake.

② Michael may not be ready for the exam.

③ There would be a temple on the corner.

④ I shouldn't have driven my car that fast.

⑤ That man must have been the suspect.

11 ① I would travel with my grandparents.

② He must leave for New York yesterday.

③ People ought to respect each other more.

④ She will not be able to do her job well.

⑤ Tom should have tried different kinds of food.

[12-13] 다음 빈칸에 공통으로 들어갈 수 있는 말을 고르시오.

12
- Jamie canceled the meeting. He _____ be sick.
- You _____ teach your child not to talk to strangers.

① can't   ② must

③ need to   ④ ought to

⑤ should

13
- I _____ go fishing many years ago.
- There _____ be an old bench around here.

① can't   ② should

③ ought to   ④ had better

⑤ used to

14 (A)와 (B)에서 알맞은 말을 골라 어법에 맞게 바꿔 문장을 완성하시오.

(A) | may | can't | had better |

(B)
go to bed earlier
prepare dinner for oneself
get cold in the evening

1) You look tired.

You _____.

2) Bring your jacket with you.

It _____.

3) I _____.

Please help me.

[15-16] 다음 우리말을 영어로 바르게 옮긴 것을 고르시오.

15
그 직원들은 오늘 지쳤음이 틀림없다.

① The staff must be exhausted today.

② The staff may have been exhausted today.

③ The staff must have been exhausted today.

④ The staff could have been exhausted today.

⑤ The staff should have been exhausted today.

16
나는 공항에 그녀를 마중 가야 할 것이다.

① I'll meet her at the airport.

② I have to meet her at the airport.

③ I'd better meet her at the airport.

④ I'd like to meet her at the airport.

⑤ I'll have to meet her at the airport.

17 다음 문장을 해석한 것 중 <u>틀린</u> 것을 모두 고르면?

① David can't have stolen the money.
→ David는 그 돈을 훔칠 수 없었다.

② She should have been more careful.
→ 그녀는 더 신중했어야 했다.

③ If you want, you may stay here.
→ 네가 원한다면 너는 여기서 머물러도 된다.

④ You don't have to buy that cap.
→ 너는 저 모자를 사서는 안 된다.

⑤ You had better change your decision.
→ 너는 네 결정을 바꾸는 게 좋겠다.

서술형 NEW 내신 기출

18 우리말과 뜻이 같도록 조건에 맞게 문장을 완성하시오.

너는 거기에 혼자 가지 않는 게 좋겠다.
→ _____

─────| 조건 |─────
• go, alone을 활용할 것
• 축약형으로 쓰지 말 것
• 7단어의 완전한 문장으로 쓸 것

서술형

[19-21] 다음 문장에서 <u>틀린</u> 부분을 찾아 바르게 고치시오.

19 He was not shocked when he heard the news.
He should have already heard about it.
(   ) → (   )

20 Those earrings are really popular. They have to be sold out.
(   ) → (   )

21 I'm too hungry to concentrate in class.
I may have had breakfast this morning.
(   ) → (   )

고난도

22 다음 중 어법상 옳은 것을 바르게 짝지은 것은?

ⓐ You ought to not avoid challenges.
ⓑ She needn't worry about losing her job.
ⓒ My baby sister will can walk next year.
ⓓ The thief can't have run far from here.
ⓔ I used to live in the Netherlands when I was a kid.

① ⓑ, ⓔ   ② ⓑ, ⓓ   ③ ⓐ, ⓒ, ⓓ
④ ⓑ, ⓓ, ⓔ   ⑤ ⓑ, ⓒ, ⓔ

서술형

[23-26] 우리말과 뜻이 같도록 조동사와 주어진 말을 사용하여 문장을 완성하시오.

23 나는 콜라를 마시느니 차라리 물을 마시겠다.
(drink, water)
→ I _____ _____ _____ _____ Coke.

24 Ted는 영화에 관심이 아주 많기 때문에 그는 그 영화를 봤을지도 모른다. (watch)
→ As Ted is very interested in movies, he _____ _____ _____ the film.

25 그녀가 나를 필요로 했을 때 나는 그녀를 도와줬어야 했다. (help)
→ I _____ _____ _____ her when she needed me.

26 나는 문제아가 될 수도 있었다. (be)
→ I _____ _____ _____ a troublemaker.

CHAPTER

06

수동태

수동태의 의미와 형태

A

수동태: 『be동사+v-ed(+by+행위자)』의 형태로, 주어가 행위의 영향을 받거나 당하는 것을 나타낸다.

The fish **was caught** by a little boy. (수동태: 행위의 대상에 주목)

A little boy **caught** the fish. (능동태: 행위의 주체에 주목)

> **Tip 주의!** happen, appear, disappear 등 목적어가 필요 없는 동사나, 소유·상태 등을 나타내는 동사 have('…을 가지다'),
> become('…에 어울리다'), belong to('…의 소유이다'), resemble('…을 닮다') 등은 수동태로 쓰지 않는다.
> All the light suddenly **disappeared**. (← All the light ~~is~~ suddenly **disappeared**.)
> Jack **resembles** his mother. (← ~~His mother is resembled by Jack.~~)

B

행위자의 생략: 행위자가 막연한 일반인을 나타낼 때, 중요하지 않을 때, 이미 누군지 알거나 분명하지 않을 때
『by+행위자』를 생략할 수 있다.

Pizza **is loved** around the world. (행위자가 막연한 일반인)

The bridge **was built** 20 years ago. (행위자가 분명하지 않음)

> **Tip 주의!** 실제로 수동태는 행위자를 밝혀야 하는 경우를 제외하고 대개 『by + 행위자』 없이 쓴다.

C

수동태의 여러 형태

1 미래시제: will be v-ed

You **will be paid** 30 dollars for your work.

2 완료형: have/had been v-ed

The baby **has been given** a lot of love by her parents.

3 진행형: 『be동사+being v-ed』

The escalator **is being repaired**.

4 조동사의 수동태: 『조동사+be v-ed』

This machine **can be operated** with ease by anybody.

> **✓ Grammar UP** 의문사가 능동태의 주어인 경우의 수동태: 『By+의문사+be동사+주어(능동태의 목적어)+v-ed?』
> **By whom was** this beautiful picture **painted**?
> (← **Who painted** this beautiful picture?)

SPEED CHECK ▶

빈칸에 알맞은 말을 고르시오.

1 The traditional clothes of Korea _____ *hanbok* in Korean.

① called   ② calls   ③ being called   ④ are calling   ⑤ are called

2 A beautiful beach _____ from my hotel room.

① can see   ② can seen   ③ can be seen   ④ can is seen   ⑤ can be seen by

PRACTICE TEST

정답 및 해설 p.17

A ( ) 안에서 알맞은 말을 고르시오.

1 The short story (wrote / was written) by an unknown author.
2 Something funny (happened / was happened) to me.
3 The robot should (fix / be fixed) by tomorrow.
4 The new idea (has / has been) suggested by Tom.
5 The song is (being / been) played by Bob on his cello.
6 Her goal will (achieve / be achieved) someday.

A
unknown [형] 알려지지 않은, 무명의
author [명] 작가
suggest [동] 제안하다
someday [부] 언젠가

B 다음 문장을 수동태 문장으로 바꿔 쓰시오.

1 The managers are discussing the problem.
→ ____________________

2 My boss has not told me about the business trip.
→ ____________________

3 The programmers must correct the errors.
→ ____________________

4 The chef will prepare the main dish.
→ ____________________

B
manager [명] 경영자, 관리자
discuss [동] …에 관해 논의하다
business trip 출장
correct [동] 바로잡다
error [명] 실수, 오류
main dish 주요리

C 우리말과 뜻이 같도록 주어진 말을 사용하여 문장을 완성하시오.

1 그 대회는 어제 취소되었어야 했다. (have to, cancel)
The contest ______ ______ ______ ______ yesterday.

2 내 교복은 지금 세탁되고 있다. (wash)
My school uniform ______ ______ ______ now.

3 이번 주말에 Robert의 생일 파티가 열릴 것이다. (hold)
Robert's birthday party ______ ______ ______ this weekend.

4 이 커피 머신은 지난해 이래로 고장 나 있다. (break)
This coffee machine ______ ______ ______ since last year.

5 이 책들은 내일 공공 도서관에 반납되어야 한다. (should, return)
These books ______ ______ ______ to the public library tomorrow.

6 나의 왼쪽 다리는 공원에서 어떤 개에게 물렸다. (bite)
My left leg ______ ______ ______ a dog in the park.

C
hold [동] (회의·시합 등을) 열다, 개최하다
return [동] 돌아오다; *반납하다
public [형] 일반인의, 대중의; *공공의
bite [동] 물다 (bit-bitten)

4형식·5형식 문장의 수동태

1 4형식 문장의 수동태 전환
- 대개 간접목적어와 직접목적어를 각각 수동태의 주어로 하는 두 가지 형태가 가능하다.
- 직접목적어를 수동태 문장의 주어로 할 때 대부분의 4형식 동사는 간접목적어 앞에 전치사 to를, make, buy, get, cook 등의 동사는 전치사 for를 쓴다.

The farmer **gave** *him a loaf of bread*.
→ *He* **was given** a loaf of bread by the farmer.
→ *A loaf of bread* **was given to him** by the farmer.

> **Tip 주의!** 전치사 for를 쓰는 동사는 직접목적어만 수동태 문장의 주어로 쓰며, 간접목적어를 주어로 쓰면 어색하다.
> My father *bought* **me a new bicycle**.
> → **A new bicycle** *was bought* **for me** by my father.
> → ~~I *was bought* a new bicycle by my father.~~

2 5형식 문장의 수동태 전환

1) 대부분 5형식 문장의 수동태 전환: 대부분 5형식 문장은 목적격 보어를 그대로 둔다.

His smile **made** me **happy**.
→ I **was made happy** by his smile.

My teacher **told** me **to be** quiet in class.
→ I **was told to be** quiet in class by my teacher.

People **consider** Shakespeare **one of the greatest writers** ever.
→ Shakespeare **is considered one of the greatest writers** ever.

2) 지각동사의 수동태: 목적격 보어로 쓰인 동사원형은 수동태 문장에서 현재분사나 to부정사로 바꾼다.

Sue **saw** him **stand** by the window.
→ He **was seen standing[to stand]** by the window by Sue.

3) 사역동사로 쓰인 make의 수동태: 목적격 보어로 쓰인 동사원형은 수동태 문장에서 to부정사로 바꾼다.

They **made** me **follow** the rules.
→ I **was made to follow** the rules by them.

SPEED CHECK

빈칸에 알맞은 말을 고르시오.

1 Becky _____ a sleeping bag by her friend for her camping trip.
① lend ② lending ③ lent ④ am lending ⑤ was lent

2 We were made _____ thirty words every day.
① memorize ② memorizes ③ memorizing ④ memorized ⑤ to memorize

PRACTICE TEST

정답 및 해설 p.18

A ( ) 안에서 알맞은 말을 고르시오.

1 She was seen (surf / surfing) the Internet.
2 He was (given / given to) no warning by anyone.
3 English was taught (to / of) me by Ms. Smith last semester.
4 The dance was made (popular / be popular) by a famous dancer.
5 Lily was made (go / to go) home early by the teacher.

A
warning [명] 경고
semester [명] 학기

B 다음 문장을 수동태 문장으로 바꿔 쓰시오.

1 She brought me a thick coat.
→ I ______________________ by her.
→ A thick coat ______________________ by her.

2 My father found me sleeping on the couch.
→ I ______________________ by my father.

3 Mr. Green allowed them to come an hour later.
→ They ______________________ by Mr. Green.

4 The king bought the princess this dress.
→ This dress ______________________ by the king.

B
thick [형] 두꺼운
couch [명] 길고 푹신한 의자

C 우리말과 뜻이 같도록 주어진 말을 사용하여 문장을 완성하시오.

1 Michael은 그 자선 단체에 100달러를 기부하도록 요청되었다. (ask, donate)
Michael _______ _______ _______ _______ $100 to the charity.

2 한 앵무새가 짧은 문장들을 말하는 것이 들렸다. (hear, speak)
A parrot _______ _______ _______ short sentences.

3 그의 사진은 나에게 보이지 않았다. (show)
His picture _______ _______ _______ _______ me.

4 직원들은 매장에서 명찰을 착용하게 되었다. (make, wear)
The employees _______ _______ _______ _______ name tags in the store.

5 그 빨간 드레스는 나를 위해 만들어졌다. (make)
The red dress _______ _______ _______ me.

C
donate [동] 기부하다
charity [명] 자선 단체
parrot [명] 앵무새
employee [명] 직원
name tag 명찰

주의해야 할 수동태

1 by 이외의 전치사를 쓸 수 있는 수동태: 이때 과거분사(v-ed)가 형용사의 성질이 강해지므로 숙어처럼 숙지한다.

- be interested in: '···에 관심이 있다'
- be satisfied with: '···에 만족하다'
- be pleased with: '···에 기뻐하다'
- be covered with[in]: '···로 덮여 있다'

- be surprised at: '···에 놀라다'
- be disappointed in[at / with]: '···에 실망하다'
- be worried about: '···에 대해 걱정하다'
- be crowded with: '···로 붐비다'

She **was pleased with** my exam result.
Are you **interested in** joining the music club?

 by 이외의 전치사를 쓰는 기타 수동태 표현

- be made of: '···로 만들어지다' (원형이 남음)
- be made from: '···로 만들어지다' (원형이 변형됨)
- be filled with: '···로 가득 차다' (= be full of)
- be known to: '···에게 알려지다'

This necklace **is made of** pure gold.
Bread **is made from** flour.

2 동사구의 수동태: 동사구 전체를 하나의 동사로 묶어 취급한다.

He **was run over** by a truck but didn't get injured.

The patient **was looked after** by his granddaughter.

3 목적어가 that절인 문장의 수동태: 가주어 it을 사용하여 『it+be동사+v-ed that ·····』의 형태로 쓴다.

They **decided that** the hospital should close.
→ **It was decided that** the hospital should close (by them).

 say, believe, think, expect, consider, report 등의 동사:
that절의 주어를 수동태 문장의 주어로 할 수도 있다. 이때 that절의 동사를 to부정사로 바꾼다.
They *say that* **this animation is** popular with children.
→ *It is said that* this animation is popular with children (by them).
→ **This animation** *is said* **to be** popular with children (by them).

SPEED CHECK

빈칸에 알맞은 말을 고르시오.

1 The sidewalk is covered _____ fallen leaves.

① with   ② of   ③ at   ④ from   ⑤ to

2 The computer was _____ Jake's father.

① turned by   ② turns off   ③ turned off by   ④ turn off   ⑤ turned by off

3 Vitamins are thought _____ many health benefits.

① had   ② has   ③ be had   ④ to have   ⑤ to having

PRACTICE TEST

정답 및 해설 p.19

A ( ) 안에서 알맞은 말을 고르시오.

1 The stadium was crowded (in / with) baseball fans.
2 The school president (is looked up / is looked up to) by students.
3 The oak tree is said (to be / it is) more than 200 years old.
4 Our trip (was put off / put off) because of the bad weather.
5 She is known (to / of) the world as the first female movie director.

A
look up to …을 존경하다
oak tree 참나무
put off …을 연기하다
female 혱 여성의
movie director 영화감독

B 다음 문장을 수동태 문장으로 바꿔 쓰시오.

1 The rabbit laughed at the tortoise.
→ _____ the rabbit.

2 They think that Sophie is a brilliant pianist.
→ It _____.
→ Sophie _____.

3 People believe that stress causes many health problems.
→ It _____.
→ Stress _____.

B
laugh at …을 비웃다, 놀리다
tortoise 혱 거북
brilliant 혱 훌륭한

C 우리말과 뜻이 같도록 주어진 말을 사용하여 문장을 완성하시오.
(단, by 이외의 전치사를 쓸 것)

1 그는 그 전화 상담 서비스에 만족했다. (satisfy)
He _____ _____ _____ the telephone counseling service.

2 Susie는 그의 무례한 행동에 놀랐다. (surprise)
Susie _____ _____ _____ his rude behavior.

3 Jim은 새로운 장소를 방문하는 데 관심이 있다. (interest)
Jim _____ _____ _____ visiting new places.

4 수백 명의 사람들이 그 행사에 참가할 것으로 예상된다. (expect, participate in)
Hundreds of people _____ _____ _____ _____ the event.

5 그 불쌍한 아이들은 자원봉사자들에 의해 돌봐졌다. (take care of)
The poor children _____ _____ _____ _____ by the volunteers.

C
counseling 혱 상담
rude 혱 무례한
behavior 혱 행동
participate in …에 참가하다
volunteer 혱 자원봉사자

REVIEW TEST

[01-03] 다음 빈칸에 들어갈 수 있는 말을 고르시오.

01

> The palace gates _____ at 7 p.m. every evening.

① locks   ② locking

③ be locked   ④ are locked

⑤ being locked

02

> This site _____ to a new server.

① moves   ② is being moving

③ has moved   ④ has been moved

⑤ is been moved

03

> David was made _____ to the English academy after school.

① go   ② gone

③ to go   ④ going

⑤ to going

서술형

[04-05] 다음 문장에서 <u>틀린</u> 부분을 찾아 바르게 고치시오.

04 A lot of funny pictures have posted on my blog.

(   ) → (   )

05 My younger sister is resembled by my grandmother.

(   ) → (   )

[06-08] 다음 문장을 수동태 문장으로 바꿀 때 빈칸에 들어갈 수 있는 말을 고르시오.

06

> They are redecorating the living room.
> → The living room _____ by them.

① redecorates   ② be redecorated

③ be redecorating   ④ has redecorated

⑤ is being redecorated

07

> The teacher told us to review the previous chapters for the exam.
> → We _____ the previous chapters for the exam by the teacher.

① told review   ② told to review

③ are told review   ④ were told review

⑤ were told to review

08

> Drivers must obey the new traffic rules.
> → The new traffic rules _____ by drivers.

① are obeyed   ② be obeyed

③ must obey   ④ must obeyed

⑤ must be obeyed

[09-10] 다음 빈칸에 들어갈 말을 바르게 짝지은 것을 고르시오.

09

> ⓐ The gift box was sent _____ him.
> ⓑ This paper carnation was made _____ my mother.

	ⓐ	ⓑ		ⓐ	ⓑ
①	to	– with	②	of	– with
③	to	– for	④	in	– for
⑤	of	– at			

10

> ⓐ They were surprised _____ the number of people at the party.
> ⓑ In summer, the beach is very crowded _____ tourists.

	ⓐ	ⓑ		ⓐ	ⓑ
①	at	– in	②	at	– with
③	of	– with	④	of	– in
⑤	by	– to			

NEW **내신 기출**

11 다음 중 빈칸에 들어갈 말이 보기와 <u>다른</u> 것은?

> —| 보기 |—
> They were asked _____ remain patient during the delays.

① My grandfather is said _____ have been a brave man.
② I was made _____ do the dishes by Mr. Jones.
③ A pair of skates was bought _____ my son by his coach.
④ The ring was given _____ her years ago by her mother.
⑤ My name will be known _____ everyone if I reach the summit of Mt. Everest.

서술형

[12-13] 주어진 말을 어법에 맞게 바꿔 쓰시오.

12 Some books in the bookstore _____ for half price last week. (sell)

13 The tiger is said _____ the king of the animals. (be)

서술형 **NEW** **내신 기출**

14 다음 대화의 빈칸에 들어갈 한 단어와 보기의 단어를 한 번씩만 사용하여 문장을 완성하시오.

> A: Are you satisfied _____ your school life?
> B: Sure. I like my teachers and classmates. We play basketball together after lunch.

> —| 보기 |—
> passengers   was   the   filled   subway

→ _____

고난도

[15-16] 다음 중 어법상 <u>틀린</u> 것을 모두 고르시오.

15 ① Your suggestion will be considered again.
② Cupcakes are being made in the kitchen.
③ He is believed that he is the only witness to the murder.
④ Henry was seen to enter the aquarium yesterday.
⑤ I was given to many farewell presents by my friends.

16
① Patrick was told to help Suji with her homework.
② The kitten was taken care by Helen.
③ Stella is said to speak more than five languages.
④ Security cameras installed in the parking lot last week.
⑤ This bracelet was made for Lia.

서술형

[17-18] 다음 그림을 보고 주어진 말을 사용하여 문장을 완성하시오.

17

The top of the mountain
_____ . _____
_____ . (cover, snow)

18

My desk _____ _____
_____ _____ .
(make, wood)

고난도

19 다음 중 어법상 옳은 것은 모두 몇 개인가?

ⓐ James was seen break the window by me.
ⓑ Jane was allowed to travel with her friends.
ⓒ All the files on my laptop disappeared due to the virus.
ⓓ His new album will release in a month.
ⓔ Claire was sent an email by her friend in Germany.

① 1개 ② 2개 ③ 3개
④ 4개 ⑤ 5개

20 다음 문장을 수동태 문장으로 바꿀 때 틀린 것은?

① You must finish your report by noon.
→ Your report must be finished by noon.
② Ava heard Tom laugh in front of the TV.
→ Tom was heard laughing in front of the TV by Ava.
③ My boyfriend made me a red sweater.
→ A red sweater was made to me by my boyfriend.
④ They will choose Anderson as the class president.
→ Anderson will be chosen as the class president.
⑤ Sam has made a model airplane for the contest.
→ A model airplane has been made for the contest by Sam.

서술형

[21-22] 우리말과 뜻이 같도록 주어진 말을 사용하여 문장을 완성하시오.

21 나는 과속으로 70달러를 지불하게 되었다.
(make, pay)
→ I _____ _____ _____ _____ $70 for speeding.

22 그 영화 포스터가 지금 인쇄되고 있다. (print)
→ The movie poster _____ _____ _____ now.

CHAPTER

07

가정법

가정법 과거, 가정법 과거완료, 혼합 가정법

1 **가정법 과거**: 현재 사실과 반대되거나 현재 또는 미래에 실현 가능성이 거의 없는 일을 가정할 때 쓴다.
- 형태: 『If+주어+were / 동사의 과거형, 주어+would[could / might]+동사원형』
- 의미: '만약 …라면 ～할 텐데'

If Eric **were** not weak, he **could lift** heavy furniture.
(→ Because Eric is weak, he can't lift heavy furniture.)

2 **가정법 과거완료**: 과거 사실과 반대되는 상황을 가정할 때 쓴다.
- 형태: 『If+주어+had v-ed, 주어+would[could / might] have v-ed』
- 의미: '만약 …했더라면 ～했을 텐데'

If I **had heard** the alarm, I **would**n't **have been** late for the appointment.
(→ Because I didn't hear the alarm, I was late for the appointment.)

3 **혼합 가정법**: 과거에 실현되지 못한 일이 현재까지 영향을 미치는 상황을 가정할 때 쓴다.
- 형태: 『If+주어+had v-ed, 주어+would[could / might]+동사원형』
- 의미: '(과거에) 만약 …했더라면 (지금) ～할 텐데'

If it **had**n't **snowed** heavily last night, the road **would** not **be** icy today.
(→ Because it snowed heavily last night, the road is icy today.)

 Grammar UP 단순 조건문과 가정법 과거

- 단순 조건문(직설법): 실제로 발생 가능한 일을 가정한다.
  If Mina **comes** to my party tomorrow, I **will be** very happy. (파티에 올 가능성이 있음)
- 가정법 과거: 실현 가능성이 거의 없는 일을 가정한다.
  If Mina **came** to my party tomorrow, I **would be** very happy. (파티에 올 가능성이 거의 없음)

SPEED CHECK

빈칸에 알맞은 말을 고르시오.

1 If I had a car, I _____ on a trip with my family.
　① go　　　　　② went　　　　　③ would go　　　　④ will go　　　　⑤ am going to go

2 If I had been there, I _____ Mr. Brown.
　① saw　　　　　② could see　　　　③ could seen　　　④ could have seen　　⑤ could had seen

3 If she had not taken that flight, she _____ here now.
　① is　　　　　② was　　　　　③ might be　　　　④ may be　　　　⑤ might have been

PRACTICE TEST

정답 및 해설 p.20

A 두 문장의 뜻이 같도록 문장을 완성하시오.

1 If Julia _______ tall, she _______ _______ the volleyball team.
→ Because Julia isn't tall, she can't join the volleyball team.

2 If Ella _______ _______ _______ her scarf at school, she _______ _______ it now.
→ Ella left her scarf at school, so she can't wear it now.

3 If I _______ _______ _______ to send her an invitation, she _______ _______ _______ _______.
→ I remembered to send her an invitation, so she could come.

A
volleyball [명] 배구
invitation [명] 초대(장)

B 보기에서 알맞은 말을 골라 어법에 맞게 바꿔 쓰시오. (단, 한 번씩만 쓸 것)

보기	be	eat	succeed	practice	follow	need

1 We could go to the amusement park if Jenny ____________ not busy.
2 If she ____________ more, she could have finished the marathon.
3 If Ryan had not believed in himself, he could not ____________.
4 If I ____________ lunch an hour ago, I wouldn't be hungry now.
5 We ____________ the police if everyone were honest.
6 If I ____________ the doctor's advice last week, I wouldn't be sick now.

B
amusement park 놀이공원
marathon [명] 마라톤
advice [명] 조언, 충고

C 우리말과 뜻이 같도록 주어진 말을 사용하여 가정법 문장을 완성하시오.

1 만약 우리가 KTX를 타면 우리는 시간을 절약할 텐데. (take, save)
If we _______ the KTX, we _______ _______ time.

2 만약 내가 노트북을 어제 고쳤더라면 나는 오늘 그것을 사용할 수 있을 텐데. (fix, use)
If I _______ _______ the laptop yesterday, I _______ _______ it today.

3 만약 내게 호박이 충분히 있었더라면 나는 호박파이를 구웠을 텐데. (have, bake)
If I _______ _______ enough pumpkin, I _______ _______ _______ a pumpkin pie.

4 만약 오늘 그 미술관이 문을 연다면 너는 거기에 갈 수 있을 텐데. (be, go)
If the gallery _______ open today, you _______ _______ there.

C
save [동] 구하다; *절약하다
pumpkin [명] 호박
gallery [명] 미술관, 화랑

I wish, as if, without[but for], it's time

1 I wish 가정법: 현재 또는 미래의 소망이나 과거 사실과 반대되는 소망을 나타낸다.

  1) 『I wish + 가정법 과거』: '…라면 좋을 텐데'

  I **wish** I **knew** all of the answers on the science test.

  (→ I'm sorry I don't know all of the answers on the science test.)

  2) 『I wish + 가정법 과거완료』: '…했더라면 좋을 텐데'

  I **wish** you **had** not **shown** him that picture.

  (→ I'm sorry you showed him that picture.)

2 as if[though] 가정법: 현재나 과거의 사실과 반대되는 내용을 가정한다.

  1) 『as if[though] + 가정법 과거』: '마치 …인 것처럼'

  Diana talks **as if** she **knew** everything about him.

  (→ In fact, Diana doesn't know everything about him.)

  2) 『as if[though] + 가정법 과거완료』: '마치 …였던 것처럼'

  Harry looks **as if** he **had** not **slept** last night.

  (→ In fact, Harry slept last night.)

3 without[but for] 가정법: '(만약) …가 없(었)다면'의 뜻으로, 가정법의 if절을 대신한다.

  Without[But for] the sun, nothing on earth *could survive*. (가정법 과거)

  (→ **If it were not for** the sun, ...)

  Without[But for] this map, we *would have been lost*. (가정법 과거완료)

  (→ **If it had not been for** this map, ...)

4 『it's time + 가정법 과거』: '(이제) …해야 할 때이다'의 뜻으로, 재촉이나 유감을 드러낸다.

  It's time we **took** a new approach. (→ It's time we should take a new approach.)

✔ **Grammar UP**   접속사 if가 생략된 가정법 문장

if절의 동사가 were, had, should일 때 접속사 if를 생략할 수 있다. 이때 if절의 주어와 동사를 도치한다.

Were I you, I wouldn't hesitate to help your neighbors. (= If I were you, ...)

Had it not been for her support, I **couldn't have finished** university.

(= If it had not been for her support, ...)

SPEED CHECK

빈칸에 알맞은 말을 고르시오.

1 I wish I _____ a cat to play with now.

  ① have   ② had   ③ will have   ④ have had   ⑤ had had

2 Jane behaves as if she _____ before.

  ① doesn't lie   ② didn't lie   ③ won't lie   ④ hasn't lied   ⑤ hadn't lied

PRACTICE TEST

정답 및 해설 p.21

A

다음 밑줄 친 부분을 가정법에 맞게 고치시오.

1 Kevin looks as if he is happy, but he's actually sad.
2 I wish it weren't so hot last summer.
3 If it were not for your help, I wouldn't have been able to write that book.
4 I really didn't enjoy the beach. I wish I didn't gone there.
5 John talks as if he watched that movie, but he didn't.
6 It's time you take responsibility for your decision.

A
take responsibility for …을 책임지다

B

두 문장의 뜻이 같도록 가정법 문장을 완성하시오.

1 ______ ______ ______ ______ more time to talk with you.
→ I'm sorry that I don't have more time to talk with you.

2 ______ ______ ______ ______ ______ ______ my assist, Joe couldn't have scored a goal.
→ But for my assist, Joe couldn't have scored a goal.

3 Kate acts ______ ______ ______ ______ ______ her own car.
→ In fact, Kate didn't have her own car.

4 ______ ______ ______ the danger, I would have changed my plans.
→ If I had realized the danger, I would have changed my plans.

B
assist [명] (스포츠의) 어시스트, 도움
score a goal 득점하다
realize [동] 깨닫다

C

우리말과 뜻이 같도록 주어진 말을 사용하여 가정법 문장을 완성하시오.

1 Jack은 마치 그가 왕자인 것처럼 행동한다. (be)
Jack acts ______ ______ ______ ______ a prince.

2 Carl은 마치 그가 직접 그 가수를 봤던 것처럼 말한다. (see)
Carl talks ______ ______ ______ ______ ______ the singer in person.

3 만약 그의 휴대용 컴퓨터가 없다면 나는 제시간에 그 과제를 끝낼 수 없을 텐데. (laptop)
______ ______ ______, I couldn't finish the task on time.

4 내가 그 웹사이트에서 예약을 했더라면 좋을 텐데. (make a reservation)
______ ______ ______ ______ ______ ______ ______ on the website.

5 너는 휴가를 가야 할 때야. 너는 열심히 일해 왔어. (go)
______ ______ ______ ______ on a vacation. You've worked hard.

C
in person 직접
task [명] 일, 과제
make a reservation 예약하다
go on a vacation 휴가를 가다

REVIEW TEST

[01-02] 다음 빈칸에 들어갈 수 있는 말을 고르시오.

01

> If I _____ a daily study plan, I could have gotten better grades.

① make
② made
③ have made
④ had made
⑤ will make

02

> If he hadn't bought a new refrigerator, he _____ some money now.

① has
② had
③ can have
④ would have
⑤ would have had

서술형

03 밑줄 친 부분과 뜻이 같도록 빈칸에 알맞은 말을 쓰시오.

> Without this flashlight, we couldn't have found the entrance in the dark.

1) _____ _____ this flashlight
2) _____ _____ _____ _____ this flashlight

서술형

[04-05] 두 문장의 뜻이 같도록 문장을 완성하시오.

04 My coworker speaks English _____ _____ _____ _____ _____ _____.

→ My coworker speaks English like he is an American. But in fact, he isn't an American.

05 If Patrick _____ _____ his medicine this morning, he would feel better now.

→ As Patrick didn't take his medicine this morning, he doesn't feel better now.

[06-07] 다음 밑줄 친 부분을 바르게 고친 것을 고르시오.

06

> James talks as if he <u>goes</u> skating last Sunday, but he didn't.

① went
② has gone
③ had gone
④ would go
⑤ will go

07

> I read your email too late yesterday. I wish I <u>checked</u> it sooner.

① check
② had checked
③ have checked
④ to check
⑤ checking

NEW 내신 기출

08 다음 대화의 빈칸에 공통으로 들어갈 수 있는 것은?

> • A: What _____ you do if you lost your bag in the subway?
> B: Well, I would go to the lost-and-found center.
>
> • A: If we built a new house, it _____ cost too much.
> B: I agree with you.

① do
② did
③ were
④ would
⑤ would be

서술형

[09-10] 우리말과 뜻이 같도록 <u>틀린</u> 부분을 찾아 바르게 고치시오.

09 만약 내가 지난 주말에 티켓을 구입했더라면 나는 지금 콘서트에 갈 수 있을 텐데.

If I bought a ticket last weekend, I could go to the concert now.

(   ) → (   )

10 만약 그 소방관이 없었다면 그 소녀는 생존하지 못했을 텐데.

It had not been for the firefighter, the girl could not have survived.

(   ) → (   )

서술형

[11-12] 다음 문장을 해석하시오.

11 If I had reviewed this chapter, I could answer your questions.

→ _____

12 Had it not been for the travel guide, we could not have visited all the tourist attractions.

→ _____

서술형 NEW 내신 기출

13 보기를 참고하여 주어진 문장을 가정법 문장으로 바꿔 쓰시오. (9단어)

―| 보기 |―
I'm sorry I don't know more about computers.
→ I wish I knew more about computers.

I'm sorry they painted the wall green.

→ _____

14 다음 빈칸에 들어갈 말을 바르게 짝지은 것은?

A: You have a fever. I told you to wear your coat!
B: I know. If I ___ⓐ___ to you, I ___ⓑ___ a fever right now.

           ⓐ   ⓑ

① listen   – didn't have

② listened   – didn't have

③ had listened – wouldn't have

④ had listened – wouldn't have had

⑤ listened   – wouldn't have had

서술형

[15-16] 다음 그림을 보고 주어진 말을 사용하여 문장을 완성하시오.

15

If Martin had woken up earlier, he _____ _____ _____ _____ the school bus.

(would, miss)

16

If Avery had enough money, she _____ _____ a sports car. (could, buy)

17 다음 두 문장이 같은 뜻이 되도록 할 때 <u>틀린</u> 것은?

① If Joe hadn't lost his pen, he could lend it to me.
→ As Joe lost his pen, he can't lend it to me.

② If I had a key, I could open the locker.
→ I don't have a key, so I can't open the locker.

③ Mike talks as if he lived in New York last year.
→ In fact, Mike didn't live in New York last year.

④ Had it not been for your assistance, I wouldn't have completed my essay.
→ But for your assistance, I wouldn't have completed my essay.

⑤ I wish I could remember your name.
→ I'm sorry I can't remember your name.

18 다음 중 어법상 <u>틀린</u> 것은?

① I wish I had had a violin when I was young.
② Henry talks as if he had gone out with Tara.
③ If I get home early, I will give you a call.
④ But for my friends, my life would be very boring.
⑤ If we had fixed the heater, we wouldn't have been cold now.

고난도

19 다음 중 어법상 옳은 것을 바르게 짝지은 것은?

> ⓐ It's time Ava stopped eating junk food.
> ⓑ If I were you, I would buy these earrings.
> ⓒ If you hurried, you could have seen your favorite singer at that time.
> ⓓ I wish you have enjoyed the concert yesterday.
> ⓔ Henry looks as if he knew about the rumor.

① ⓐ, ⓑ   ② ⓑ, ⓔ   ③ ⓐ, ⓑ, ⓔ
④ ⓑ, ⓒ, ⓔ   ⑤ ⓑ, ⓓ, ⓔ

서술형

[20-22] 우리말과 뜻이 같도록 주어진 말을 사용하여 가정법 문장을 완성하시오.

20 Leo는 훌륭한 배우이다. 이제 그가 상을 받아야 할 때이다. (win)
→ Leo is a great actor. _____ _____ _____ _____ an award.

21 만약 군인들이 없다면 우리는 안전하지 않을 텐데. (the soldiers)
→ _____ _____ _____ _____ _____ _____, we wouldn't be safe.

22 만약 내가 Nancy와 친했더라면 나는 그녀를 너에게 소개했을 텐데. (be close with)
→ _____ _____ _____ _____ _____ _____ Nancy, I would have introduced her to you.

CHAPTER

08

관계사

관계대명사

○ **관계대명사**: 『접속사＋대명사』의 역할을 하며, 형용사처럼 앞의 명사(선행사)를 수식한다.

Emily is **the author**. + **She** wrote ten books on English education. (the author = She)

→ Emily is *the author* **who** wrote ten books on English education.

선행사

선행사	관계대명사의 격	주격	소유격	목적격
사람		who[that]	whose	who(m)[that]
동물, 사물		which[that]	whose	which[that]
선행사 포함		what	×	what

Tip 주의! 선행사가 『사람 + 사물』, 『사람 + 동물』, all, none, any, some, ‑thing 등이거나, 최상급, 서수, the only, the very, the same, the last, all, no, any, some, every 등의 수식을 받을 때 주로 관계대명사 that을 쓴다.

Bianca yelled at *the boy and the dog* **that** were crossing her garden.

1 **주격 관계대명사**: 관계대명사가 관계사절 내에서 주어 역할을 한다.

I know *a girl* **who**[**that**] can speak Spanish very well.

The package **which**[**that**] is on the table is Kelly's.

2 **소유격 관계대명사**: 관계대명사가 관계사절 내에서 수식하는 명사의 소유격 역할을 한다.

I have *a neighbor* **whose** dog barks all the time.

I have met *a man* **whose** job is composing pop music.

3 **목적격 관계대명사**: 관계대명사가 관계사절 내에서 목적어 역할을 한다.

The woman **who**(**m**)[**that**] you met yesterday owns a café.

The handbag **which**[**that**] I bought at the mall is expensive.

4 **관계대명사 what**

- 선행사를 포함한 관계대명사로, '…한 것'이라는 뜻을 가지며 the thing(s) which[that]로 바꿔 쓸 수 있다.
- what이 이끄는 명사절은 주어, 목적어, 보어 역할을 한다.

  What surprised me *was* her bad attitude. (주어)
  (= **The thing which**[**that**])
  Can you tell me **what** you want for Christmas? (목적어)
  This is **what** we wanted to eat. (보어)

SPEED CHECK

빈칸에 알맞은 말을 고르시오.

1 The magic show _____ I saw last Sunday was very interesting.

① who ② whose ③ whom ④ which ⑤ what

2 I can't understand _____ you said to me.

① who ② whose ③ that ④ which ⑤ what

PRACTICE TEST

정답 및 해설 p.22

A ( ) 안에서 알맞은 말을 고르시오.

1 The sci-fi movie is about a boy and a robot (which / that) live together.
2 These picture books are (that / what) I read when I was a child.
3 Julia has a phone (which / whose) screen is twice as big as mine.
4 This is the wine (who / which) I bought for you in France.
5 The man (who / which) gave me this necklace became my husband.

A
sci-fi movie
공상 과학 영화
screen 똉 화면
necklace 똉 목걸이

B 관계대명사를 사용하여 두 문장을 한 문장으로 만드시오.

1 I have a friend. He wants to be an astronaut in the future.
→ I have a friend _____ in the future.

2 That is the pear tree. It was planted by my grandfather.
→ That is the pear tree _____ by my grandfather.

3 What was the first movie? The director made it.
→ What was the first movie _____ ?

4 Juliana has a younger brother. I can't remember his name.
→ Juliana has a younger brother _____ .

B
astronaut 똉 우주 비행사
pear tree 배나무
plant 똉 심다

C 우리말과 뜻이 같도록 관계대명사와 주어진 말을 사용하여 문장을 완성하시오.

1 그 왕은 욕심 많고 이기적인 사람들을 좋아하지 않는다. (people, be)
The king doesn't like _____ _____ _____ greedy and selfish.

2 내가 어제 빌린 그 소설은 재미있다. (borrow)
The novel _____ _____ _____ yesterday is interesting.

3 나는 취미가 사진 찍는 것인 친구가 한 명 있다. (hobby)
I have _____ _____ _____ _____ is taking pictures.

4 내 딸이 원하는 것은 이 스웨터이다. (daughter, want, be)
_____ _____ _____ _____ _____ this sweater.

5 그녀는 내게 동의하지 않은 유일한 사람이었다. (agree with)
She was the only person _____ _____ _____ _____ me.

C
greedy 똉 욕심 많은
selfish 똉 이기적인
agree with
…에게 동의하다

관계부사

○ **관계부사**: 『접속사＋부사(구)』의 역할을 하며, 형용사처럼 앞의 명사(선행사)를 수식한다.

I know **the year**. + The first World Cup was held **then**.

→ I know *the year* **when** the first World Cup was held.

선행사 ↑

Tip 주의! 관계부사는 『전치사 + 관계대명사』로 바꿔 쓸 수 있다.

• when: at[on / in / during] which	• where: at[on / in / to] which
• why: for which	• how: the way (in which) (보통 the way로만 씀)

There are three elevators in *the building* **where** I work.

(= **in which**)

1 when: 때를 나타내는 명사(the day, the time, the year 등)를 선행사로 한다.

Summer is *the time* **when** peaches taste most delicious.

(= during which)

2 where: 장소를 나타내는 명사(the place, the town, the city 등)를 선행사로 한다.

This is *the place* **where** my friends and I used to play hide-and-seek.

(= at which)

3 why: 이유를 나타내는 명사(the reason)를 선행사로 한다.

Do you know *the reason* **why** James and his family left his hometown?

(= for which)

4 how: 방법을 나타내는 명사(the way)를 선행사로 한다. 단, 선행사 the way와 관계부사 how는 함께 쓰지 않는다.

Can you show me **how** this copier works? (← ~~Can you show me **the way how** this copier works?~~)

(= the way)

✓ **Grammar UP** 선행사나 관계부사의 생략

관계부사의 선행사가 time, place, reason 등 시간, 장소, 이유를 나타내는 일반적인 명사일 때 관계부사와 선행사 중 하나를 생략하는 경우가 많으며, 주로 선행사를 생략한다.

Kevin recalls **when[the time / the time when]** he first met his best friend.

This is **where[the place / the place where]** I waited for Mike last Sunday.

Tell me **why[the reason / the reason why]** you were absent from school.

SPEED CHECK

빈칸에 알맞은 말을 고르시오.

1 The town _____ I grew up has changed a lot.

① when ② where ③ why ④ how ⑤ which

2 There is no reason _____ I should apologize to him.

① when ② where ③ why ④ how ⑤ which

PRACTICE TEST

정답 및 해설 p.23

A ( ) 안에서 알맞은 말을 고르시오.

1 Spring is the season (where / when) everything begins to grow.
2 The zoo is a place (where / when) you can see many wild animals.
3 I don't know (which / why) Jake was punished at school.
4 Tell me (the way how / how) I can get to City Hall from here.
5 The town (in which / for which) I was born is near a beautiful mountain.

A
punish [동] 처벌하다
City Hall 시청

B 두 문장의 의미가 같도록 빈칸에 알맞은 관계부사를 쓰시오.

1 This is the middle school at which my father teaches physics.
→ This is the middle school _______ my father teaches physics.

2 I don't know the way he makes the pasta so quickly.
→ I don't know _______ he makes the pasta so quickly.

3 I'll never forget the year in which I entered university.
→ I'll never forget the year _______ I entered university.

4 That is the reason for which Eric canceled his appointment with her.
→ That is the reason _______ Eric canceled his appointment with her.

B
physics [명] 물리학
cancel [동] 취소하다
appointment [명] 약속

C 우리말과 뜻이 같도록 관계부사와 주어진 말을 사용하여 문장을 완성하시오.

1 나는 Ken에게 그가 그렇게 빨리 그의 보고서를 완성한 방법을 물었다. (complete)
I asked Ken _______ _______ _______ his reports so quickly.

2 내일은 내가 나의 운전면허 시험을 치르는 날이다. (the day)
Tomorrow is _______ _______ _______ I take my driver's license test.

3 나에게 네가 우리와 함께 갈 수 없는 이유를 말해 줘. (the reason)
Tell me _______ _______ _______ you can't go with us.

4 교토는 내가 일본 문화에 관해 배운 장소이다. (the place)
Kyoto is _______ _______ _______ I learned about Japanese culture.

C
complete [동] 완성하다
driver's license test 운전면허 시험
culture [명] 문화

복합 관계사

A

복합 관계대명사: 『관계대명사+-ever』의 형태로 명사절이나 부사절을 이끈다.

복합 관계대명사	명사절('…든지')	부사절('…라도')
whoever	anyone who ('…하는 사람은 누구든지')	no matter who ('누가[누구를] …하더라도')
whichever	anything which ('…하는 것은 어느 것이든지')	no matter which ('어느 것이[을] …하더라도')
whatever	anything that ('…하는 것은 무엇이든지')	no matter what ('무엇이[을] …하더라도')

Jane loves **whatever** her mother cooks for her. (목적어로 쓰인 명사절)

Whatever happens, I will achieve my goal. (부사절)

Grammar UP **복합 관계형용사 whatever와 whichever**: 뒤에 오는 명사를 수식하는 형용사 역할을 하기도 한다.

• whatever: '무슨 …든지' (명사절), '무슨 …라도' (부사절)

  You may read **whatever** *book* you like.

• whichever: '어느 …든지' (명사절), '어느 …라도' (부사절)

  Whichever *road* you will take, you can get to the post office.

B

복합 관계부사: 『관계부사+-ever』의 형태로 부사절을 이끈다.

복합 관계부사	'…든지', '…나'	'…라도'
whenever	any time (that)/at any time ('…할 때는 언제나')	no matter when ('언제 …하더라도')
wherever	at/in/to any place (that) ('…하는 곳은 어디든지')	no matter where ('어디서 …하더라도')
however	·	no matter how ('어떤 방법으로[아무리] …하더라도')

Come to my house **whenever** you want.

Whenever you come, you'll be welcomed.

The singer attracts a crowd **wherever** he goes.

However hard I tried, I couldn't remove the stains from my shirt.

SPEED CHECK

빈칸에 알맞은 말을 고르시오.

1 _____ wants the map may take it.

① Whoever ② Whichever ③ Whatever ④ Wherever ⑤ However

2 _____ carefully I read this poem, I couldn't understand its meaning.

① Whoever ② Whatever ③ Whenever ④ Wherever ⑤ However

PRACTICE TEST

정답 및 해설 p.24

A ( ) 안에서 알맞은 말을 고르시오.

1 (Whoever / Whichever) sees this house wants to purchase it.
2 Steve takes his smartphone (wherever / whatever) he goes.
3 (Whichever / Wherever) shirt you buy, you will get a 20% discount.
4 (Wherever / Whatever) they may say, I will not change my mind.
5 (Whenever / Whoever) I stopped by his office, he was out.
6 (However / Whoever) rich people are, they always want more.

A
purchase [동] 사다, 구입하다
get a discount 할인을 받다
stop by …에 들르다
be out (집 등을) 비우다

B 두 문장의 뜻이 같도록 빈칸에 알맞은 말을 쓰시오.

1 No matter where the actress goes, her fan club members follow her.
→ _______ the actress goes, her fan club members follow her.

2 Anyone who visits our store today gets a free donut.
→ _______ visits our store today gets a free donut.

3 No matter how much Kevin eats, he never gains weight.
→ _______ much Kevin eats, he never gains weight.

4 No matter what you wear, you will look awesome.
→ _______ you wear, you will look awesome.

B
gain weight 체중이 늘다
awesome [형] 아주 멋진, 굉장한

C 우리말과 뜻이 같도록 복합 관계사와 주어진 말을 사용하여 문장을 완성하시오.

1 네가 무엇을 하더라도 항상 최선을 다하려고 노력해라. (do)
_______ _______ _______, always try to do your best.

2 6시 전에 오는 사람들은 누구든지 그 콘서트홀에 입장할 수 있다. (come)
_______ _______ before six can enter the concert hall.

3 나는 스트레스를 받을 때는 언제나 내가 가장 좋아하는 음악을 듣는다. (feel stressed)
_______ _______ _______ _______, I listen to my favorite music.

4 아무리 그 차의 가격이 높을지라도 나는 그것을 살 것이다. (high, the car's price)
_______ _______ _______ _______ _______ _______, I will buy it.

5 네가 무슨 결정들을 하더라도 나는 너를 지지할 거야. (decisions)
_______ _______ you make, I will support you.

C
price [명] 가격
support [동] 지지하다

주의해야 할 관계사의 용법

A

관계사의 계속적 용법: 관계사 앞에 콤마를 쓰며, 선행사에 대한 부가적인 설명을 덧붙인다.

1 **관계대명사의 계속적 용법**: who와 which만 가능하며, that은 쓸 수 없다. 『접속사＋대명사』로 바꿔 쓸 수 있다.

I called Anna, **who**(= **but she**) didn't answer the phone.

He wrote a lot of songs, **which**(= **and they**) are loved by many people.

> **Grammar UP** **계속적 용법으로 쓰인 관계대명사 which**: 앞서 나온 구나 절을 선행사로 하기도 한다.
> We tried *to open the door*, **which** was impossible. (선행사: to부정사구)
> *I saw my boss at the hospital*, **which** I didn't expect. (선행사: 앞 절 전체)

2 **관계부사의 계속적 용법**: when과 where만 가능하며, 『접속사＋부사』로 바꿔 쓸 수 있다.

The school festival will be held next week, **when**(= **and then**) the final exam is over.

I went to San Francisco, **where**(= **and there**) I met Ms. Brown.

B

관계대명사의 생략

1 **목적격 관계대명사의 생략**: 동사 및 전치사의 목적어로 쓰인 관계대명사는 생략할 수 있다.

I can't remember the bookstore (**which**[**that**]) you mentioned.

> **Tip 주의!** 계속적 용법으로 쓰인 목적격 관계대명사는 생략할 수 없다.
> The earphones, **which** I wanted to buy, are already sold out.

2 **『주격 관계대명사＋be동사』의 생략**: 『주격 관계대명사＋be동사』는 뒤에 형용사구나 분사구가 올 때 생략할 수 있다.

The woman (**who**[**that**] **is**) *drinking coffee over there* is my cousin.

C

『전치사＋관계대명사』: 관계대명사가 전치사의 목적어일 때, 전치사를 관계대명사 바로 앞에 쓰거나 관계사절 끝에 쓴다.
단, 관계대명사를 생략할 경우 전치사를 반드시 관계사절 끝에 쓴다.

This is the house **in which** the sports star lives.

→ This is the house (**which**[**that**]) the sports star lives **in**.

> **Tip 주의!** 전치사 뒤에는 관계대명사 that이나 who를 쓸 수 없다.
> → ~~This is the house **in that** the sports star lives.~~

> **Grammar UP** **전치사를 주로 관계사절 끝에 쓰는 경우**
> 관계사절의 동사가 look at, ask for, laugh at, look up to 등의 동사구이거나, be proud/afraid/
> aware of, be responsible for 등 형용사와 전치사의 결합이 강한 경우 주로 전치사를 관계사절 뒤에 쓴다.
> This is the gold medal **which** I'm most *proud of*.
> This is the gold medal *of which* I'm most *proud*. (매우 딱딱한 표현)

SPEED CHECK

빈칸에 알맞은 말을 고르시오.

I wasn't interested in the things about ＿＿＿＿＿ they were talking.

① whom   ② which   ③ that   ④ what   ⑤ 필요 없음

정답 및 해설 p.24

PRACTICE TEST

A ( ) 안에서 알맞은 말을 고르시오.

1 The child (climbing / is climbing) the tree is so cute.
2 What is the name of the man with (whom / that) you were jogging?
3 Ava wore my skirt without my permission, (which / that) made me angry.
4 Our class will go to the zoo, (where / when) we will see lots of animals.

A
climb [동] 오르다
permission [명] 허락

B 다음 문장에서 생략할 수 있는 말에 ○ 표시하시오.
(단, 생략할 부분이 없으면 X 표시할 것)

1 My father ate the apple pies that I baked this morning.
2 David visited the country in which his relatives lived.
3 People need someone whom they can rely on.
4 The armchair, which she sat on this morning, is broken.
5 Look at the boys who are pushing the rock with all their might.
6 We saw the beautiful stars that were shining brightly in the sky.

B
relative [명] 친척
rely on …에 의지하다
armchair [명] 안락의자
with all one's might 전력을 다하여, 힘껏
brightly [부] 밝게

C 두 문장의 뜻이 같도록 빈칸에 알맞은 관계사를 쓰시오.

1 Lily is close with Adam, and he is from New Zealand.
→ Lily is close with Adam, _______ is from New Zealand.

2 Julia was very busy, and this made her skip dinner.
→ Julia was very busy, _______ made her skip dinner.

3 Matt went to Busan, and he stayed there for a week.
→ Matt went to Busan, _______ he stayed for a week.

4 I sent an email to the girl, and she hasn't answered me.
→ The girl to _______ I sent an email hasn't answered me.

REVIEW TEST

[01-02] 다음 빈칸에 들어갈 수 있는 말을 고르시오.

01

> Mia said that she stayed home all day,
> _____ is not true.

① who   ② what

③ which   ④ why

⑤ that

02

> The town is beautiful in winter, _____ it
> is covered in snow.

① who   ② what

③ when   ④ where

⑤ how

NEW 내신 기출

03 다음 우리말을 영어로 옮겨 쓸 때 사용되지 <u>않는</u> 표현은?

> 그녀가 무엇을 말하더라도 그것은 항상 모두를
> 미소 짓게 한다.

① says   ② smile

③ makes   ④ however

⑤ everybody

서술형

[04-05] 두 문장의 뜻이 같도록 문장을 완성하시오.

04 No matter how brilliant she is, she can't know everything about the universe.

→ _____ brilliant she is, she can't know everything about the universe.

05 Daniel went to Guam, and there he enjoyed beautiful beaches and sunshine.

→ Daniel went to Guam, _____ he enjoyed beautiful beaches and sunshine.

06 다음 빈칸에 들어갈 말이 나머지와 <u>다른</u> 것은?

① This is the pool _____ celebrities often visit.

② July is the month _____ my grandfather passed away.

③ Do you remember the day _____ you won the prize?

④ 2012 is the year _____ my daughter entered elementary school.

⑤ Today is the day _____ the shopping season starts at this mall.

07 다음 밑줄 친 부분 중 생략할 수 <u>없는</u> 것은?

① I knew the woman <u>who was</u> walking past me.

② The man <u>whom</u> Alice is talking to is her teacher.

③ The nurse <u>who is</u> taking care of her patient is my sister.

④ This is the watch <u>that</u> the customer has been looking for.

⑤ Joseph was the student <u>that</u> finished the quiz first.

[08-09] 다음 빈칸에 공통으로 들어갈 수 있는 말을 고르시오.

08

> • Never put off till tomorrow _____ you can do today.
> • This isn't _____ I ordered yesterday.

① who   ② why   ③ that
④ what   ⑤ which

09

> • Please feel free to invite _____ you like.
> • Be polite to _____ you meet online.

① that   ② what   ③ whoever
④ whichever   ⑤ however

서술형 **NEW** **내신 기출**

10 보기를 참고하여 두 문장을 한 문장으로 만드시오. (8단어)

> ┤ 보기 ├
> My roommate wore a pair of white skates.
> They looked great.
> → My roommate wore a pair of white skates which looked great.

Here are the plates. We bought them today.
→ _____

서술형

11 네 문장의 뜻이 같도록 문장을 완성하시오.

I remember the log cabin. I was born there.
→ I remember the log cabin _____ I was born.
→ I remember the log cabin _____ _____ I was born.
→ I remember the log cabin _____ I was born in.

12 다음 밑줄 친 that의 성격이 나머지와 다른 것은?

① The gift box that is on the table is empty.
② I'll send you some pictures that I took in Venice.
③ Sue has a small garden that is full of flowers.
④ I believe that Wendy is responsible for the accident.
⑤ Tina is the only person in my class that is from Canada.

서술형

13 Alex가 참여할 다음 여행 계획표를 보고 문장을 완성하시오.

> **Day**
> **Trip**
> **Schedule**
>
> Date: March 3
> Place: Lake Louise
> Main Activity: fishing

1) March 3 is _____ _____ _____ Alex will go on a trip.
2) Lake Louise is _____ Alex will go.
3) Alex will learn _____ people fish.

14 다음 빈칸에 들어갈 말을 바르게 짝지은 것은?

> ⓐ _____ attends our event can get free samples.
> ⓑ _____ cookie you try, it'll be delicious.
> ⓒ _____ you go, respect local customs.

     ⓐ   ⓑ   ⓒ
① However – Whenever – Wherever
② However – Whichever – Whenever
③ Whoever – Whichever – Whatever
④ Whoever – Whoever – Whatever
⑤ Whoever – Whichever – Wherever

15 다음 대화의 빈칸에 들어갈 수 <u>없는</u> 것은?

> A: Does Jacob come from Seoul?
> B: Yes. _____

① Seoul is where he was born.

② Seoul is the city where he was born.

③ Seoul is the city which he was born in.

④ Seoul is the city he was born in.

⑤ Seoul is the city in that he was born.

18 다음 중 어법상 옳은 것은 모두 몇 개인가?

> ⓐ He can sing whatever songs you like.
> ⓑ Joy adopted a dog which tail is black.
> ⓒ Table tennis is the sport Diana likes most.
> ⓓ I want to introduce you to Roy, that is my coworker.
> ⓔ This is the movie I'm interested in.

① 1개   ② 2개   ③ 3개

④ 4개   ⑤ 5개

서술형 고난도

[16-17] 다음 중 어법상 **틀린** 것을 모두 골라 바르게 고치시오.

16 ① No one knows what he wants.

② The technician taught us the way how the heater works.

③ Wherever Jenny has free time, she goes to the park.

④ Call whoever you trust, and ask them for help.

⑤ However challenging the task is, I will finish it.

서술형

[19-21] 우리말과 뜻이 같도록 관계사와 주어진 말을 사용하여 문장을 완성하시오.

19 춤추는 것을 즐기는 사람은 누구든지 우리 댄스 동아리에 가입할 수 있다. (enjoy, dance)

→ _____ _____ _____ can join our dance club.

20 Serena는 단추들이 사각형인 코트를 입고 있다. (a coat, buttons)

→ Serena is wearing _____ _____ _____ _____ are square.

17 ① Have you found the wallet which you lost?

② I took a picture of the man and the dog which were sleeping under the tree.

③ Here is the tag on which you can write your name.

④ The airplane taking off is leaving for Beijing.

⑤ I went to the aquarium, which I saw baby penguins.

21 Steven은 나에게 내가 나의 집을 팔기로 결정한 이유를 물었다. (decide, sell)

→ Steven asked me _____ _____ _____ _____ my house.

CHAPTER

09

비교 구문

비교 구문

1 『as+형용사/부사의 원급+as』: '…만큼 ~한/하게'

Kelly swims **as well as** Jenny (does).

Bad eating habits can be **as dangerous as** stress.

This armchair is **not as[so] comfortable as** that one.

2 『형용사/부사의 비교급+than』: '…보다 더 ~한/하게'

· 비교급 만드는 법: 일반적으로 원급 뒤에 -(e)r를 붙이며, 2음절 단어 중 -ful / -less / -ous 등으로 끝나는 단어와 3음절 이상의 단어는 앞에 more를 쓴다.

My house is **larger than** his.

Sam is **more humorous than** Joe.

 『less + 원급 + than』: '…보다 덜 ~한/하게'

Taking a bus is **less expensive than** taking a taxi.

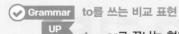 to를 쓰는 비교 표현

1 -or로 끝나는 형용사: superior('우수한'), inferior('열등한'), prior('이전의') 등

Our army was **superior to[than]** the enemy's.

2 prefer A to B: 'B보다 A를 더 좋아하다'

I **prefer** staying home **to[than]** going out on such a rainy day.

3 『the+형용사/부사의 최상급』: '가장 …한/하게'

· 최상급 만드는 법: 일반적으로 원급 뒤에 -(e)st를 붙이며, 2음절 단어 중 -ful / -less / -ous 등으로 끝나는 단어와 3음절 이상의 단어는 앞에 most를 쓴다.

· 최상급 뒤에 주로 『in+장소·범위를 나타내는 단수명사』나 『of+비교 대상이 되는 명사』를 쓴다.

· 최상급이 수식하는 명사는 문맥상 뜻이 분명할 때 생략할 수 있다.

· 부사의 최상급 앞에는 the를 붙이지 않기도 한다.

Ted is **the most talented** (*student*) **in** my class.

Diana is **the youngest** (*cheerleader*) **of** all the school's cheerleaders.

Liz can hold her breath underwater (*the*) **longest**.

SPEED CHECK

빈칸에 알맞은 말을 고르시오.

1 Michael is not as _____ as his younger sister Emily.

① calm　　② calmer　　③ calmest　　④ more calm　　⑤ most calm

2 Joe's Bakery is _____ than Tommy's.

① crowded　　② crowdeder　　③ crowdedest　　④ more crowded　　⑤ most crowded

3 That is the _____ watch in this store.

① expensive　　② expensiver　　③ expensivest　　④ more expensive　　⑤ most expensive

PRACTICE TEST

정답 및 해설 p.26

A ( ) 안에서 알맞은 말을 고르시오.

1 Your suitcase is as (heavy / heavier) as mine.

2 Last night I went to bed (earlier / earliest) than usual.

3 Peter hates chemistry (more / most) of all.

4 He is the (more / most) popular architect in England.

5 Jim prefers watching dramas (than / to) playing outside.

6 I am the (stronger / strongest) person of all my relatives.

A
suitcase 몡 여행 가방
chemistry 몡 화학
architect 몡 건축가
relative 몡 친척

B 다음 문장과 뜻이 통하도록 주어진 말을 사용하여 문장을 완성하시오.

1 My dog is 3 kg. My cat is 5 kg. (light)
→ My cat is _____ _____ _____ as my dog is.

2 I was very busy today. I am not usually that busy. (busy)
→ I was _____ _____ usual today.

3 The red cap is $10. The blue cap is $34. The grey cap is $50. (cheap)
→ The red cap is _____ _____ _____ the three caps.

B
light 몡 밝은; *가벼운

C 우리말과 뜻이 같도록 주어진 말을 사용하여 문장을 완성하시오.

1 내 새 소파가 네 것보다 더 딱딱하다. (hard)
My new sofa _____ _____ than yours.

2 Susan은 그녀의 남동생만큼 사려 깊지는 않다. (thoughtful)
Susan is _____ _____ _____ _____ her brother.

3 이 사원은 이 나라에서 가장 오래된 건물이다. (old, building)
This temple is _____ _____ _____ in this country.

4 나는 영어 수업이 역사 수업만큼 즐겁다는 것을 알게 되었다. (enjoyable)
I found English class _____ _____ _____ history class.

5 그 파란색 드레스는 흰 것보다 덜 아름답다. (beautiful)
The blue dress is _____ _____ _____ the white one.

C
thoughtful 몡 생각에 잠긴;
*사려 깊은
temple 몡 절, 사원
enjoyable 몡 즐거운

여러 가지 최상급 표현

1 원급과 비교급을 사용한 최상급 표현
- 원급과 비교급을 사용하여 최상급의 뜻을 나타낼 수 있다.
- 형태

> 『the＋최상급』
> → 『No (other)＋명사＋…＋as[so]＋원급＋as』
> → 『No (other)＋명사＋…＋비교급＋than』
> → 『비교급＋than any other＋단수명사』
> → 『비교급＋than all the other＋복수명사』

Emma is **the funniest student** in my school.
→ **No (other) student** in my school is **as[so] funny as** Emma.
→ **No (other) student** in my school is **funnier than** Emma.
→ Emma is **funnier than any other student** in my school.
→ Emma is **funnier than all the other students** in my school.

2 『one of the＋최상급＋복수명사』: '가장 …한 것[사람]들 중 하나'
Thanksgiving Day is **one of the biggest holidays** in America.
Picasso was **one of the greatest artists** in the world.
The mayor is **one of the most respected men** in our city.

3 『the＋최상급(＋that)＋주어＋have ever v-ed』: '지금까지 …한 것[사람] 중 가장 ～한'
It is **the longest** river (**that**) **we have ever seen**.
Jill is **the most honest** girl (**that**) **I have ever met**.
This is **the most horrible** movie (**that**) **I've ever watched**.

SPEED CHECK

두 문장의 뜻이 같도록 할 때 빈칸에 알맞은 말을 고르시오.

1 Russia is the largest country in the world.
→ Russia is _____ any other country in the world.
① large ② larger than ③ the largest ④ as large as ⑤ larger

2 The last question was the most difficult one on the science test.
→ No question on the science test was _____ the last one.
① as difficult as ② more difficult ③ difficult than
④ more difficult as ⑤ the most difficult

PRACTICE TEST

정답 및 해설 p.27

A ( ) 안에서 알맞은 말을 고르시오.

1 No one's idea is as (good / better) as Lisa's.
2 It's (bigger / the biggest) mistake he's ever made.
3 Busan is one of the most crowded (city / cities) in Korea.
4 Joey has (many / more) books than any other member of our club.
5 Brian is faster than all the other (athlete / athletes) in the game.

B 주어진 문장과 뜻이 같도록 빈칸에 알맞은 말을 쓰시오.

1 Garlic cream pasta is the most delicious dish at this restaurant.

→ No other dish at this restaurant is _____ _____ _____ garlic cream pasta.
→ No other dish at this restaurant is _____ _____ _____ garlic cream pasta.
→ Garlic cream pasta is _____ _____ _____ _____ at this restaurant.
→ Garlic cream pasta is _____ _____ _____ _____ _____ at this restaurant.

2 This novel is more boring than any other book in the library.

→ No other book in the library is _____ _____ _____ this novel.
→ No other book in the library is _____ _____ _____ this novel.
→ This novel is _____ _____ _____ _____ _____ _____ in the library.
→ This novel is _____ _____ _____ _____ in the library.

C 우리말과 뜻이 같도록 주어진 말을 사용하여 문장을 완성하시오.

1 한라산은 내가 지금까지 등반한 것 중 가장 높은 산이다. (high, mountain, climb)
Mt. Halla is _____ _____ _____ _____ _____ _____ _____.

2 장미꽃은 세계에서 가장 인기 있는 꽃들 중 하나이다. (popular, flower)
Roses are _____ _____ _____ _____ _____ in the world.

A
athlete 몡 운동선수

B
dish 몡 접시; *요리, 음식

비교 구문을 이용한 표현

1 『much / even / far / a lot + 비교급 + than』: '…보다 훨씬 더 ~한/하게' (비교급 강조)

Happiness is **much more important than** money.

Jack eats **a lot fewer** vegetables **than** I do.

> **Tip 주의!** 부사 very는 비교급을 강조할 수 없다.
> The new smartphone is **very more expensive** than the old one.

2 『as + 원급 + as possible』: '가능한 한 …한/하게' (= 『as + 원급 + as + 주어 + can』)

Paul ran to the bus stop **as fast as possible**.

= Paul ran to the bus stop **as fast as he could**.

3 『비교급 + and + 비교급』: '점점 더 …한/하게'

The world is getting **smaller and smaller**.

As time went by, my English got **better and better**.

> **Tip 주의!** 비교급이 『more + 원급』인 경우에는 『more and more + 원급』으로 쓴다.
> The basketball game is getting **more and more exciting**.

4 『the + 비교급, the + 비교급』: '…(하면) 할수록 더 ~하다'

The harder you study, **the higher** your scores will be.

The warmer the weather gets, **the better** I feel.

5 『배수사 + as + 원급 + as』: '…의 몇 배로 ~한/하게' (= 『배수사 + 비교급 + than』)

His garden is **twice as large as** yours.

Your hair is **three times as long as** mine.

= Your hair is **three times longer than** mine.

SPEED CHECK

빈칸에 알맞은 말을 고르시오.

1 Sarah is _____ more interested in politics than I am.

① very   ② much   ③ many   ④ only   ⑤ most

2 _____ I went up the mountain, the more I sweated.

① High   ② Higher   ③ The higher   ④ Highest   ⑤ The highest

3 This luggage is _____ as heavy as that one.

① two   ② twice   ③ second   ④ two time   ⑤ times

PRACTICE TEST

正답 및 해설 p.27

A ( ) 안에서 알맞은 말을 고르시오.

1 I think I can sing (very / far) better than Amy.

2 Chris goes hiking as often as (possible / can) to stay healthy.

3 The (much / more) you exercise, the more calories you burn.

4 This bed is three times (as expensive as / the most expensive) that one.

5 People are becoming (many and many / more and more) selfish.

B 두 문장의 뜻이 같도록 문장을 완성하시오.

1 As you get to know Abby better, you will like her more.

→ _____ _____ you get to know Abby, _____ _____ you will like her.

2 He entered the classroom as quietly as possible.

→ He entered the classroom _____ _____ _____ _____ _____.

3 This cheesecake is four times bigger than that chocolate cake.

→ This cheesecake is _____ _____ _____ _____ _____ that chocolate cake.

C 우리말과 뜻이 같도록 주어진 말을 사용하여 문장을 완성하시오.

1 모든 상황이 점점 더 나빠지고 있다. (bad)

The whole situation is getting _____ _____ _____.

2 내 공책은 그녀의 것보다 다섯 배로 두껍다. (thick)

My notebook is _____ _____ _____ _____ _____ hers.

3 네가 컴퓨터 게임들을 더 오래 할수록 너는 더 많이 피곤해질 것이다. (long, tired)

_____ _____ you play computer games, _____ _____ _____ you will get.

4 우리는 가능한 한 빨리 햄버거를 먹었다. (quickly)

We ate the hamburgers _____ _____ _____ _____.

5 그의 부상은 우리가 생각했던 것보다 훨씬 더 심각했다. (serious)

His injury was _____ _____ _____ than we thought.

A
calorie 몡 칼로리 (열량의 단위)
burn 통 태우다; *소모하다
selfish 몡 이기적인

B
get to-v …하게 되다
quietly 빈 조용히

C
whole 몡 전체의, 모든
situation 몡 상황
thick 몡 두꺼운, 굵은
serious 몡 심각한
injury 몡 부상

CHAPTER 09 비교 구문 **97**

REVIEW TEST

[01-02] 다음 빈칸에 들어갈 수 있는 말을 고르시오.

01

> The hotter people get, _____ they use their air conditioners.

① much
② more
③ the more
④ as much as
⑤ the most

02

> As time went on, he grew _____.

① as nervous as
② much nervous
③ the most nervous
④ more and more nervous
⑤ more nervous and nervous

`NEW` `내신 기출`

03 다음 우리말을 영어로 옮겨 쓸 때 사용되지 <u>않는</u> 표현은?

> 새 약은 복통에 훨씬 더 효과적이다.

① very
② more
③ effective
④ medicine
⑤ stomachache

04 두 문장의 뜻이 같도록 할 때 빈칸에 들어갈 수 있는 것은?

> February is the shortest month of the year.
> → February is _____ month of the year.

① shorter than all the other
② shorter than any other
③ most short than any other
④ shortest than any other
⑤ most shortest than any other

`서술형`

[05-06] 다음 문장에서 <u>틀린</u> 부분을 찾아 바르게 고치시오.

05 The music outside became loudest and loudest.

(_____) → (_____)

06 This tablet is more convenient one I've ever used.

(_____) → (_____)

`서술형`

07 다음 빈칸에 공통으로 들어갈 수 있는 말을 쓰시오.

> • Our product is superior _____ our competitor's.
> • Jessica prefers walking _____ riding a car for short distances.

08 다음 중 학생들의 성적표와 일치하지 <u>않는</u> 것은?

	English	Music	History
Mia	90	50	50
Max	50	70	40
Harry	70	90	70

① Mia got the highest score of all three students in English.
② Max got a lower score than Harry in music.
③ Harry got a higher score than Mia in history.
④ Max got the lowest history score of all the students.
⑤ Harry's music score is not higher than Mia's.

[09-10] 두 문장의 뜻이 같도록 문장을 완성하시오.

09 The roller coaster is the scariest ride in the amusement park.

→ _____ ride in the amusement park is _____ _____ _____ the roller coaster.

10 Most people want to look as attractive as possible.

→ Most people want to look _____ _____ _____ _____ _____.

11 우리말과 뜻이 같도록 조건에 맞게 문장을 완성하시오.

> 그것은 볼링공의 세 배로 무겁다.
> → (A) _____
> → (B) _____

> ─── | 조건 | ───
> • 문장 (A)는 비교급을, 문장 (B)는 원급을 사용하
>   여 쓸 것
> • heavy, a bowling ball을 활용하여 쓸 것
> • 각각 9단어, 10단어의 완전한 문장으로 쓸 것

12 다음 밑줄 친 부분을 바르게 고친 것 중 <u>어색한</u> 것은?

① She is <u>one of the great teacher</u> I've ever known. (→ one of the greatest teachers)

② Try to laugh <u>as much as you possible</u>.
(→ as much as possible)

③ This magazine <u>is as not interesting as</u> that one. (→ is not as interesting as)

④ Tom is <u>busy than any other members</u> of our team. (→ busier than any other member)

⑤ He had three times as <u>much money as</u> I did.
(→ more money than)

13 다음 메뉴판을 보고 주어진 말을 사용하여 대화를 완성하시오.

A: I'll have a cheese sandwich. It is (1) _____ _____ food on the menu. (cheap) How about you?

B: Well, I'd like a chicken burger, but it's (2) _____ _____ _____ a cheese sandwich. (twice, expensive)

A: Then how about a bacon sandwich? It's (3) _____ _____ a chicken burger. (cheap)

B: Okay. I'll get that.

14 다음 우리말을 영어로 옮긴 것 중 <u>틀린</u> 것은?

> 너의 건강이 가장 중요하다.

① Nothing is as important as your health.

② Your health is the most important thing.

③ Nothing is less important than your health.

④ Nothing is more important than your health.

⑤ Your health is more important than any other thing.

15 다음 문장을 읽고 키가 작은 순서대로 이름을 쓰시오.

> - Alex is shorter than David.
> - James is taller than David.
> - No boy in the class is taller than Nate.

_____ < _____ < _____ < _____

16 다음 표를 보고 문장을 완성하시오.

Gallery	Ivy's	Eve's	Carl's	Ben's
Number of visitors	50	50	80	20

1) Ivy's gallery had _____ many visitors _____ Eve's.

2) _____ gallery had _____ visitors _____ Carl's.

3) Carl's gallery had _____ _____ _____ many visitors _____ Ben's.

17 다음 중 어법상 옳은 것은 모두 몇 개인가?

> ⓐ It's the most beautiful place I've ever seen.
> ⓑ He is one of the most famous conductor in Korea.
> ⓒ Serana is much more outgoing than Joel.
> ⓓ His homework is getting more and more difficult.
> ⓔ No book in the library is more interesting as *The Old Man and the Sea*.

① 1개   ② 2개   ③ 3개
④ 4개   ⑤ 5개

[18-19] 다음 중 어법상 <u>틀린</u> 것을 고르시오.

18 ① Jimmy is the smartest of his four sons.
② It is the most impressive story that I've ever heard.
③ Liam always stays longest in the office.
④ The more carefully you drive, the safe you are.
⑤ Ian called his parents as often as possible.

19 ① My son weighed twice as much as her son.
② I tried to speak as slower as possible.
③ Briana runs faster than any other girl in her class.
④ Mr. Kim's lecture was not as difficult as I expected.
⑤ The days are getting longer and longer.

[20-21] 우리말과 뜻이 같도록 주어진 말을 사용하여 문장을 완성하시오.

20 Ella는 파리에서 가장 성공한 디자이너들 중 하나이다. (successful, designer)

→ Ella is _____ _____ _____ _____ _____ _____ in Paris.

21 이 신발은 이전보다 덜 편안하다. (comfortable)

→ These shoes are _____ _____ than before.

CHAPTER

10

접속사

시간·이유를 나타내는 접속사

1 while: '…하는 동안에'

Sam did his homework **while** I was taking an English class online.

> **Tip 비교!** 접속사 while의 다른 뜻: '…하는 반면에'; '…지만'
> The first drink is free, **while** the second costs $7. ('…하는 반면에')
> **While** I agree with him, I still think my idea is a good one. ('…지만')

2 as: '(동시에) …할 때', '…하면서'; '…함에 따라'; '… 때문에'

As we were having lunch, we talked about our summer plans. ('(동시에) …할 때', '…하면서')
As Nicole got older, she became more responsible. ('…함에 따라')
We were late for the meeting, **as** the traffic was very heavy. ('… 때문에')

3 since: '… 이래로'; '… 때문에'

I've felt much better **since** I started working out. ('… 이래로')
Since spaghetti is easy to cook, it is very popular. ('… 때문에')

4 until[till]: '…할 때까지'

Add chocolate and wait **until**[**till**] it is completely melted.

5 every time: '…할 때마다' (= each time / whenever)

Every time Alex visits Chicago, he stays at the same hotel.

6 as soon as: '…하자마자'

As soon as Carrie entered the laboratory, she fell down.
(→ **On entering** the laboratory, Carrie fell down.)
(→ **The moment**[**minute / instant**] Carrie entered the laboratory, she fell down.)
(→ **No sooner** had Carrie entered the laboratory **than** she fell down.)

> **Tip 주의!** 시간을 나타내는 부사절에서는 미래를 나타내더라도 미래시제 대신 현재시제를 쓴다.
> I will leave when the rain **stops**.
> (← I will leave when the rain **will stop**.)

SPEED CHECK

빈칸에 알맞은 말을 고르시오.

1 Danny broke his left arm _____ he was playing soccer.
① until ② while ③ as soon as ④ since ⑤ every time

2 It has been a long time _____ I watched a play.
① as ② since ③ as soon as ④ while ⑤ when

PRACTICE TEST

정답 및 해설 p.29

A

(　　) 안에서 알맞은 말을 고르시오.

1 Her husband was cooking (while / until) she was doing laundry.

2 It has been three years (since / every time) the program was launched.

3 (As / while) the population increases, our city will need more electricity.

4 (As soon as / Until) the talk show ended, he turned off the TV.

5 I'll call you as soon as I (hear / will hear) the results of the contest.

A
do laundry 빨래하다
launch [동] 시작하다
population [명] 인구
increase [동] 증가하다
electricity [명] 전기
result [명] 결과

B

두 문장의 뜻이 같도록 빈칸에 알맞은 접속사를 쓰시오.

1 On seeing the school bus, I began to run.
→ _______ _______ _______ I saw the school bus, I began to run.

2 I post pictures on my blog whenever I travel abroad.
→ I post pictures on my blog _______ _______ I travel abroad.

3 It is raining heavily, so we won't go shopping downtown.
→ _______ it is raining heavily, we won't go shopping downtown.

4 Hailey moved to Canada four years ago.
→ It has been four years _______ Hailey moved to Canada.

B
post [동] (우편물을) 발송하다; *게시하다
abroad [부] 해외로
downtown [부] 시내로

C

우리말과 뜻이 같도록 주어진 말을 사용하여 문장을 완성하시오.

1 Tina는 그녀의 딸이 잠들 때까지 노래했다. (daughter, fall asleep)
Tina sang _______ _______ _______ _______ _______.

2 다른 학생들이 공부하고 있는 동안에 시끄럽게 하지 마라. (other students, study)
Don't make noise _______ _______ _______ _______ _______.

3 나는 별똥별을 볼 때마다 소원을 빈다. (see, a shooting star)
_______ _______ _______ _______ _______ _______ _______, I make a wish.

4 그가 나에게 사과하지 않았기 때문에 나는 그에게 말을 걸고 싶지 않다. (apologize)
_______ _______ _______ _______ to me, I don't want to talk to him.

C
shooting star 별똥별
wish [명] 소원

조건·양보·결과를 나타내는 접속사

1 if: '만약 …라면'

If it snows tomorrow, I'll make a snowman with my children.

> ✓ **Grammar** 명사절을 이끄는 접속사 if[whether]: '…인지'
> **UP** I don't know **if[whether]** Jean will join our study group (or not).

2 unless: '…하지 않으면' (= if ... not)

Unless we protect wild animals, they will become extinct.

(→ **If** we **don't** protect wild animals, they will become extinct.)

> **Tip 주의!** 조건을 나타내는 부사절에서는 미래를 나타내더라도 미래시제 대신 현재시제를 쓴다.
> I will get an autograph *if* I **meet** my favorite novelist.
> (← I will get an autograph *if* I **will meet** my favorite novelist.)

3 『although[though] / even though + 사실』: '비록 …지만'

Although[Though] Lucas studied math hard, he couldn't get good scores on the exams.

He is the company's best reporter, **even though** he has the least experience. (though 강조)

4 『even if + 가상의 일』: '설령 …할지라도'

Even if you take a taxi, you'll miss your flight.

5 『so + 형용사/부사 + that』 『such(+a[an]) + 형용사 + 명사 + that』: '매우 …해서 ~하다'

The coffee was **so** good **that** I had another cup.

It was **such** a foggy day **that** I drove very carefully.

> **Tip 비교!** 『so (that) + 주어 + 동사』: '…가 ~하기 위하여', '…가 ~하도록' (= 『in order that + 주어 + 동사』)
> Speak more loudly **so that** *the audience can hear* you.
>   (= **in order that** *the audience can hear* you)

> ✓ **Grammar** 명사절을 이끄는 접속사 that: '…하는 것'
> **UP** *It* is true **that** Annie will leave the company. (가주어 it, 진주어 that절)
> I think **that** she is the best singer in the UK. (목적어)
> The problem is **that** we are short of time. (보어)

SPEED CHECK ▶

빈칸에 알맞은 말을 고르시오.

1 _____ the air conditioner is on, it is still hot.

① If   ② Unless   ③ Though   ④ Whether   ⑤ That

PRACTICE TEST

정답 및 해설 p.29

A 보기에서 알맞은 접속사를 골라 빈칸에 쓰시오.

| 보기 | that though unless if

1 Don't get a pet _______ you can care for it.
2 _______ I was in a bad mood, I tried to keep smiling.
3 _______ you park here, the police officer will give you a ticket.
4 The topic was so difficult _______ I often had to stop reading.

A
care for …을 보살피다
be in a bad mood 기분이 나쁘다
give a ticket 딱지를 끊다

B 다음 문장에서 틀린 부분을 찾아 바르게 고치시오.

1 Bianca will give you a ride if she will drive tomorrow.
2 If Jack has lived in Korea for a long time, he can't speak Korean well.
3 I wonder if I get a pay raise next year.
4 Santorini Island was so a beautiful place that I wanted to go there again.

B
give A a ride A를 차에 태워 주다
wonder [동] 궁금하다
get a pay raise 임금이 오르다

C 우리말과 뜻이 같도록 주어진 말을 사용하여 문장을 완성하시오.

1 설령 내가 사과할지라도 그녀는 나를 용서하지 않을 것이다. (apologize)
_______ _______ _______ _______, she wouldn't forgive me.

2 그녀가 메모하지 않으면 나의 여동생은 사소한 일들을 잊어버린다. (take notes)
My sister forgets small things _______ _______ _______ _______.

3 비록 그가 그것을 표현하지 않지만, Ethan은 너를 사랑한다. (express)
Ethan loves you, _______ _______ _______ _______ _______ it.

4 그 이야기는 무척 무서워서 그는 그것을 더 이상 읽을 수 없었다. (scary)
The story was _______ _______ _______ he couldn't read anymore of it.

5 그 사고에서 아무도 다치지 않은 것은 다행이다. (fortunate)
_______ _______ _______ _______ nobody was hurt in the accident.

6 Cindy는 그것을 이해할 수 있도록 그 수업을 주의 깊게 들었다. (understand)
Cindy listened carefully to the lesson _______ _______ _______ _______ _______ _______.

C
forgive [동] 용서하다
take notes 메모하다
express [동] 표현하다
anymore [부] 더 이상
fortunate [형] 운 좋은, 다행인

짝으로 이루어진 접속사

1 both A and B: 'A와 B 둘 다'

My parents **both** trust **and** support me.

Danny cooks **both** fried rice **and** fried noodles very well.

2 either A or B: 'A와 B 중 하나'

Cathy is **either** a fool **or** a genius.

Add **either** sugar **or** honey to the soup.

3 neither A nor B: 'A도 B도 아닌'

Paul is interested in **neither** dancing **nor** singing.

Neither my husband **nor** I have been to New Zealand.

4 not only A but also B: 'A뿐만 아니라 B도' (≒ B as well as A)

The homeless need **not only** food **but also** shelter.

(→ The homeless need shelter **as well as** food.)

The lecture was **not only** boring **but also** difficult.

(→ The lecture was difficult **as well as** boring.)

✓ **Grammar UP** 짝으로 이루어진 접속사의 수 일치

both A and B는 복수 취급하며, 나머지는 B에 동사의 수를 일치시킨다.

Both you *and* Jack **are** nice to people.

Either Alex *or* **I am** wrong.

Neither Ben *nor* **you were** invited to her wedding.

Not only you *but also* **I am** fond of classical music.

(→ **I**, *as well as* you, **am** fond of classical music.)

SPEED CHECK

빈칸에 알맞은 말을 고르시오.

1 Both price _____ quality are important in shopping.

① but   ② and   ③ or   ④ nor   ⑤ as

2 _____ she nor I have any experience in this field.

① As well as   ② Not only   ③ Both   ④ Neither   ⑤ Either

3 His dog is not only friendly _____ also faithful.

① and   ② or   ③ but   ④ so   ⑤ nor

PRACTICE TEST

정답 및 해설 p.30

A ( ) 안에서 알맞은 말을 고르시오.

1 Visitors can choose (either / neither) a mug or a towel as a free gift.

2 Both Olivia and you (need / needs) to save money for your trip.

3 (Neither / Both) Daisy and I cried when we watched the sad movie.

4 Not only Chris but also I (are / am) going to run for school president.

A
run for …에 출마하다
school president
학생회장

B 두 문장의 뜻이 같도록 빈칸에 알맞은 접속사를 쓰시오.

1 Sue can help you with your work today. Or she can help you tomorrow.
→ Sue can help you with your work ＿＿＿＿ today ＿＿＿＿ tomorrow.

2 Mike likes to read books. And I like to read books, too.
→ ＿＿＿＿ Mike ＿＿＿＿ I like to read books.

3 We need time as well as money to take a vacation.
→ We need ＿＿＿＿ ＿＿＿＿ money ＿＿＿＿ ＿＿＿＿ time to take a vacation.

4 This guidebook was not cheap. It was not useful, either.
→ This guidebook was ＿＿＿＿ cheap ＿＿＿＿ useful.

B
guidebook
(명) (여행) 안내서
useful (형) 유용한

C 우리말과 뜻이 같도록 주어진 말을 사용하여 문장을 완성하시오.

1 우리는 오늘 밤에 역사와 생물 둘 다 공부할 것이다. (history, biology)
We'll study ＿＿＿＿ ＿＿＿＿ ＿＿＿＿ ＿＿＿＿ tonight.

2 이 박물관은 크지도 붐비지도 않았다. (big, crowded)
This museum was ＿＿＿＿ ＿＿＿＿ ＿＿＿＿ ＿＿＿＿.

3 너는 여기에 머무를 수도 나와 함께 갈 수도 있다. (stay here, go)
You can ＿＿＿＿ ＿＿＿＿ ＿＿＿＿ ＿＿＿＿ ＿＿＿＿ with me.

4 그 스타는 돈뿐만 아니라 명성도 원했다. (money, fame)
The star wanted ＿＿＿＿ ＿＿＿＿ ＿＿＿＿ ＿＿＿＿ ＿＿＿＿ ＿＿＿＿.

5 이 드라마는 1990년대뿐만 아니라 현재를 배경으로 펼쳐질 것이다. (in the 1990s)
This drama will be set in the present ＿＿＿＿ ＿＿＿＿ ＿＿＿＿ ＿＿＿＿
＿＿＿＿ ＿＿＿＿.

6 나의 남동생도 나도 용돈을 받지 못한다. (get an allowance)
Neither my brother ＿＿＿＿ ＿＿＿＿ ＿＿＿＿ ＿＿＿＿ ＿＿＿＿.

C
biology (명) 생물학
fame (명) 명성
set (동) 놓다; *배경을 설정
하다(set-set)
allowance (명) 용돈

REVIEW TEST

[01-02] 다음 빈칸에 들어갈 수 있는 말을 고르시오.

01
> Search the Internet _____ you need any information.

① if　　　　　　② until

③ while　　　　　④ unless

⑤ though

02
> _____ Henry was putting on his uniform, he looked in the mirror.

① If　　　　　　② As

③ But　　　　　④ Until

⑤ Though

NEW　내신 기출

03 다음 문장 (A)와 (B)에 대해 <u>잘못</u> 설명한 학생은?

> (A) The man didn't become either a vet _____ an animal trainer.
> (B) Either Jason _____ his brothers are going to visit me in Seoul.

① 보은: (A)와 (B)의 빈칸에 공통으로 or를 써야 해.

② 찬우: (A)는 '그 남자는 수의사도 조련사도 되지 않았다.'라고 해석해.

③ 다슬: (A)는 The man neither became a vet nor an animal trainer.로 바꿔 쓸 수 있어.

④ 규민: (B)의 are는 is로 고쳐야 해.

⑤ 혜인: (B)는 이전에 계획된 미래의 일을 나타내.

서술형

[04-05] 다음 문장에서 <u>틀린</u> 부분을 찾아 바르게 고치시오.

04 Both my boss and I am going on a business trip next week.

(　　　　　　) → (　　　　　　)

05 I'll wait until I will get the ticket.

(　　　　　　) → (　　　　　　)

서술형　NEW　내신 기출

06 주어진 말을 바르게 배열하여 문장을 완성하고 해석하시오.

(wanted, that, to, hot, it, I, go for a swim, so, was).

→ _____

→ _____

[07-08] 다음 빈칸에 들어갈 수 있는 말을 모두 고르시오.

07
> _____ you read the same book again, you may find something new in it.

① Although　　　② Even if

③ Until　　　　④ Whenever

⑤ Every time

08
> _____ I get to Hawaii, I will send you a photo.

① While　　　　② The moment

③ Since　　　　④ Even if

⑤ As soon as

서술형

09 우리말과 뜻이 같도록 빈칸에 알맞은 접속사를 쓰시오.

설령 그것이 하루 종일 걸릴지라도 나는 이 프로젝트를 끝낼 것이다.

→ _____ _____ it takes the whole day, I'll finish this project.

108

서술형

10 다음 학생들의 프로필을 보고 빈칸에 알맞은 접속사를 쓰시오.

	Place	Hobby	Future Job
Jeff	L.A.	painting	lawyer
Karen	Houston	painting	artist
Carl	Atlanta	swimming	lawyer

1) _____ Jeff _____ Karen enjoy painting as a hobby.

2) _____ Karen _____ Carl lives in L.A.

3) _____ _____ Jeff _____ _____ Carl wants to be a lawyer in the future.

[11-12] 다음 빈칸에 들어갈 말을 바르게 짝지은 것을 고르시오.

11

> ⓐ Don't call me _____ something urgent comes up.
> ⓑ _____ summer approaches, mosquitoes begin to appear.

	ⓐ	ⓑ		ⓐ	ⓑ
①	if	– While	②	so	– Since
③	if	– Till	④	unless	– As
⑤	unless	– Till			

12

> ⓐ Ellie woke up _____ the alarm clock started going off.
> ⓑ _____ Brian wants to get promoted, he works very hard.

	ⓐ	ⓑ		ⓐ	ⓑ
①	as	– Until	②	as	– Unless
③	until	– Since	④	as soon as	– Unless
⑤	as soon as	– Since			

서술형

[13-14] 두 문장의 뜻이 같도록 문장을 완성하시오.

13 If he doesn't eat less and exercise more, he will gain weight.

→ _____ _____ _____ _____ _____ _____ _____ , he will gain weight.

14 Mia gave her sister not only a cap but also blue jeans.

→ Mia gave her sister _____ _____ _____ _____ _____ _____ _____ .

[15-17] 다음 빈칸에 공통으로 들어갈 수 있는 말을 고르시오.

15

> • I wonder _____ you've heard the rumor about her.
> • _____ you get hungry later, order pizza.

① as[As] ② even if[Even if]
③ though[Though] ④ as if[As if]
⑤ if[If]

16

> • _____ she won the gold medal in the Olympics, she has been on TV often.
> • Noah has lived alone _____ he entered the university.

① While[while] ② If[if]
③ Though[though] ④ Since[since]
⑤ Unless[unless]

17

> • I burned my hand _____ I was baking muffins.
>
> • _____ Jack is good at snowboarding, he is not good at skiing.

① as[As] ② until[Until]

③ while[While] ④ since[Since]

⑤ unless[Unless]

18 다음 밑줄 친 부분 중 어법상 틀린 것은?

① He took care of Emily's dog <u>while she was away</u>.

② Do you know <u>if she will come to the seminar</u>?

③ We'll postpone the soccer game <u>if it will rain tomorrow</u>.

④ The soldiers stayed in the woods <u>until it got dark</u>.

⑤ You can't use the room <u>unless you reserve it</u>.

19 다음 밑줄 친 부분의 쓰임이 나머지와 다른 것은?

① Anderson stepped into the house <u>as</u> he talked on the phone.

② <u>As</u> Michael was fixing his bicycle, Jessica stopped by.

③ <u>As</u> Ms. Green was crossing the street, she bumped into her old friend.

④ <u>As</u> I left the bookstore, someone touched my shoulder.

⑤ <u>As</u> the novel was boring, I couldn't read it from beginning to end.

서술형 고난도

[20-21] 다음 중 쓰임이 <u>어색한</u> 부분을 모두 골라 바르게 고치시오.

20 ① They neither like nor dislike Van Gogh's paintings.

② Either Patrick or you has to explain the whole situation.

③ Both Jennifer and Selena are my favorite singers.

④ Betty, as well as her friends, wants to visit the resort.

⑤ I will not meet you again if you stop teasing me.

21 ① Neither Ian nor I wasn't satisfied with the food.

② I'll rest at home until I feel better.

③ Either you or he has lied to me.

④ Not only you but also Harry write in a diary every day.

⑤ There is a toy museum as well as several kids cafés.

서술형

[22-23] 우리말과 뜻이 같도록 접속사와 주어진 말을 사용하여 문장을 완성하시오.

22 나는 그가 내일 돌아올지 아닐지 확신할 수 없다. (come back)

→ I am not sure _____ _____ _____ _____ _____ tomorrow or not.

23 나는 남아메리카로 여행할 수 있도록 돈을 모으는 중이다. (travel)

→ I am saving money _____ _____ _____ _____ _____ to South America.

CHAPTER

11

일치와 화법

수의 일치

1 단수 취급하는 경우

1) each, every, -thing, -one, -body

Every student in my class **is** learning how to swim.

Is there *anybody* who can help me?

2) (복수형의) 학문명, 국가명

Economics **is** his favorite subject.

The Philippines **is** composed of thousands of islands.

3) 시간, 거리, 금액, 무게 등의 단위

Seven hours **is** enough time to sleep.

Fifty dollars **was** given to me as prize money.

4) 명사구[절]

Drinking soda **is** not good for your health.

What the world wants **is** peace.

2 복수 취급하는 경우

1) (both) A and B

Caitlin and I **are** the same age.

> A and B가 하나의 개념을 나타내는 경우는 단수 취급한다.
> *Curry and rice* **is** very delicious.

2) 『the+형용사』: '…한 사람들'

The injured **were** taken to the hospital immediately.

3) 『a number of+복수명사』: '많은 …'

A number of people **are** standing in line at the bus stop.

> 『the number of+복수명사』: '…의 수'라는 뜻으로, 단수 취급한다.
> *The number of newborn babies* **is** decreasing every year.

 『부분 표현+of+명사』의 수 일치

『부분 표현(분수, most, half, some, the rest 등)+of+명사』가 주어일 때, 명사에 동사의 수를 일치시킨다.

Three fourths of *the earth's surface* **is** water.

Some of *the oranges* **have** gone bad.

SPEED CHECK

(   ) 안에서 알맞은 말을 고르시오.

1 Each student (has / have) a locker.

2 Mathematics (is / are) very hard for me to understand.

3 A number of children (was / were) playing on the playground.

4 Mark and my brother (is / are) going to take rock climbing lessons.

PRACTICE TEST

정답 및 해설 p.32

A

주어진 말을 어법에 맞게 바꿔 쓰시오. (단, 현재시제로 쓸 것)

1 Each athlete _______ around the track every morning. (run)
2 Of all of our classes, statistics _______ the most interesting. (be)
3 Kate and Peter _______ in the same building. (work)
4 What you think about them _______ important to me. (be)
5 The blind _______ able to read using a special kind of writing. (be)
6 Forty dollars _______ expensive for a meal. (be)
7 Most of the basketball players _______ taller than you. (be)
8 The number of unemployed people _______ risen. (have)

A
athlete [명] 운동선수
statistics [명] 통계학
blind [형] 시각장애인의
unemployed [형] 실업자의
rise [동] 오르다, 증가하다 (rose-risen)

B

밑줄 친 부분이 어법상 맞으면 ○ 표시하고, 틀리면 바르게 고치시오.

1 Almost half of the watermelon <u>are</u> rotten.
2 A number of spelling errors <u>have been found</u> in his report.
3 Thirteen kilometers <u>are</u> too far for me to walk.
4 Every citizen <u>have</u> the right to vote.
5 The rich <u>pays</u> more taxes than the poor.
6 <u>Are</u> anything wrong with your bicycle?

B
rotten [형] 썩은
spelling error 철자 오류
citizen [명] 시민
right [명] 권리
vote [동] 투표하다
tax [명] 세금

C

우리말과 뜻이 같도록 주어진 말을 사용하여 문장을 완성하시오.

1 다음에 어떤 일이 일어날지 아무도 모른다. (nobody, know)
_______ _______ what will happen next.

2 내 친구들과 이야기하는 것은 내가 스트레스를 완화하도록 도와준다. (chat with, help)
_______ _______ _______ _______ _______ me relieve stress.

3 젊은 사람들이 나이 든 사람들보다 항상 덜 현명한 것은 아니다. (young)
_______ _______ _______ not always less wise than the old.

4 폭우 때문에 많은 학생들이 학교에 늦었다. (number, student)
_______ _______ _______ _______ _______ late for school because of the heavy rain.

C
relieve [동] (스트레스를) 완화하다
heavy rain 폭우

시제의 일치

1 시제의 일치: 주절의 시제에 따라 종속절의 시제를 다르게 쓰는데, 그 원칙을 시제의 일치라 한다.

주절의 시제	종속절의 시제
현재	모든 시제가 가능
과거	현재(진행) → 과거(진행)
	현재완료, 과거(진행) → 과거완료(진행)
	will → would, can → could, may → might, must → must[had to]

1) 주절의 시제가 현재일 때

We *think* that he **is** healthy now.
He *knows* that I **have been** looking for a new apartment.
My mom *knows* that I **will need** her help.

2) 주절의 시제가 과거일 때

I *thought* that he **was** worried about me. (종속절과 주절이 같은 시점)
He *knew* that she **had missed** the school bus. (종속절이 주절보다 앞선 시점)
She *knew* that I **had been working** at a bank. (종속절이 주절보다 앞선 시점)

2 시제 일치의 예외

1) 종속절이 변하지 않는 사실, 격언·속담, 과학적 사실일 때 주절의 시제와 관계없이 현재시제를 쓴다.

Josh *learned* that Seoul **is** the capital of Korea.
My parents *said* that honesty **is** the best policy.

2) 종속절이 역사적 사실일 때 주절의 시제와 관계없이 과거시제를 쓴다.

I *learned* that Gandhi **was born** in 1869.
(← ~~I learned that Gandhi **had been born** in 1869.~~)

3) 종속절이 현재에도 지속되는 사실이나 습관일 때 주절의 시제와 관계없이 현재시제를 쓸 수 있다.

I *found out* that the lemon tree **is** still there in my old neighborhood.
Kate *said* that she **starts** her day with a cup of coffee.

SPEED CHECK

빈칸에 알맞은 말을 고르시오.

1 Alice sang the song that her boyfriend _____ for her.
　① write　　　　② writes　　　　③ had written　　④ will write　　⑤ has written

2 I told my daughter that four plus six _____ 10.
　① was　　　　　② is　　　　　③ would be　　　④ will be　　　⑤ has been

3 My history teacher said that James Watt _____ the steam engine.
　① invents　　　② invented　　③ has invented　④ had invented　⑤ would invent

PRACTICE TEST

정답 및 해설 p.32

A

주어진 말을 어법에 맞게 바꿔 쓰시오.

1 We learned that water _______ from a high point to a low point. (flow)
2 Cathy told us that many Korean soldiers _______ in the Vietnam War. (fight)
3 Peter heard that Korea _______ many beautiful mountains. (have)
4 Mr. Brown told his students that walls _______ ears. (have)

A
point [명] (특정한) 지점, 장소
flow [동] 흐르다
Vietnam War 베트남 전쟁

B

다음 문장을 보기와 같이 바꿔 쓰시오.

| 보기 | Susan wonders how you feel about the film.
→ Susan wondered how you felt about the film.

1 We think that Jack planted the red roses in the garden.
→ We thought that _________________________ in the garden.

2 I believe that Luke will break up with her soon.
→ I believed that _________________________ soon.

3 Do you know that Heo Gyun wrote *Hong Gildong jeon*?
→ Did you know that _________________________ *Hong Gildong jeon*?

B
plant [동] 심다
break up with …와 결별하다

C

우리말과 뜻이 같도록 주어진 말을 사용하여 문장을 완성하시오.

1 나는 어제 Dana가 그녀의 일을 그만두었다는 것을 알게 되었다. (quit)
Yesterday I found out that Dana _______ _______ her job.

2 엄마는 일찍 일어나는 새가 벌레를 잡는다고 말씀하시곤 했다. (the early bird, catch)
Mom used to say that _______ _______ _______ _______ the worm.

3 Nancy는 Joe가 매일 아침 식사를 거른다고 들었다. (skip breakfast)
Nancy heard that Joe _______ _______ every day.

4 나는 1945년 일본 히로시마에 미국이 폭탄 하나를 투하했다는 것을 배웠다. (drop a bomb)
I learned that the USA _______ _______ _______ on Hiroshima, Japan, in 1945.

5 나의 조카는 그가 초조하다고 말했다. (say, nervous)
My nephew _______ _______ _______ _______ _______.

C
worm [명] (땅속에 사는) 벌레
skip [동] 거르다
drop a bomb 폭탄을 투하하다

화법

- **직접화법**: 다른 사람이 한 말을 인용 부호(" ")로 묶어 그대로 전달하는 것
- **간접화법**: 다른 사람이 한 말을 전달자의 입장에 맞게 바꿔서 전달하는 것

1 평서문의 간접화법 전환: 『say[tell+목적어](+that)+주어+동사』

John **said to** me, "I want to get some air."

→ John **told** me (**that**) **he wanted** to get some air.

> **Tip 주의!** 간접화법으로 전환 시 주의 사항
> 1. 시제 일치의 원칙에 맞춰 종속절의 시제를 바꾸고, 전달자에 맞춰 인칭대명사를 바꾼다.
> 2. 부사와 지시대명사는 전달하는 날짜, 시간, 장소 등이 다를 때 바꾼다.

now → at that time, then	today → that day	tomorrow → the next[following] day
yesterday → the day before, the previous day	ago → before	here → there
this[these] → that[those]	last week → the previous week	next week → the next week

2 의문문의 간접화법 전환

1) 의문사가 있는 경우: 『ask(+목적어)+의문사+주어+동사』

The coach **asked** me, "How tall are you?"

→ The coach **asked** me **how tall I was**.

> **Tip 주의!** 의문사가 주어일 때 『ask(+목적어)+의문사+동사』의 어순으로 쓴다.
> Everyone **asked** me, "Who saved you?" → Everyone **asked** me **who had saved** me.

2) 의문사가 없는 경우: 『ask(+목적어)+if[whether]+주어+동사』

Hans **asked** me, "Will you go jogging with me?"

→ Hans **asked** me **if[whether] I would go** jogging with him.

3 명령문의 간접화법 전환: 『tell[ask, order, advise 등]+목적어+to-v』

Jill **said to** me, "Please call me back immediately."

→ Jill **asked** me **to call** her back immediately.

> **Tip 주의!** 부정 명령문을 간접화법으로 전환할 때는 don't나 never를 없애고 동사원형을 not to-v로 바꾼다.
> She **said to** her child, "**Don't shout.**" → She **told** her child **not to shout**.

 Grammar UP 간접의문문: 의문문이 다른 문장에서 주어, 목적어, 보어로 쓰인 것을 말한다.

1 의문사가 있는 간접의문문: 『의문사+주어+동사』

Do you know **where she is going**? (← Do you know? + Where is she going?)

2 의문사가 없는 간접의문문: 『if[whether]+주어+동사』

I'm not sure **if[whether] she will like my present**. (← I am not sure. + Will she like my present?)

SPEED CHECK

다음 문장을 간접화법으로 바꿔 쓰시오.

Arnold said to Emma, "I will be back tomorrow."

→ Arnold told Emma _____.

PRACTICE TEST

정답 및 해설 p.33

A ( ) 안에서 알맞은 말을 고르시오.

1 Carl (said / told) me he was very shocked to see the crime scene.
2 Ben asked me (that / if) I had special plans for the new school year.
3 Dr. Davis told me (not to drink / don't drink) too many soft drinks.
4 When Tom woke up, he asked me what time (was it / it was).
5 Tell me (what you / what do you) want for Christmas.

B 우리말과 뜻이 같도록 틀린 부분을 찾아 바르게 고치시오.

1 Jacob은 나에게 그의 전화번호를 기억하라고 말했다.
   Jacob told me remember his phone number.

2 나는 그 웨이터에게 언제 우리의 테이블이 준비될지 물었다.
   I asked the waiter when would our table be ready.

3 우리는 약간의 돈을 발견했지만 그것이 누구의 것인지 몰랐다.
   We found some money, but we didn't know whose money was it.

4 나는 내가 다음에 무엇을 해야 할지 모르겠다.
   I don't know if I have to do next.

C 다음 문장을 간접화법으로 바꾸시오.

1 My mother said to my brother, "Take your umbrella."
   → My mother told _____.

2 Nicole asked him, "Where did you buy this tablet?"
   → Nicole asked him _____.

3 Aiden asked Lauren, "Have you ever been to Hawaii?"
   → Aiden asked Lauren _____.

4 Bob said, "I don't know how to play the guitar."
   → Bob said _____.

5 Jane said to Harry, "I will show you the pictures tomorrow."
   → Jane told Harry _____.

6 Jackson asked his friend, "Did I do something wrong?"
   → Jackson asked his friend _____.

A
crime 몡 범죄
scene 몡 현장
school year (교육) 학년
soft drink 청량음료

B
ready 휑 준비가 된

CHAPTER 11 일치와 화법 117

REVIEW TEST

[01-02] 다음 빈칸에 들어갈 수 있는 말을 고르시오.

01

> We learned that Jupiter _____ the biggest of all the planets.

① is   ② be   ③ will be

④ has been   ⑤ would be

02

> I rang the doorbell several times, but nobody _____ home.

① is   ② was   ③ are

④ were   ⑤ has been

NEW 내신 기출

03 주어진 문장과 의미가 같은 것을 2개 고르면?

> Robin asked me, "Are you ready to go?"

① Robin asked me if I was ready to go.

② Robin asked me if he was ready to go.

③ Robin asked me when I was ready to go.

④ Robin asked me whether I was ready to go.

⑤ Robin asked me whether he was ready to go.

[04-06] 다음 빈칸에 들어갈 말을 바르게 짝지은 것을 고르시오.

04

> ⓐ One third of my friends _____ from Canada.
> ⓑ We saw that every house in the area _____ decorated with Christmas lights.

	ⓐ	ⓑ		ⓐ	ⓑ
①	is	were	②	are	were
③	are	was	④	is	was
⑤	are	is			

05

> ⓐ The doctor said that the number of lung cancer patients _____ increasing.
> ⓑ A number of people _____ around the movie star.

	ⓐ	ⓑ		ⓐ	ⓑ
①	was	gather	②	were	gathers
③	was	gathers	④	were	gather
⑤	is	gathers			

06

> A: Do you know where Adam is now? He's not answering his phone.
> B: Adam ___ⓐ___ me that he ___ⓑ___ at the senior center every Sunday.

	ⓐ	ⓑ
①	told	volunteers
②	says	volunteers
③	told	volunteer
④	said	volunteered
⑤	said	volunteers

서술형

[07-09] 다음 문장에서 <u>틀린</u> 부분을 찾아 바르게 고치시오.

07 My uncle thought politics were easy and fun to learn when he was in university.

(   ) → (   )

08 Christine asked me that she could use my battery charger.

(   ) → (   )

09 Ava learned that the Joseon Dynasty had been founded in 1392.

( ) → ( )

[10-11] 다음 문장을 간접화법으로 바꿀 때 **틀린** 부분을 고르시오.

10 Mark said to me, "Open the window now."

→ Mark ① told ② me ③ open ④ the window ⑤ at that time.

11 I said to my mother, "Can you buy me a new dress?"

→ I ① asked my mother ② if ③ she ④ can buy ⑤ me a new dress.

고난도

12 다음 중 간접화법으로의 전환이 **틀린** 것은?
(단, 시간과 장소가 다름)

① My teacher said to me, "Don't be late again."
  → My teacher told me not to be late again.
② Sue said, "I want to stay here."
  → Sue told that she wanted to stay here.
③ Jane asked me, "Is this book yours?"
  → Jane asked me if that book was mine.
④ Ms. Scott said to us, "Hand in your essays by tomorrow."
  → Ms. Scott told us to hand in our essays by the next day.
⑤ I asked Blake, "When did you receive my email?"
  → I asked Blake when he had received my email.

서술형

[13-15] 다음 문장을 간접화법으로 바꿔 쓰시오.

13 Daniel said to me, "Don't make noise in the library."

→ Daniel told me _____

_____.

14 The woman asked him, "Where can I wash my hands?"

→ The woman asked him _____

_____.

15 He says, "I want to join the newspaper club."

→ He says _____

_____.

[16-17] 다음 대화의 빈칸에 들어갈 수 있는 말을 고르시오.

16

A: What are you reading?
B: I'm reading a book about Beethoven. I just read that he _____ the *Moonlight Sonata* in 1801.

*the *Moonlight Sonata* 월광 소나타

① composes   ② composed
③ have composed   ④ had composed
⑤ would compose

17

A: How about meeting at the department store at 9 a.m. tomorrow?
B: That's too early. I heard it _____ at 10:30 a.m.

① opens
② is opening
③ has opened
④ had opened
⑤ would open

서술형

18 다음은 전학생 Miranda에게 친구들이 한 질문이다. 각각의 질문을 간접화법으로 바꿔 쓰시오.

Mia : Do you live with your grandparents?

Dave : What is your favorite song?

Roy : Can you play the piano?

1) Mia asked Miranda _____
_____ .

2) Dave asked Miranda _____
_____ .

3) Roy asked Miranda _____
_____ .

19 다음 중 어법상 틀린 것을 모두 고르면?

① My brother and sister are cheerful.
② He thinks physics is the study of nature.
③ I wonder whose cat it is.
④ Only the disabled is allowed to park here.
⑤ My homeroom teacher reminded us that haste made waste.

고난도

20 다음 중 어법상 옳은 것은 모두 몇 개인가?

ⓐ Smoking cigarettes are harmful to your health.
ⓑ I realized that I hadn't brought my textbook.
ⓒ Paul told me he brushes his teeth three times a day.
ⓓ Are there anything you want to ask me?
ⓔ Seven months is not enough time to finish the project.

① 1개
② 2개
③ 3개
④ 4개
⑤ 5개

서술형

[21-22] 우리말과 뜻이 같도록 주어진 말을 사용하여 문장을 완성하시오. (단, 시제, 화법에 주의할 것)

21 Sarah는 그녀의 여동생이 그녀와 쇼핑을 갈 거라고 생각했다. (will, go shopping)
→ Sarah thought that _____ _____ _____
_____ _____ with her.

22 그 점원은 나에게 무엇을 찾고 있는지 물었다.
(what, look for)
→ The clerk asked me _____ _____ _____
_____ _____ .

서술형 NEW 내신기출

23 우리말과 뜻이 같도록 주어진 철자로 시작하여 문장을 완성하시오.

그 학생들 대부분이 수학을 공부하고 있었다.
→ M_____ o_____ t_____ s_____ w_____
s_____ m_____ .

CHAPTER

12

특수 구문

강조, 부정 구문, 병렬

A 강조

1 do를 이용한 강조: '정말 …하다'의 뜻으로, 동사를 강조하며 『do / does / did＋동사원형』의 형태로 쓴다.

I believed what Brian told me.

→ I **did** *believe* what Brian told me.

This mushroom soup tastes salty.

→ This mushroom soup **does** *taste* salty.

2 it is / was ... that 강조 구문: '～한 것은 바로 …이다[였다]'의 뜻으로, 강조하고자 하는 말(주어, 목적어, 부사(구/절) 등)을 it is / was와 that 사이에 둔다.

I saw Joe on the subway yesterday.

→ **It was I that[who]** saw Joe on the subway yesterday. (주어 강조)

→ **It was** *Joe* **that[who(m)]** I saw on the subway yesterday. (목적어 강조)

→ **It was** *on the subway* **that** I saw Joe yesterday. (부사구 강조)

→ **It was** *yesterday* **that** I saw Joe on the subway. (부사 강조)

> **Tip 주의!** 강조하는 말이 사람일 때 that 대신 who(m)를 쓸 수 있다.
> **It was** *Anthony* **who[that]** bought a small blue car.

B 부정 구문

1 부분부정: 『not＋all, every, always 등』의 형태로 '모두/항상 …인 것은 아니다'의 뜻을 나타낸다.

Not all of the questions on the test were easy.

Hugo does **not always** work hard.

2 전체부정: no, none, neither, never 등으로 '아무도/결코 …하지 않다'의 뜻을 나타낸다.

None of the students had visited this theme park before. (all의 전체부정)

Neither of them has a plan to study abroad. (both의 전체부정)

C 병렬: 등위접속사(and / but / or) 또는 짝으로 이루어진 접속사(both A and B, either A or B, neither A nor B, not only A but also B, B as well as A 등)에서 A와 B는 문법적으로 동일한 형태와 구조를 쓴다.

Erica is **smart**, **pretty**, *and* **funny**.

You can *either* **use** a computer *or* **read** a magazine in the lounge.

SPEED CHECK

빈칸에 알맞은 말을 고르시오.

1 My cousin _____ to see me last weekend.

① do come   ② does come   ③ did come   ④ does came   ⑤ did came

2 It was in Pyeongchang _____ the Winter Olympics was held.

① which   ② that   ③ what   ④ when   ⑤ who

PRACTICE TEST

정답 및 해설 p.35

A 다음 밑줄 친 부분을 강조하는 문장을 완성하시오.

1 David takes part in the winter camp.
→ It ______________ takes part in the winter camp.

2 Joy started to learn to swim in March.
→ It ______________ Joy started to learn to swim.

3 Jenny took pictures of the movie star at the cinema.
→ Jenny ______________ of the movie star at the cinema.

A
cinema [명] 영화관, 극장

B 두 문장의 뜻이 같도록 문장을 완성하시오.

1 Natalie is not married, and Jenny isn't either.
→ _______ of them is married.

2 Most of the customers liked our new products, but some didn't.
→ _______ _______ of the customers liked our new products.

3 I'm usually home on Sundays, but I sometimes go out.
→ I'm _______ _______ home on Sundays.

4 There were five people in the building, and they weren't injured.
→ _______ of the people in the building was injured.

B
either [부] (부정문에서) …도 또한 그렇다
product [명] 상품, 제품

C 우리말과 뜻이 같도록 주어진 말을 사용하여 문장을 완성하시오.

1 모든 미국인이 영어를 완벽하게 말하는 것은 아니다. (every, American)
_______ _______ _______ speaks English perfectly.

2 그녀를 놀라게 한 것은 바로 그 높은 가격이었다. (the high price)
_______ _______ _______ _______ _______ _______ surprised her.

3 우리들 중 아무도 올해 새 스마트폰을 사지 않았다. (us)
_______ _______ _______ bought a new smartphone this year.

4 Henry와 Kelly는 여름 방학이 끝나기 전에 놀이공원에 정말 가고 싶어 한다. (want)
Henry and Kelly _______ _______ to go to the amusement park before the summer vacation is over.

5 Lucy는 그림을 잘 그릴 뿐만 아니라 피아노도 잘 친다. (draw, play)
Lucy is good at not only _______ pictures but also _______ the piano.

C
perfectly [부] 완벽하게
surprise [동] 놀라게 하다
amusement park 놀이공원

도치

도치: 문법상의 이유나 특정 어구를 강조하기 위해 『주어+동사』의 어순을 『동사+주어』로 바꾸는 것이다.

1 방향·장소의 부사(구)를 강조하기 위한 도치: 『부사(구)+동사+주어』

Down **came the rain**.

Next to the door **was a big box**.

> **Tip 비교!** 주어가 대명사인 경우 부사를 문장 맨 앞에 써도 보통 도치하지 않는다.
> *Up* **he climbed**. (← *Up* climbed he.)

2 부정어(구)를 강조하기 위한 도치

- **일반동사가 있는 문장**: 『부정어(구)(never, little, no, not, hardly, rarely 등)+do / does / did+주어+동사원형』
- **be동사 / 조동사가 있는 문장**: 『부정어(구)(never, little, no, not, hardly, rarely 등)+be동사 / 조동사+주어』

Never **does she ask** others for help.

Rarely **does Joe show** his feelings on his face.

Little **did I realize** that I had gained 10 kg.

Not only **was the concert** exciting, but it was also very cheap.

Hardly **could I trust** his promises.

> **Tip 주의!** 부정의 뜻을 포함하는 부사: hardly, rarely, seldom, scarcely, barely '거의[좀처럼] … 않다'

> **Tip 비교!** 부정에 가까운 의미를 갖는 only를 문장 맨 앞에 써도 주어와 동사를 도치한다.
> *Only* recently **did I learn** the truth.

3 『so / neither[nor]+do / does / did / be동사 / 조동사+주어』: '(앞서 한 말에 대해) …도 또한 그렇다 / 그렇지 않다'의 뜻으로, 『so+동사+주어』는 긍정문 뒤에, 『neither[nor]+동사+주어』는 부정문 뒤에 쓴다.

I went to the Seoul Arts Center last weekend. – **So did I**.

Never have I won the lottery. – **Neither[Nor] have I**.

✔ Grammar UP not A until B가 있는 문장의 강조

Alice did **not** come home **until** midnight. (not A until B: 'B하고 나서야 비로소 A하다')

→ **Not until midnight** *did Alice come* home. (부정어구 강조를 위한 도치)

→ *It was* **not until midnight** *that* Alice came home. (it is / was ... that 강조 구문)

SPEED CHECK

빈칸에 알맞은 말을 고르시오.

1 Rarely _____ last winter.

① it did snow ② did it snow ③ snowed it ④ it did snowed ⑤ did it snowed

2 I write in my diary every day. – So _____.

① I ② I do ③ do I ④ I did ⑤ did I

PRACTICE TEST

정답 및 해설 p.35

A ( ) 안에서 알맞은 말을 고르시오.

1 Out (came the sun / the sun came).
2 My name was on the waiting list. — So (hers was / was hers).
3 I'm not interested in rock music. — (So / Neither) am I.
4 Never (she will / will she) forget the day her daughter was born.
5 Little (did Eva / Eva did) understand what her student had told her.

A
waiting list 대기자 명단

B 다음 밑줄 친 부분을 강조하는 문장을 완성하시오.

1 A crow sat on the branch.
→ On the branch ______________________.

2 The department store closes only on Mondays.
→ Only on Mondays ______________________.

3 I have never watched such a thrilling action movie.
→ Never ______________________ such a thrilling action movie.

4 The boat passes under the bridge.
→ Under the bridge ______________________.

B
crow [명] 까마귀
branch [명] 나뭇가지
thrilling [형] 스릴 있는, 짜릿한

C 우리말과 뜻이 같도록 주어진 말을 사용하여 문장을 완성하시오.

1 나는 외국에 결코 가 본 적이 없다. 내 여동생도 그렇다. (neither)
I have never been abroad. ______ ______ ______ ______.

2 바위 뒤에 백호가 한 마리 있었다. (a white tiger)
Behind the rock ______ ______ ______ ______.

3 Stella는 그녀의 행운을 거의 믿을 수 없었다. (hardly, believe)
______ ______ ______ ______ her good luck.

4 나는 스쿠버 다이빙 가는 것을 정말 좋아해. — 나도 또한 그래.
I really love to go scuba diving. — ______ ______ ______.

5 나는 결코 내가 수의사가 될 것을 꿈꾸지 않았다. (never, dream)
______ ______ ______ ______ that I would be a vet.

C
abroad [부] 해외에(서), 해외로
vet [명] 수의사

REVIEW TEST

[01-02] 다음 빈칸에 들어갈 수 있는 말을 고르시오.

01

It was _____ that was run over by the car.

① unexpected ② last night
③ terrible ④ on the road
⑤ a statue

02

Michael was chewing gum after lunch, and
_____.

① so is his coworker
② so was his coworker
③ so his coworker was
④ neither was his coworker
⑤ neither his coworker was

[03-04] 다음 밑줄 친 부분의 쓰임이 나머지와 다른 것을 고르시오.

03 ① Ted did break the school rules again.
② I did my history homework last night.
③ She does respect Mr. Adams.
④ Joan does look good in the red dress.
⑤ The elderly woman does look like my grandmother.

04 ① It was English that she liked most.
② It was the white plate that Cindy broke.
③ It was shocking that he died suddenly.
④ Was it Nick who picked you up at the airport?
⑤ It was last Saturday that I went to the flea market.

서술형

[05-06] 도치 구문을 사용하여 다음 밑줄 친 부분을 강조하는 문장으로 바꿔 쓰시오.

05 A thick layer of dust lay on the bookshelves.
→ _____

06 I hardly expected that I would get stuck in traffic.
→ _____

[07-08] 다음 대화의 빈칸에 들어갈 수 있는 말을 고르시오.

07

A: I didn't hand in my art report yesterday.
B: _____

① So I was. ② So did I.
③ Neither did I. ④ Neither I did.
⑤ Neither was I.

08

A: Is there anyone in your classroom?
B: _____ of my classmates are there now. They all went to the science room.

① All ② Both
③ Neither ④ None
⑤ Never

NEW 내신 기출

09 다음 우리말을 영어로 옮겨 쓸 때 사용되지 않는 표현은?

모든 만화책이 쓸모없는 것은 아니다.

① is ② none
③ every ④ useless
⑤ comic book

서술형

[10-11] 두 문장의 뜻이 같도록 문장을 완성하시오.

10 I have never thought of changing my major.

→ Never _____ _____ _____ _____
changing my major.

11 John didn't finish the marathon. I didn't
finish the marathon either.

→ _____ _____ us finished the marathon.

서술형

[12-13] 다음 그림을 보고 주어진 말을 사용하여 문장을
완성하시오.

12

_____ _____ _____ _____ wore caps.

(boy)

13

_____ _____ _____ _____ _____ are
sitting on the bench. (girl)

14 다음 대화의 빈칸에 들어갈 말을 바르게 짝지은 것
은?

> ⓐ A: Why didn't Leah come to the school
>   festival?
>   B: She _____ come. I saw her.
> ⓑ A: I thought Jennifer was very rude
>   yesterday.
>   B: _____ I don't know why
>   she talked to him that way.

	ⓐ	ⓑ
①	does	– Nor did I.
②	do	– So does I.
③	did	– So did I.
④	did	– Neither did I.
⑤	didn't	– Neither does I.

[15-16] 다음 밑줄 친 부분을 강조하는 문장으로 옳은 것
을 고르시오.

15

> I have never been to San Francisco before.

① Never I have been to San Francisco before.

② Never have I been to San Francisco before.

③ Never have been I to San Francisco before.

④ Never did I have been to San Francisco
before.

⑤ Never have I be to San Francisco before.

16

> He dropped the vase <u>in the living room</u>.

① It was that in the living room he dropped the vase.

② It was in the living room who he dropped the vase.

③ It was in the living room that he dropped the vase.

④ It was in the living room which he dropped the vase.

⑤ It was in the living room he dropped the vase.

17 다음 강조 표현 중 자연스럽지 <u>않은</u> 것은?

① Seldom did Lisa have a chance to talk with him.

② On the screen was a warning message.

③ Ben is afraid of pigeons, and so am I.

④ Into the cafeteria came my English teacher.

⑤ Only then I realized that I had made a silly mistake.

고난도

18 다음 중 어법상 옳은 것은 모두 몇 개인가?

ⓐ My wallet is neither in my bag nor my car.
ⓑ Rarely does Julia go out late at night.
ⓒ It is Paul who runs the laundry shop.
ⓓ I don't like skating. So does my girlfriend.
ⓔ Only in the morning did Ava find out that her earrings were missing.

① 1개　　　② 2개　　　③ 3개
④ 4개　　　⑤ 5개

서술형

19 다음 중 어법상 <u>틀린</u> 것을 모두 골라 바르게 고치시오.

① Next to the fountain stood a man holding some flowers.

② Most of the students did answered the question correctly.

③ Grace likes writing songs as well as to sing them.

④ Seldom did Logan go shopping with his wife.

⑤ It was last year that my cousin entered the university.

서술형

[20-21] 우리말과 뜻이 같도록 주어진 말을 사용하여 문장을 완성하시오. (단, 강조, 부정, 도치 구문을 사용할 것)

20 탁자 위에 세 개의 컵이 있다. (cup)
→ On the table _____.

21 그의 소설들이 항상 재미있는 것은 아니다. (interesting)
→ His novels _____.

서술형　NEW　내신 기출

22 다음 세 문장 중 어법상 <u>틀린</u> 문장을 찾아 바르게 고쳐 다시 쓰시오.

• Seldom is he late for class.
• Rarely does Ms. Bartel work on Sunday.
• Little I can imagine living without electricity.

→ _____

반   이름   맞은 개수

정답 및 해설 p.37

[01-05] 다음 빈칸에 들어갈 수 있는 말을 고르시오.

01
Do I have to pay to have this washing machine _____?

① repair
② repaired
③ repairing
④ to repair
⑤ being repaired

02
The film will show you _____ the natives of Alaska lived at that time.

① when
② which
③ how
④ who
⑤ what

03
My father let my sister _____ a bicycle.

① have
② has
③ had
④ to have
⑤ having

04
If it had not been for your help, I _____ up.

① give
② gave
③ will give
④ had given
⑤ would have given

05
When I arrived at the party, Jack wasn't there. He _____ home.

① goes
② go
③ was going
④ has gone
⑤ had gone

서술형 **NEW** **내신 기출**

06 다음 대화의 빈칸에 들어갈 한 단어와 보기의 단어를 한 번씩만 사용하여 문장을 완성하시오.

A: Mom, I want to go out and play.
B: It's raining heavily now. You will get wet _____ you go out.

| 보기 |
he   I   will   wonder
a   new   release   album

→ _____

서술형

07 다음 문장에서 틀린 부분을 찾아 바르게 고치시오.

Do you know the man who talking with her?
(   ) → (   )

[08-10] 다음 대화의 빈칸에 들어갈 수 있는 말을 고르시오.

08
A: How long has Jessica worked in this restaurant?
B: About two years. She has worked here _____ she was 20.

① for
② after
③ at
④ from
⑤ since

09
A: What would you do if you _____ more free time?
B: I'd take dancing lessons.

① have
② had
③ will have
④ had had
⑤ have had

10

> A: She is mad because I didn't tell the truth.
> B: You _____ have lied.

① must   ② can't

③ should   ④ shouldn't

⑤ could

[11-12] 두 문장의 뜻이 같도록 문장을 완성하시오.

11 Without his advice, his son couldn't have succeeded.

→ If it _____ his advice, his son couldn't have succeeded.

12 No matter what she sings, it will sound great.

→ _____ she sings, it will sound great.

[13-14] 다음 ( ) 안의 말을 바르게 고친 것을 고르시오.

13

> I feel like (go) to the beach.

① went   ② to go

③ go   ④ going

⑤ having gone

14

> They were planning (visit) their cousins.

① visit   ② to visit

③ visiting   ④ visited

⑤ having visited

[15-16] 우리말과 뜻이 같도록 문장을 완성하시오.

15 비가 아무리 많이 올지라도 우리는 그곳에 가야 한다.

→ _____ hard it may rain, we must go there.

16 언덕을 달려 내려가고 있는 그 여자는 나의 고등학교 친구들 중 한 명이다.

→ The woman _____ down the hill is one of my high school friends.

17 다음 중 어법상 틀린 것은?

① We do believe what you said.

② It was Sam that broke the glass.

③ Neither of them goes to college.

④ I didn't hear it, and neither did he.

⑤ Never finished she her homework on time.

18 다음 밑줄 친 부분 중 어법상 틀린 것은?

① Compared with him, she is old.

② While talking to him, I drank a Coke.

③ Knowing not what to do, he stood still.

④ I was walking down the street singing songs.

⑤ Generally speaking, boys are taller than girls.

19 다음 표를 보고 가정법을 사용하여 문장을 완성하시오.

Wish
to have a girlfriend
to get better grades in science
to be a soccer team captain

1) I wish _____ _____ _____ _____.

2) I wish _____ _____ _____ _____

_____ _____.

3) I wish _____ _____ _____ _____

_____ _____.

[20-21] 다음 문장을 간접화법으로 바꿀 때 빈칸에 들어
갈 수 있는 말을 고르시오.

20
> The policeman said to him, "Where do you
> live?"
> → The policeman asked him _____.

① where you live

② where you lived

③ where he lives

④ where he lived

⑤ where he had lived

21
> Mike said to me, "Can you go with me?"
> → Mike asked me _____.

① if I could go with him

② that I can go with him

③ if you could go with me

④ whether I can go with him

⑤ that you could go with me

22 주어진 말을 어법에 맞게 배열할 때 네 번째 오는 말
은?

> (an old man, up, was, by, he, brought).

① by   ② he

③ up   ④ was

⑤ brought

23 두 문장의 뜻이 같도록 할 때 빈칸에 들어갈 수 있는
것은?

> Some books are interesting, but others are
> not.
> → _____ book is interesting.

① Neither   ② None

③ All   ④ Both

⑤ Not every

[24-25] 우리말과 뜻이 같도록 주어진 말을 사용하여 문장
을 완성하시오.

24 그는 내가 지금까지 만난 사람 중 가장 재미있는 사람이다.
(funny, person, meet)

→ He is _____ _____ _____ _____

_____ _____ _____ _____.

25 이 가게에서 사과보다 더 인기 있는 과일은 없다.
(fruit, popular, apples)

→ _____ _____ _____ _____ _____

_____ _____ in this store.

[01-05] 다음 빈칸에 들어갈 수 있는 말을 고르시오.

01

London has a famous clock _____ "Big Ben."

① call   ② calling
③ to call   ④ called
⑤ be called

02

Do you know _____ he felt tired today?

① who   ② why
③ what   ④ which
⑤ whom

03

_____ Mary washed the shirt twice, it still wasn't clean.

① As   ② Though
③ If   ④ Because
⑤ Since

04

A: Which is my bed, this one or that one?
B: You can sleep in _____ you like.

① it   ② which
③ that   ④ whichever
⑤ wherever

05

It was nice _____ you to help the old lady.

① to   ② for
③ of   ④ about
⑤ with

NEW 내신 기출

06 다음 문장에 대해 잘못 설명한 학생은?

There _____ be some pine trees near my school, but they were cut down years ago.

① 민주: 빈칸에 조동사 used to가 와야 자연스러워.
② 세윤: 빈칸에 조동사 would를 쓸 수 있어.
③ 다인: but 이하는 수동태가 쓰인 문장이야.
④ 해찬: but 이하 문장에는 『by+행위자』가 생략 되어 있어.
⑤ 나라: ago는 명백하게 과거를 나타내는 말이야.

서술형

[07-08] 우리말과 뜻이 같도록 문장을 완성하시오.

07 Roy가 TV를 켰을 때 그 프로그램은 이미 끝난 뒤였다.
→ When Roy turned on the TV, the program _____ already _____.

08 내가 여기 있는 모든 사람의 이름을 아는 것은 아니다.
→ I _____ know _____ person's name here.

서술형 **NEW** 내신 기출

09 우리말과 뜻이 같도록 주어진 철자로 시작하여 문장을 완성하시오.

한국 학생들이 항상 바쁜 것은 아니다.
→ K_____ s_____ a_____ n_____
a_____ b_____ .

10 다음 밑줄 친 부분 중 생략할 수 있는 것은?

He had no ① money ② which ③ he could ④ buy bread ⑤ with.

11 다음 빈칸에 들어갈 수 <u>없는</u> 것은?

> Mr. Kim _____ me to go home early.

① had   ② told

③ asked   ④ ordered

⑤ advised

서술형

[12-13] 다음 빈칸에 공통으로 들어갈 수 있는 말을 보기에서 고르시오.

> —| 보기 |—
> as   after   since   while   because

12 • _____ I have no money, I can't buy it.
  • I haven't seen her _____ she came back from Canada.

13 • I saw him _____ he was leaving the party.
  • He fell asleep on the sofa, _____ he was tired.

[14-16] 우리말과 뜻이 같도록 할 때 빈칸에 들어갈 수 있는 말을 고르시오.

14

> 그가 말한 것을 고려해 보면, 그는 영리함이 틀림없다.
> → _____ what he said, he must be smart.

① Thinking   ② Considering

③ Compared   ④ Speaking

⑤ Taken

15

> 그녀는 눈을 감은 채로 앉아 있다.
> → She sat _____.

① her eyes closing

② with close eyes

③ with closing eyes

④ with her eyes closed

⑤ with her eyes closing

16

> Mike가 집 청소를 시작해야 할 때이다.
> → It's time Mike _____.

① start cleaning the house

② starts cleaning the house

③ started cleaning the house

④ will start cleaning the house

⑤ have started cleaning the house

17 다음 밑줄 친 부분 중 어법상 <u>틀린</u> 것은?

① He is <u>sleeping</u> now.

② <u>Have you</u> ever been to America?

③ She <u>came back</u> to Korea yesterday.

④ I've <u>known</u> her since she was a kid.

⑤ He <u>was watching</u> TV since two o'clock.

서술형

[18-19] 두 문장의 뜻이 같도록 문장을 완성하시오.

18 As he is honest, he is loved by everybody.

  → _____ _____, he is loved by everybody.

19 After he had finished his work, he went home.

  → _____ _____ his work, he went home.

20 다음 문장을 간접화법으로 바꿔 쓰시오.

The man said to them, "Don't bring any food into the pool."

→ _____

21 다음 밑줄 친 부분 중 어법상 틀린 것을 바르게 고치시오.

I ① found ② the necklace ③ that I ④ have lost ⑤ the day before.

22 보기의 밑줄 친 if와 쓰임이 같은 것은?

| 보기 |
Do you know if he bought a new backpack yesterday?

① If you need help, come and see me.
② If I were you, I would stay home.
③ If you need the book, I'll lend it to you.
④ I'm not sure if he went to see his parents.
⑤ I won't see you again if you don't stop lying.

[23-24] 주어진 말을 어법에 맞게 바꿔 쓰시오.

23 If it _____ a nice day today, we would play baseball. (be)

24 If I _____ a pencil, I would have sketched the view. (have)

25 다음 빈칸에 들어갈 말을 바르게 짝지은 것은?

ⓐ The number of people _____ increasing rapidly.
ⓑ The poor _____ helped by the charity.

	ⓐ	ⓑ		ⓐ	ⓑ
①	is	– is	②	is	– are
③	are	– is	④	am	– are
⑤	are	– are			

26 다음 두 문장을 한 문장으로 만들 때 빈칸에 들어갈 수 있는 것은?

It began snowing three hours ago. It is snowing now.
→ It _____ for three hours.

① is snowing
② was snowing
③ had snowed
④ has been snowing
⑤ had been snowing

27 중학생들이 통학하는 방법에 대한 다음 표를 보고, 주어진 말을 사용하여 문장을 완성하시오

1) Taking a bus is _____ _____ _____ any other way of getting to school. (popular)

2) Taking the subway is _____ _____ _____ _____ riding a bike. (common)

3) Riding a bike is _____ _____ _____ way of getting to school. (common)

MEMO

지은이

NE능률 영어교육연구소

NE능률 영어교육연구소는 혁신적이며 효율적인 영어 교재를 개발하고
영어 학습의 질을 한 단계 높이고자 노력하는 NE능률의 연구조직입니다.

1316 GRAMMAR 〈LEVEL 3〉

펴 낸 이	주민홍
펴 낸 곳	서울특별시 마포구 월드컵북로 396(상암동) 누리꿈스퀘어 비즈니스타워 10층
	(주)NE능률 (우편번호 03925)
펴 낸 날	2024년 1월 5일 개정판 제1쇄 발행
	2024년 6월 15일 제2쇄
전　　화	02 2014 7114
팩　　스	02 3142 0356
홈페이지	www.neungyule.com
등록번호	제 1-68호
I S B N	979-11-253-4286-1
정　　가	14,500원

NE 능률

고객센터

교재 내용 문의 : contact.nebooks.co.kr (별도의 가입 절차 없이 작성 가능)
제품 구매, 교환, 불량, 반품 문의 : 02-2014-7114
☎ 전화문의는 본사 업무시간 중에만 가능합니다.

MEMO

기초부터 내신까지 중학 영문법 완성

1316

1316 GRAMMAR

WORKBOOK

LEVEL
3

UNIT 1 to부정사의 명사적 용법

[1-3] 두 문장의 뜻이 같도록 문장을 완성하시오.

1 To wear a helmet is important.

→ _____ is important _____ _____ a helmet.

2 Please let me know what I should do next.

→ Please let me know _____ _____ _____ next.

3 To make friends with her is easy.

→ _____ is easy _____ _____ friends with her.

[4-9] 우리말과 뜻이 같도록 주어진 말을 사용하여 문장을 완성하시오.

4 애완동물을 키우는 것은 아주 좋다. (have a pet)

_____ is great _____ _____ _____ _____.

5 어머니께서는 프랑스에 가고 싶어 하신다. (want, go)

My mother _____ _____ _____ to France.

6 나의 직업은 커피를 만드는 것이다. (make coffee)

My job is _____ _____ _____.

7 아버지께서는 내게 돈을 현명하게 사용하는 법을 가르치셨다. (use money)

My father taught me _____ _____ _____ _____ wisely.

8 그는 금요일까지 그 프로젝트를 끝내는 게 힘들다는 것을 깨달았다. (difficult, finish)

He found _____ _____ _____ _____ the project by Friday.

9 나는 돈을 낭비하지 않기로 결심했다. (waste)

I decided _____ _____ _____ money.

[10-12] 우리말과 뜻이 같도록 주어진 말을 바르게 배열하시오.

10 진정한 친구를 갖는 것은 좋다. (have, a true friend, is, it, good, to)

→ _____

11 그녀는 어느 것을 선택할지 결정할 수 없었다. (decide, which, she, choose, couldn't, to)

→ _____

12 그들은 매일 밤 산책하는 것을 규칙으로 정했다. (made, every night, they, a rule, it, to, take a walk)

→ _____

UNIT 2 to부정사의 형용사적 용법, 부사적 용법

[1-4] 두 문장을 한 문장으로 만들 때 빈칸에 알맞은 말을 쓰시오.

1 You must be foolish. You believe his lie.
→ You must be foolish _____ _____ his lie.

2 He missed his favorite TV program. He was disappointed.
→ He was disappointed _____ _____ his favorite TV program.

3 If he knew that, he would be very shocked.
→ He would be very shocked _____ _____ _____.

4 She went to the drugstore but found it closed.
→ She went to the drugstore only _____ _____ it closed.

[5-8] 우리말과 뜻이 같도록 주어진 말을 사용하여 문장을 완성하시오.

5 Mick은 말을 걸기에 쉽지 않다. (talk to)
Mick is not easy _____ _____ _____.

6 너는 오늘 오후에 Brown 씨를 방문해야 한다. (visit)
_____ _____ _____ _____ Mr. Brown this afternoon.

7 너는 이 노래를 들어 볼 기회가 있었니? (listen to)
Have you ever had the chance _____ _____ _____ _____ _____?

8 Brian은 새 자전거 한 대를 사기 위해 돈을 모았다. (buy, bicycle)
Brian saved money _____ _____ _____ _____ _____.

[9-12] 다음 문장을 해석하시오.

9 I need some warm clothes to wear.
→ _____

10 The actor woke up to find himself a superstar.
→ _____

11 If you are to stay healthy, you should not eat junk food.
→ _____

12 They were very happy to win first prize.
→ _____

UNIT 3 to부정사의 의미상 주어, 시제, 수동태

[1-5] 다음 밑줄 친 부분을 바르게 고치시오.

1 He seems to <u>leaving</u> his wallet on the bus this morning.

2 <u>She</u> seemed that she missed her boyfriend.

3 It is stupid <u>for</u> you to lie.

4 It is uncomfortable <u>of</u> me to wear skinny jeans.

5 It was generous <u>for</u> her to help homeless people.

[6-8] 두 문장의 뜻이 같도록 문장을 완성하시오.

6 They seem to have been angry.
   → It seems _____ _____ _____ angry.

7 It seems that Mary was a teacher.
   → Mary seems _____ _____ _____ a teacher.

8 It seems that he is in a bad mood today.
   → He seems _____ _____ in a bad mood today.

[9-13] 우리말과 뜻이 같도록 주어진 말을 사용하여 문장을 완성하시오.

9 너는 그 파티에서 즐거운 시간을 보내는 것 같았다. (enjoy oneself)
   You _____ _____ _____ _____ at the party.

10 그녀가 나의 가방을 찾아 준 것은 친절했다. (nice, find)
   It was _____ _____ _____ _____ _____ my bag.

11 그녀가 모든 사람에게 사랑받는 것은 당연하다. (natural, love)
   It is _____ _____ _____ _____ _____ _____ by everyone.

12 네가 미리 예약을 한 것은 현명했다. (wise, make a reservation)
   It was _____ _____ _____ _____ _____ _____ _____ in advance.

13 그 음식은 며칠 전에 요리된 것처럼 보였다. (cook)
   The food _____ _____ _____ _____ _____ a few days ago.

UNIT 4 목적격 보어로 쓰이는 to부정사와 원형부정사

[1-5] 다음 밑줄 친 부분을 바르게 고치시오.

1 My grandfather had me <u>to bring</u> him a blanket.

2 He saw me <u>to talking</u> with her.

3 They asked Mr. Taylor <u>play</u> the piano.

4 She ordered the boy <u>going</u> home.

5 She wanted me <u>sing</u> for her.

[6-9] 주어진 말을 필요시 어법에 맞게 바꿔 쓰시오.

6 They got me _____ Jane home. (take)

7 My father allowed me _____ camping with my friends. (go)

8 Mr. Lee made the students _____ their homework by Wednesday. (do)

9 We saw Natalie _____ at the bus stop. (stand)

[10-14] 우리말과 뜻이 같도록 주어진 말을 사용하여 문장을 완성하시오.

10 나는 내 남동생에게 파티 음식을 준비하게 했다. (have, prepare)
   I _____ _____ _____ _____ food for the party.

11 사랑은 우리가 좀 더 나은 세상을 만들도록 도와준다. (make)
   Love _____ _____ _____ a better world.

12 나는 그 고양이가 내 옆에 눕는 것을 느꼈다. (the cat, lie)
   I _____ _____ _____ _____ beside me.

13 그들은 내가 저녁을 사기를 기대했다. (expect, buy)
   They _____ _____ _____ _____ dinner.

14 우리는 차고에서 누군가가 비명을 지르는 것을 들었다. (someone, scream)
   We _____ _____ _____ in the garage.

UNIT 5 to부정사를 이용한 주요 구문, 독립부정사

[1-4] 다음 밑줄 친 부분을 바르게 고치시오.

1 It took me an hour <u>finding</u> a parking spot.

2 Strange <u>saying</u>, I hoped to fail that audition.

3 The cell phone was so expensive that I <u>could</u> buy it.

4 It is <u>enough cold</u> to freeze the lake.

[5-6] 두 문장의 뜻이 같도록 문장을 완성하시오.

5 I was so scared that I couldn't watch the movie.
   → I was _____ scared _____ watch the movie.

6 The child is so clever that she can speak three languages.
   → The child is _____ _____ _____ _____ three languages.

[7-9] 우리말과 뜻이 같도록 주어진 말을 사용하여 문장을 완성하시오.

7 네가 거기에 가는 데 20분이 걸릴 것이다. (take, get)
   It'll _____ _____ _____ _____ _____ _____ there.

8 사실대로 말하면, 나는 네 헤어스타일이 마음에 들지 않는다. (tell)
   _____ _____ _____ _____, I don't like your hairstyle.

9 설상가상으로, 그들은 또한 충분한 돈이 없었다. (matters, worse)
   _____ _____ _____ _____, they also didn't have enough money.

[10-13] 우리말과 뜻이 같도록 주어진 말을 바르게 배열하시오.

10 나는 스파게티를 요리하는 데 두 시간이 걸렸다. (took, the spaghetti, to, it, two hours, me, cook)
    → _____

11 솔직히 말해서, 저 셔츠는 너에게 어울리지 않는다. (frank, with, you, be, to)
    → _____, that shirt does not look good on you.

12 그들은 너무 기뻐서 가만히 앉아 있을 수 없었다. (to, too, glad, still, sit)
    → They were _____.

13 그녀는 그 롤러코스터를 탈 수 있을 만큼 충분히 나이가 들었다.
    (ride, to, enough, the roller coaster, old)
    → She is _____.

UNIT **1** 동명사의 역할

[1-6] 다음 밑줄 친 부분이 어법상 맞으면 ○ 표시하고, 틀리면 바르게 고치시오.

1 He enjoys <u>to have</u> adventures.

2 My biggest problem is <u>waking up</u>.

3 <u>Traveling</u> by train is cheaper.

4 We went to sleep instead of <u>watch</u> TV.

5 She is not good at <u>being hidden</u> her feelings.

6 I am worried about <u>she missing</u> the class today.

[7-10] 두 문장의 뜻이 같도록 문장을 완성하시오.

7 I'm worried that you might catch a bad cold.
→ I'm worried about _____ _____ a bad cold.

8 I'm proud that you won first prize.
→ I'm proud of _____ _____ _____ first prize.

9 He was sorry that he didn't remember my birthday.
→ He was sorry for _____ _____ my birthday.

10 Do you mind if I open the window?
→ Do you mind _____ _____ the window?

[11-15] 우리말과 뜻이 같도록 주어진 말을 바르게 배열하시오.

11 그는 자신의 직업에 대해 계속해서 불평했다. (about, his job, he, complaining, kept)
→ _____

12 균형 잡힌 식사를 하는 것이 중요하다. (having, is, important, a balanced diet)
→ _____

13 당신과 함께 있지 못해서 미안합니다. (not, you, sorry, being, for, I'm, with)
→ _____

14 나는 점심으로 샌드위치를 먹는 것에 싫증이 난다. (am tired, eating, for lunch, I, of, sandwiches)
→ _____

15 내가 가장 좋아하는 활동은 강가를 따라 자전거를 타는 것이다. (along, a bicycle, the riverside, riding)
→ My favorite activity is _____.

UNIT 2 목적어로 쓰이는 동명사와 to부정사

[1-5] 다음 밑줄 친 부분을 바르게 고치시오.

1 Justin promised <u>lending</u> me his jacket.

2 She gave up <u>to learn</u> Chinese.

3 He denied <u>to commit</u> the crime.

4 They wanted <u>going</u> to an amusement park.

5 Do you mind <u>to turn</u> off the radio?

[6-10] 우리말과 뜻이 같도록 문장을 완성하시오.

6 나는 그녀를 기쁘게 만들려고 노력했다.
   I tried _____ her happy.

7 우리는 여러분을 우리 집에 초대하고 싶습니다.
   We hope _____ you to our house.

8 나는 청바지와 같이 캐주얼한 옷을 즐겨 입는다.
   I enjoy _____ casual clothes such as jeans.

9 그 개는 그 소년을 따라가는 것을 멈췄다.
   The dog stopped _____ the boy.

10 그는 그녀를 처음으로 만났던 것을 기억한다.
   He remembers _____ her for the first time.

[11-14] 우리말과 뜻이 같도록 주어진 말을 사용하여 문장을 완성하시오.

11 그녀는 의사의 진찰을 받을 것을 잊어버렸다. (forget, see a doctor)
   She _____ _____ _____ _____ _____.

12 그는 Veronica에게 계속 전화했다. (keep, call)
   He _____ _____ _____.

13 그 남자는 그의 신분증을 보여 주는 것을 거부했다. (refuse, show his ID)
   The man _____ _____ _____ _____ _____.

14 Jack은 그의 첫사랑을 언급하는 것을 피했다. (avoid, mention, his first love)
   Jack _____ _____ _____ _____ _____.

UNIT 3 동명사를 이용한 주요 구문

[1-5] 다음 밑줄 친 부분을 바르게 고치시오.

1 Ms. Jones is used to <u>handle</u> complaints.

2 Mr. Baker is worth <u>trust</u>.

3 What about <u>join</u> the school band?

4 I feel like <u>to drink</u> something hot.

5 He is having trouble <u>train</u> his new pet.

[6-10] 우리말과 뜻이 같도록 문장을 완성하시오.

6 나는 그 뮤지컬 보는 것을 고대하고 있다.

   I am _____ _____ _____ seeing the musical.

7 우리는 내일 스케이트를 타러 갈 것이다.

   We will _____ _____ tomorrow.

8 그는 크리스마스 카드를 쓰느라 바쁘다.

   He _____ _____ _____ Christmas cards.

9 방에 들어오자마자 나는 TV를 켰다.

   _____ _____ the room, I turned on the TV.

10 나는 그에게 "미안해."라고 말하지 않을 수 없다.

   I _____ _____ _____ "I'm sorry" to him.

[11-14] 우리말과 뜻이 같도록 주어진 말을 사용하여 문장을 완성하시오.

11 아빠는 내가 밤에 외출하는 것을 막으신다. (go out)

   Dad _____ _____ _____ _____ _____ at night.

12 이 장소는 여러 번 방문할 만한 가치가 있다. (visit)

   This place _____ _____ _____ many times.

13 그녀는 새 수영복 하나를 사는 데 두 시간을 썼다. (shop for)

   She _____ _____ _____ _____ _____ a new swimsuit.

14 너의 결정에 대해 후회해 봐야 소용없다. (regret)

   _____ _____ _____ _____ your decision.

UNIT 1 분사의 역할

[1-5] 주어진 말을 어법에 맞게 바꿔 쓰시오.

1 The boy _____ brightly is Chloe's brother. (smile)

2 The end of the movie was _____. (disappoint)

3 He bought a picture _____ by a young artist. (paint)

4 There are pieces of _____ glass on the floor. (break)

5 My mother looked at the children _____ toward her. (run)

[6-10] 두 문장의 뜻이 같도록 문장을 완성하시오.

6 The students are shouting. They are my classmates.
   → The students _____ are my classmates.

7 The story was written by Harry. It was really interesting.
   → The story _____ _____ _____ was really interesting.

8 She has a watch. It was made in Switzerland.
   → She has a watch _____ _____ _____.

9 The police have found the car. It was stolen from Scott.
   → The police have found the car _____ _____ _____.

10 The flowers are growing in the garden. They are very beautiful.
   → The flowers _____ _____ _____ _____ are very beautiful.

[11-14] 우리말과 뜻이 같도록 주어진 말을 사용하여 문장을 완성하시오.

11 무대 위에서 노래를 부르는 그 소녀는 행복해 보인다. (sing, on the stage)
   The girl _____ _____ _____ _____ looks happy.

12 나는 내 사진을 찍었다. (have, picture, take)
   I _____ _____ _____ _____.

13 그녀는 한 아이가 모형 비행기를 만드는 것을 보았다. (watch, a child, make)
   She _____ _____ _____ _____ a model plane.

14 바이올린을 켜고 있는 그 아이는 다섯 살이다. (the child, play the violin)
   _____ _____ _____ _____ _____ is five years old.

UNIT 2 분사구문

[1-5] 다음 밑줄 친 부분을 부사절로 바꿔 쓰시오.

1 <u>Having nothing to do</u>, I stayed in bed all day.

2 <u>Being very busy</u>, he didn't have time for breakfast.

3 <u>Though having a car</u>, I often walk to work.

4 <u>Breaking your promise</u>, you will lose her trust.

5 <u>Taking a walk with my family</u>, I came across my girlfriend.

[6-10] 다음 밑줄 친 부분을 분사구문으로 바꿔 쓰시오.

6 <u>If you take bus number 33</u>, you can get there.
   → _____, you can get there.

7 <u>As he took off his coat</u>, he said hello to everyone in the room.
   → _____, he said hello to everyone in the room.

8 <u>As soon as he saw his mother</u>, the child ran to her.
   → _____, the child ran to her.

9 <u>Because she knew how to do it</u>, she finished the work very quickly.
   → _____, she finished the work very quickly.

10 <u>Although they got poor grades</u>, they were not disappointed.
   → Although _____, they were not disappointed.

[11-14] 우리말과 뜻이 같도록 주어진 말을 바르게 배열하시오. (단, 분사구문을 문두에 쓸 것)

11 우리는 일찍 출발해서 정시에 도착했다. (we, early, leaving, on time, arrived)
   → _____

12 나는 서둘렀기 때문에 실수를 많이 했다. (I, many mistakes, in a hurry, made, being)
   → _____

13 커피 한 잔을 마시면서 나는 그 잡지를 읽었다. (drinking, read, the magazine, I, a cup of coffee)
   → _____

14 이 셔츠를 사면 당신은 하나를 공짜로 얻게 될 것이다. (this, free, you'll, shirt, buying, get, one)
   → _____

UNIT 3 분사구문의 부정, 시제, 수동태

[1-3] 두 문장의 뜻이 같도록 문장을 완성하시오.

1 After I read his letter, I couldn't sleep at all.
   → _____ his letter, I couldn't sleep at all.

2 Because he didn't like to stay home, he went out.
   → _____ _____ to stay home, he went out.

3 Although she saw me, she pretended not to see me.
   → _____ _____ _____, she pretended not to see me.

[4-7] 우리말과 뜻이 같도록 주어진 말을 바르게 배열하시오.

4 다리를 다쳐서 그는 축구하는 것을 그만두었다. (injured, his leg, having)
   → _____, he stopped playing soccer.

5 어디로 가야 할지 몰랐기 때문에 나는 한참 동안 거기에 서 있었다. (go, not, to, knowing, where)
   → _____, I stood there for a long time.

6 가난한 집에서 태어났기 때문에 그는 대학에 갈 수 없었다. (having, born, a poor family, into, been)
   → _____, he wasn't able to go to a college.

7 바리스타로 일했기 때문에 그는 맛있는 커피를 만들 수 있다. (worked, as, having, a barista)
   → _____, he can make delicious coffee.

[8-11] 우리말과 뜻이 같도록 주어진 말을 사용하여 문장을 완성하시오.

8 그 드라마를 보지 않아서 나는 그 줄거리를 모른다. (watch)
   _____ _____ the drama, I don't know the plot.

9 50년 전에 지어져서 그 집은 수리가 필요했다. (build)
   _____ _____ _____ _____, the house needed repairing.

10 전에 거기에 가 본 적이 있기 때문에 나는 그것을 찾는 데 어려움을 겪지 않았다. (be)
   _____ _____ there before, I had no difficulty finding it.

11 그의 아버지에 비해 그는 훨씬 더 키가 크다. (compare to)
   _____ _____ his father, he is much taller.

UNIT 4 주의해야 할 분사구문

[1-4] 우리말과 뜻이 같도록 주어진 말을 사용하여 문장을 완성하시오.

1 그는 팔짱을 낀 채 소파에 앉아 있었다. (fold)

He sat on the sofa with his arms _____.

2 대강 말하자면 오천 명이 넘는 사람들이 매년 그곳을 방문한다. (speak)

_____ _____, over 5,000 people visit the place every year.

3 그의 목소리로 판단하건대 그는 낙담했음이 틀림없다. (judge)

_____ _____ his voice, he must be depressed.

4 남은 티켓이 없었기 때문에 우리는 그 경기를 보지 못했다. (be)

There _____ no tickets left, we couldn't watch the game.

[5-7] 다음 문장을 해석하시오.

5 The baby falling asleep, I turned off the TV.

→ _____

6 Strictly speaking, she is not good at math.

→ _____

7 The alarm ringing loudly, he woke up.

→ _____

[8-11] 우리말과 뜻이 같도록 주어진 말을 사용하여 분사구문을 완성하시오.

8 날이 화창해서 우리는 소풍을 갔다. (the day, sunny)

_____ _____ _____ _____, we went on a picnic.

9 나의 상사는 다리를 꼰 채 앉아 있었다. (legs, cross)

My boss was sitting _____ _____ _____ _____.

10 그의 개가 그를 뒤따르는 채 그는 밖으로 나갔다. (follow)

He went out _____ _____ _____ _____ _____.

11 어두워졌기 때문에 우리는 집에 있기로 결정했다. (it, get dark)

_____ _____ _____, we decided to stay home.

UNIT 1 현재완료

[1-4] 두 문장의 뜻이 같도록 문장을 완성하시오.

1 He went to Australia, and he's still there.
   → He _____ _____ to Australia.

2 I started to take yoga in 2012. I still take it.
   → I _____ _____ yoga since 2012.

3 The alarm began to ring ten minutes ago. It is still ringing.
   → The alarm _____ _____ _____ for ten minutes.

4 I forgot his phone number, and I can't remember it now.
   → I _____ _____ his phone number.

[5-8] 우리말과 뜻이 같도록 주어진 말을 사용하여 문장을 완성하시오.

5 나는 Eddie를 위한 선물을 이미 샀다. (buy)
   I _____ _____ _____ a present for Eddie.

6 그녀는 하루 종일 방에서 노래를 불러 오고 있다. (sing)
   She _____ _____ _____ in her room all day.

7 나는 여름 방학 때 어디를 갈지 아직 결정하지 못했다. (decide)
   I _____ _____ where to go for summer vacation yet.

8 우리는 전에 그렇게 아름다운 섬을 결코 본 적이 없다. (see)
   We _____ _____ _____ such a beautiful island before.

[9-12] 다음 문장을 해석하시오.

9 I have just finished cleaning the house.
   → _____

10 She has not been feeling well since last Sunday.
   → _____

11 Tim has not arrived the station yet.
   → _____

12 We have been waiting for you for an hour.
   → _____

UNIT 2 과거완료, 미래완료

[1-5] 다음 밑줄 친 부분을 바르게 고치시오.

1 They lost the game because they <u>haven't</u> practiced enough.

2 When we arrived at the theater, the movie had already <u>begin</u>.

3 They <u>have</u> been talking for an hour when I went to see them.

4 Maria looked at the painting that she <u>has</u> seen in the books.

5 I <u>have</u> changed my clothes before I went to Tom's party.

[6-10] 우리말과 뜻이 같도록 밑줄 친 부분을 바르게 고치시오.

6 우리는 거기에 전에 가 본 적이 있었기 때문에 그 장소를 잘 알고 있었다.
We knew the place well, for we <u>were</u> there before.

7 그는 그저께 교통사고를 당했어서 어제 오지 못했다.
He <u>has</u> a car accident the day before yesterday, so he couldn't come yesterday.

8 내가 그녀에게 전화했을 때 그녀는 이미 숙제를 마쳤었다.
She <u>has already finished</u> her homework when I called her.

9 내가 시애틀에 도착했을 때 일주일 째 비가 내리고 있었다.
It <u>has rained</u> for a week when I arrived in Seattle.

10 20분 후면 그녀는 그를 3시간째 기다리고 있는 게 될 것이다.
In 20 minutes, she <u>is waiting</u> for him for three hours.

[11-14] 우리말과 뜻이 같도록 주어진 말을 사용하여 문장을 완성하시오.

11 우리가 몇 주 동안 집을 청소하지 않았어서 집이 매우 더러웠다. (clean the house)
_____ _____ _____ _____ _____ for weeks, so it was very dirty.

12 그녀는 체중이 늘었어서 그 빨간 드레스를 입을 수 없었다. (gain weight)
_____ _____ _____ _____, so she couldn't wear the red dress.

13 지금쯤이면 심판들이 우승자를 결정했을 것이다. (decide on)
By now, the judges _____ _____ _____ _____ a winner.

14 내가 집에 갔을 때는 모두 이미 잠자리에 든 뒤였다. (go to bed, already)
Everybody _____ _____ _____ _____ when I got home.

UNIT **1** can, must, should / ought to, may, need

[1-3] 두 문장의 뜻이 같도록 문장을 완성하시오.

1 You must wear a helmet for your safety.
→ You _____ _____ wear a helmet for your safety.

2 They are able to speak Chinese.
→ They _____ speak Chinese.

3 Can I use your phone?
→ _____ I use your phone?

[4-8] 우리말과 뜻이 같도록 문장을 완성하시오.

4 내가 이 프로젝트를 마치면 나는 휴가를 갈 수 있을 것이다.
If I finish this project, I will _____ _____ _____ take a vacation.

5 나는 그 사무실을 다시 방문해야 했다.
I _____ _____ visit the office again.

6 너는 그 일을 지금 당장 할 필요가 없다.
You _____ _____ _____ do the work right now.

7 그것은 다이아몬드일 리가 없다. 그것은 너무 싸다.
It _____ _____ a diamond. It is too cheap.

8 여기에 주차하면 안 됩니다.
You _____ _____ park here.

[9-12] 우리말과 뜻이 같도록 조동사와 주어진 말을 사용하여 문장을 완성하시오.

9 그것은 사실일지도 모른다. (be, true)
_____ _____ _____ _____.

10 우리는 미래를 준비해야 한다. (prepare, for the future)
_____ _____ _____ _____ _____ _____.

11 제가 거기에 가야 하나요? (do, go, there)
_____ _____ _____ _____ _____ _____?

12 너는 너의 부모님께 순종해야 한다. (obey, your parents)
_____ _____ _____ _____ _____.

[1-5] 다음 밑줄 친 부분을 바르게 고치시오.

1 You have better drink some water.

2 I would better wash the dishes myself than have Tim do it.

3 Susan would have long, blonde hair.

4 We used to playing soccer after school.

5 That necklace is too expensive. I would not rather buy it.

[6-9] 우리말과 뜻이 같도록 문장을 완성하시오.

6 나는 그의 차를 타느니 차라리 그곳에 걸어가겠다.
I _____ _____ _____ there _____ take his car.

7 너는 점심에 과식을 하지 않는 게 좋겠다.
You had _____ _____ overeat at lunch.

8 그 아기는 밤에 울곤 했다.
The baby _____ _____ cry at night.

9 너는 따뜻한 코트를 입는 게 좋겠어.
You had _____ _____ a warm coat.

[10-13] 우리말과 뜻이 같도록 조동사와 주어진 말을 사용하여 문장을 완성하시오.

10 너는 네 자신을 잘 돌보는 게 좋겠다. (had, take care of)
You _____ _____ _____ _____ _____ yourself.

11 그녀는 하루에 다섯 시간씩 TV를 보곤 했다. (watch TV)
She _____ _____ _____ five hours a day.

12 나는 사람들 앞에서 노래를 부르느니 차라리 춤을 추겠다. (dance, sing a song)
I _____ _____ _____ _____ _____ _____ in front of people.

13 나는 그를 다시 안 보는 편이 낫겠다. (would, see)
I _____ _____ _____ _____ him again.

UNIT **3** 조동사 + have v-ed

[1-5] 주어진 말을 문맥에 맞게 바꿔 쓰시오.

1 She may (call) me yesterday. She wanted to ask me something.

2 He must (write) the report in a hurry the other day. It had many errors.

3 She can't (wash) her hair. She said she was busy this morning.

4 I should (visit) my grandparents last month. They said they missed me.

5 I could (win) first prize, but I finished in second place.

[6-9] 우리말과 뜻이 같도록 주어진 말을 사용하여 문장을 완성하시오.

6 우리는 지하철을 탔어야 했다. (take)

We _____ _____ _____ the subway.

7 그는 그렇게 멀리 갔을 리 없다. (go)

He _____ _____ _____ that so far.

8 Jack이 그 컵을 깨뜨렸음이 틀림없다. (break)

Jack _____ _____ _____ the cup.

9 그녀는 지난달에 시험에 불합격했을지도 모른다. (fail)

She _____ _____ _____ the test last month.

[10-14] 다음 문장을 해석하시오.

10 They can't have gone out together last night.

→ _____

11 He shouldn't have signed the contract.

→ _____

12 We could have helped each other.

→ _____

13 They must have fought each other.

→ _____

14 She might have been a reporter long ago.

→ _____

UNIT **1** 수동태의 의미와 형태

[1-5] 다음 밑줄 친 부분을 바르게 고치시오. (단, 시제를 유지할 것)

1 Tom <u>has invited</u> to dinner by Linda.

2 <u>Did</u> the music composed by her?

3 This orchard <u>is belonged to</u> Ms. Kim.

4 The World Cup <u>held</u> in Qatar in 2022.

5 The speech <u>is being making</u> by Sally.

[6-10] 다음 문장을 수동태 문장으로 바꿔 쓰시오.

6 They will find me.

→ _____

7 My father is washing the dog.

→ _____

8 We must not waste money.

→ _____

9 Who made this delicious pasta?

→ _____

10 They have displayed new clothes since last week.

→ _____

[11-14] 우리말과 뜻이 같도록 주어진 말을 사용하여 문장을 완성하시오.

11 그녀는 그들에 의해 가르침을 받을 것이다. (teach)

She _____ _____ _____ by them.

12 그 남자는 다리에 부상을 입었다. (wound)

The man _____ _____ in his leg.

13 이 블라우스는 세탁기에서 세탁되어서는 안 된다. (must, wash)

This blouse _____ _____ _____ _____ in the washing machine.

14 새로운 기술이 그 기업에 의해 개발되었다. (develop)

The new technology _____ _____ by the company.

UNIT 2 4형식·5형식 문장의 수동태

[1-5] ( ) 안에서 알맞은 말을 고르시오.

1 Robin was made (washing / to wash) the fruit by his mother.

2 He was asked (stop / to stop) smoking.

3 She was told (to cook / cooking) dinner.

4 The boy is expected (become / to become) a scientist.

5 A beggar was seen (enter / entering) the hotel.

[6-10] 두 문장의 뜻이 같도록 문장을 완성하시오.

6 We called him Little Joe.
  → He _____ Little Joe by us.

7 The people elected him president.
  → He _____.

8 She saw them swim in the river.
  → They _____.

9 My mother made me a pink dress.
  → A pink dress _____.

10 We named our daughter Amy.
  → Our daughter _____.

[11-14] 우리말과 뜻이 같도록 주어진 말을 사용하여 문장을 완성하시오.

11 그가 중국어를 유창하게 하는 것이 들렸다. (hear, speak)
  _____ _____ _____ _____ _____ fluently.

12 그 정보는 경찰에게 주어졌다. (the information, give, the police)
  _____ _____ _____ _____ _____ _____.

13 그녀는 그녀의 남자친구로부터 선물을 받았다. (give, a present)
  _____ _____ _____ _____ _____ _____ _____.

14 꽃 한 바구니가 나에게 보내졌다. (a basket of flowers, send, me)
  _____ _____ _____ _____ _____.

UNIT **3** 주의해야 할 수동태

[1-5] 빈칸에 by 이외의 전치사 중 알맞은 말을 쓰시오.

1 We were satisfied _____ their good service.

2 Is he interested _____ space science?

3 I was pleased _____ his success.

4 The bat was made _____ wood.

5 The doctor is known _____ the whole country.

[6-10] 두 문장의 뜻이 같도록 문장을 완성하시오.

6 My family depends on me.
   → I _____ by my family.

7 His team will carry out the project.
   → The project _____ by his team.

8 It is said that the Jessica's 3rd album was successful.
   → The Jessica's 3rd album is said _____.

9 We should look after the patient.
   → The patient _____ by us.

10 Mom turned off the TV.
   → The TV _____ by Mom.

[11-15] 우리말과 뜻이 같도록 주어진 말을 사용하여 문장을 완성하시오. (단, by 이외의 전치사를 쓸 것)

11 그의 가면이 벗겨졌다. (take off)
   His mask _____ _____ _____.

12 그녀의 눈은 눈물로 가득 차 있었다. (filled)
   Her eyes _____ _____ _____ tears.

13 그 백화점은 쇼핑객들로 붐빈다. (crowded)
   The department store _____ _____ _____ shoppers.

14 나는 수학 시험이 걱정된다. (worried)
   I _____ _____ _____ the math exam.

15 Michael은 모든 사람에게 친절하다고 일컬어진다. (say, friendly)
   Michael _____ _____ _____ _____ _____ to everyone.

UNIT **1** 가정법 과거, 가정법 과거완료, 혼합 가정법

[1-5] 주어진 말을 가정법에 맞게 바꿔 쓰시오.

1 If I _____ you, I would accept his proposal. (be)

2 If we _____ time, we could have watched the show. (have)

3 If the actor _____ good at acting, he would be more popular. (be)

4 If he _____ smoking, he could have lived longer. (stop)

5 If Jason had practiced more, he _____ a driver's license now. (will have)

[6-10] 다음 문장을 if절로 시작하는 가정법 문장으로 바꿔 쓰시오.

6 As they didn't do their homework, the teacher was disappointed.
   → _____

7 As she doesn't know his phone number, she can't call him.
   → _____

8 The concert tickets were sold out, so I couldn't go to the show.
   → _____

9 As he didn't know me well, he didn't lend me his books.
   → _____

10 I'm allergic to dogs, so I can't have one.
   → _____

[11-14] 우리말과 뜻이 같도록 주어진 말을 사용하여 가정법 문장을 완성하시오.

11 만약 그녀가 현명했더라면 그녀는 그 문제를 해결했을 텐데. (solve)
   If she had been wise, _____ _____ _____ _____ the problem.

12 만약 나의 할아버지께서 살아계시다면 무척 행복하실 텐데. (be, alive)
   _____ _____ _____ _____, he would be very happy.

13 만약 내가 휴대 전화를 떨어뜨리지 않았더라면 나는 지금 그것을 사용할 수 있을 텐데. (use)
   If I had not dropped my cell phone, _____ _____ _____ _____ now.

14 만약 네가 바쁘지 않다면 어디로 가겠니? (busy)
   Where would you go _____ _____ _____ _____?

UNIT **2** I wish, as if, without[but for], it's time

[1-6] 다음 밑줄 친 부분을 바르게 고치시오.

1 I wish I <u>can</u> go on a vacation this winter.

2 Jane talks as if she <u>had</u> a date with Roy, but she didn't.

3 I wish I <u>watched</u> the musical yesterday.

4 Tina lives in Seattle, but she acts as if she <u>had not lived</u> there.

5 If it <u>were not</u> for my friends, I would have quit the team last year.

6 It's time you <u>face</u> the truth.

[7-11] 두 문장의 뜻이 같도록 문장을 완성하시오.

7 Without water, we would die.
→ _____ _____ _____ _____ water, we would die.

8 I am sorry I didn't take your advice.
→ I _____ I _____ _____ your advice.

9 In fact, they didn't win the game.
→ They look as if they _____ _____ the game.

10 But for her efforts, she wouldn't have succeeded.
→ If it _____ _____ _____ _____ her efforts, she wouldn't have succeeded.

11 I am sorry I don't know how to play the game.
→ I _____ I _____ how to play the game.

[12-15] 우리말과 뜻이 같도록 주어진 말을 사용하여 문장을 완성하시오.

12 우리가 더 일찍 집에서 나왔더라면 좋을 텐데. (leave)
I wish _____ _____ _____ home earlier.

13 Wendy는 마치 그녀가 그 배우를 만났던 것처럼 말한다. (meet)
Wendy talks _____ _____ _____ _____ _____ the actor.

14 그 열쇠가 없었다면 우리는 문을 열 수 없었을 것이다. (the key, open)
_____ _____ _____ _____, _____ _____ _____ _____ _____
the door.

15 지금이 여름이라면 좋을 텐데. (be)
_____ _____ _____ _____ summer now.

UNIT 1 관계대명사

[1-4] 우리말과 뜻이 같도록 빈칸에 알맞은 관계대명사를 쓰시오.

1 나는 LA에 사는 친구가 한 명 있다.

I have a friend _____ lives in LA.

2 이것이 그가 가진 돈 전부이다.

This is all the money _____ he has.

3 우리가 가장 하고 싶은 것은 영화 보러 가는 것이다.

_____ we want to do most is to go to a movie.

4 그 감독은 머리가 금발인 소녀를 찾고 있다.

The director is looking for a girl _____ hair is blonde.

[5-8] 관계대명사를 사용하여 두 문장을 한 문장으로 만드시오.

5 This is the cat. I found it in the park.

→ _____

6 The boy is my brother. He is playing the drums on the stage.

→ _____

7 I moved to a house. Its roof is blue.

→ _____

8 I interviewed the actor. I've liked him for a long time.

→ _____

[9-12] 우리말과 뜻이 같도록 관계대명사와 주어진 말을 사용하여 문장을 완성하시오.

9 이것은 내가 가지고 있는 가장 오래된 책이다. (the oldest book, have)

This is _____ _____ _____ _____ _____ _____.

10 저 사람이 자녀가 천재인 그 여자이다. (a genius, the woman, child)

That's _____ _____ _____ _____ _____ _____.

11 그것들은 일본에서 온 원숭이들이다. (the monkeys)

They are _____ _____ _____ came from Japan.

12 그가 필요한 것은 진정한 친구이다. (need)

_____ _____ _____ _____ a true friend.

UNIT 2 관계부사

[1-5] 빈칸에 알맞은 관계부사를 쓰시오.

1   10 years ago today was the day _____ they married.

2   No one knows the reason _____ he did it.

3   Tell me _____ you spell your first name.

4   We work two miles away from the town _____ we live.

5   It was last New Year's Day _____ we first met.

[6-10] 두 문장의 뜻이 같도록 문장을 완성하시오.

6   This is the way in which they built the tower.
    → This is _____ they built the tower.

7   That café is the place in which we first met.
    → That café is the place _____ we first met.

8   Wednesday is the day on which the exhibition starts.
    → Wednesday is the day _____ the exhibition starts.

9   That is the reason for which she left Brian.
    → That is the reason _____ she left Brian.

10 We don't know how Mike found the answer.
    → We don't know _____ _____ Mike found the answer.

[11-14] 우리말과 뜻이 같도록 관계부사와 주어진 말을 사용하여 문장을 완성하시오.

11 겨울은 눈이 오는 계절이다. (the season)
    Winter is _____ _____ _____ it snows.

12 너희는 그가 학교에 결석한 이유를 들었니? (be absent from)
    Did you hear _____ _____ _____ _____ _____ school?

13 방콕은 우리가 우리의 휴가를 보낸 도시이다. (the city, spend, vacation)
    Bangkok is _____ _____ _____ _____ _____ _____.

14 그는 우리에게 그가 양초들을 만드는 방법을 보여 주었다. (make, candles)
    He showed us _____ _____ _____ _____.

UNIT 3 복합 관계사

[1-4] 우리말과 뜻이 같도록 빈칸에 알맞은 복합 관계사를 쓰시오.

1 여행 중에 우리가 가는 곳은 어디든지 비가 내렸다.
During our trip, it rained _____ we went.

2 Robin이 아무리 세심하게 설명해도 그의 남동생은 여전히 이해하지 못했다.
_____ carefully Robin explained, his little brother still didn't understand.

3 내가 보고 싶을 때는 언제나 여기에 와도 좋다.
You can come here _____ you want to see me.

4 표를 원하는 사람은 누구든지 이곳에 일찍 와야 한다.
_____ wants a ticket should come here early.

[5-8] 두 문장의 뜻이 같도록 문장을 완성하시오.

5 Anyone who comes to the concert can get an autograph.
→ _____ comes to the concert can get an autograph.

6 No matter where he goes, he will be loved by everyone.
→ _____ he goes, he will be loved by everyone.

7 She calls me at any time when she has a question.
→ She calls me _____ she has a question.

8 However hard I tried, I couldn't solve that problem.
→ _____ _____ _____ hard I tried, I couldn't solve that problem.

[9-11] 우리말과 뜻이 같도록 복합 관계사와 주어진 말을 사용하여 문장을 완성하시오.

9 그들은 여기에서 구입하는 것은 무엇이든지 만족할 것이다. (buy)
They will be satisfied with _____ _____ _____ here.

10 나는 네가 어디에 가더라도 너를 찾을 수 있다. (go)
I can find you _____ _____ _____.

11 아무리 오래 걸릴지라도 나는 그 일을 끝마칠 것이다. (long, it, take)
_____ _____ _____ _____ _____ _____, I'll finish the job.

UNIT 4 주의해야 할 관계사의 용법

[1-5] 다음 문장에서 생략된 말을 쓰시오.

1 It is the watch she has wanted to get.

2 This is the student I have told you about.

3 He is talking to the man selling fruits.

4 The skirt I'm wearing is my sister's.

5 I'd like to read the new novel written by Paulo Coelho.

[6-10] 두 문장의 뜻이 같도록 문장을 완성하시오.

6 It was Sophia's birthday party. They met him at the party.
   → The birthday party _____ _____ they met him was Sophia's.

7 We have money. We can travel with the money.
   → We have money _____ _____ we can travel.

8 This is the playground. My kids often play on it.
   → This is the playground _____ _____ my kids often play.

9 This is a friend of mine. I've talked about her before.
   → This is the friend of mine _____ _____ I've talked before.

10 I don't like the man. Lisa fell in love with him.
   → I don't like the man _____ _____ Lisa fell in love.

[11-14] 두 문장의 뜻이 같도록 관계사를 사용하여 문장을 완성하시오.

11 I went to the tourist information center, and there I got a city map.
   → I went to the tourist information center, _____ I got a city map.

12 Little boys danced on the stage, and it was very fun to watch.
   → Little boys danced on the stage, _____ was very fun to watch.

13 We visited Brazil in 2016, and at that time the Olympics were held.
   → We visited Brazil in 2016, _____ the Olympics were held.

14 I met Jack, and he taught me how to ride a bicycle.
   → I met Jack, _____ taught me how to ride a bicycle.

UNIT 1 비교 구문

[1-3] 두 문장의 뜻이 같도록 문장을 완성하시오.

1 I like baseball more than soccer.

→ I _____ baseball _____ soccer.

2 The theater is very crowded, and it is not usually as crowded as this.

→ The theater is _____ _____ _____ usual.

3 English is difficult, but math is more difficult.

→ English is _____ _____ _____ math.

[4-12] 우리말과 뜻이 같도록 주어진 말을 사용하여 문장을 완성하시오.

4 우리는 회의 전에 Jill에게 이야기했다. (prior, the meeting)

We talked to Jill _____ _____ _____ _____ .

5 나는 나의 오빠보다 더 많은 돈을 모았다. (money)

I saved _____ _____ _____ my brother did.

6 여름에 런던은 서울만큼 덥지는 않다. (hot)

London is _____ _____ _____ _____ Seoul in summer.

7 Amy는 우리 학교에서 가장 키가 큰 소녀이다. (tall)

Amy is _____ _____ _____ _____ my school.

8 John은 Kate보다 덜 활동적이다. (energetic)

John is _____ _____ _____ Kate.

9 그 쇼는 한국에서 가장 인기 있는 TV 프로그램이다. (popular, TV program)

The show is _____ _____ _____ _____ _____ in Korea.

10 그 연구는 책상이 변기보다 더 더러울 수 있다는 것을 보여 준다. (dirty)

The study shows that desks _____ _____ _____ _____ toilets.

11 나는 너보다 피아노를 더 잘 치지는 못한다. (well)

I can't play the piano _____ _____ _____ .

12 그녀는 세 아이들 중에 가장 재미있다. (fun)

She is _____ _____ _____ the three children.

UNIT 2 여러 가지 최상급 표현

[1-3] 다음 문장과 뜻이 같도록 문장을 완성하시오.

> This is the oldest house in my town.

1 _____ other house in my town is _____ _____ this one.

2 No other house in my town is _____ _____ _____ this one.

3 This house is _____ _____ _____ _____ _____ in my town.

[4-7] 다음 문장과 뜻이 같도록 ( ) 안의 지시대로 문장을 완성하시오.

> Time is the most precious thing of all.

4 Time is _____. (비교급 이용)

5 Time is _____. (비교급 이용)

6 Nothing is _____. (원급 이용)

7 Nothing is _____. (비교급 이용)

[8-13] 우리말과 뜻이 같도록 주어진 말을 사용하여 문장을 완성하시오.

8 브로콜리는 가장 몸에 좋은 음식들 중 하나이다. (healthy, foods)
   Broccoli is _____ _____ _____ _____ _____.

9 그는 그의 학교에서 다른 모든 학생들보다 더 높은 점수를 받았다. (good, student)
   He had _____ grades _____ _____ _____ _____ _____ in his school.

10 이 방에서 Jake만큼 키가 큰 소년은 없다. (tall)
   No boy in this room is _____ _____ _____ Jake.

11 이것이 내가 지금까지 마셔 본 것 중 가장 맛있는 커피이다. (good, coffee, have)
   This is _____ _____ _____ _____ _____ _____ _____.

12 아마존 강은 세계에서 가장 긴 강들 중 하나이다. (long, river)
   The Amazon River is _____ _____ _____ _____ _____ in the world.

13 이 휴대 전화보다 더 가벼운 휴대 전화는 없다. (cell phone, light)
   No other _____ _____ _____ _____ _____ this cell phone.

UNIT 3 비교 구문을 이용한 표현

[1-3] 주어진 말을 사용하여 문장을 완성하시오.

1 The situation is getting _____ and _____. (good)

2 He got paid twice _____ _____ _____ I did. (much)

3 The harder I try to understand this book, _____ _____ _____ it becomes. (difficult)

[4-8] 우리말과 뜻이 같도록 주어진 말을 사용하여 문장을 완성하시오.

4 그 강은 한강보다 약 3배 더 길다. (long)
   The river is about _____ _____ _____ _____ _____ the Han River.

5 점점 더 많은 손님들이 그의 가게에 왔다. (many)
   _____ _____ _____ customers came to his store.

6 그녀와 더 많은 시간을 보낼수록, 나는 그녀가 더 좋아진다. (much)
   _____ _____ _____ I spend with her, _____ _____ I like her.

7 그 영화배우는 점점 더 유명해지고 있다. (famous)
   The movie actor is becoming _____ _____ _____ _____.

8 제 컴퓨터를 가능한 한 빨리 고쳐 주세요. (soon)
   Please fix my computer _____ _____ _____ _____.

[9-13] 우리말과 뜻이 같도록 주어진 말을 바르게 배열하시오.

9 우리는 그들보다 다섯 배 더 많은 책들을 가지고 있다. (than, books, more, five times)
   → We have _____ they do.

10 네가 늦게 올수록 네가 저녁 먹을 시간은 더 적어진다. (have, less, will, time, you, the)
    → The later you come, _____ for dinner.

11 Tim은 가능한 한 빨리 집에 돌아가려고 노력했다. (could, as, he, as, soon)
    → Tim tried to come back home _____.

12 그 질병은 우리가 생각한 것보다 훨씬 더 위험하다. (much, dangerous, the disease, more, is, than)
    → _____ we thought.

13 나는 날이 점점 더 어두워지자 무서웠다. (darker, it, darker, and, got)
    → I felt scared as _____.

UNIT 1 시간·이유를 나타내는 접속사

[1-3] 우리말과 뜻이 같도록 문장을 완성하시오.

1   내가 그녀의 얼굴을 볼 때마다 나는 기분이 좋다.

＿＿＿＿＿ ＿＿＿＿＿ I see her face, I feel good.

2   그녀가 마지막으로 나가기 때문에 나는 그녀가 불을 끄도록 했다.

＿＿＿＿＿ she leaves last, I made her turn off the light.

3   폭풍우가 다가옴에 따라 사람들은 더 안전한 곳으로 이동했다.

＿＿＿＿＿ the storm approached, people moved to safer places.

[4-5] 두 문장의 뜻이 같도록 문장을 완성하시오.

4   She came back when it grew dark.

→ She did not come back ＿＿＿＿＿ it grew dark.

5   He met a lot of interesting people during his vacation.

→ He met a lot of interesting people ＿＿＿＿＿ he was on vacation.

[6-9] 우리말과 뜻이 같도록 문장을 완성하시오.

그녀는 나를 보자마자 울기 시작했다.

6   The ＿＿＿＿＿ she saw me, she began to cry.

7   As ＿＿＿＿＿ ＿＿＿＿＿ she saw me, she began to cry.

8   On ＿＿＿＿＿ me, she began to cry.

9   ＿＿＿＿＿ ＿＿＿＿＿ ＿＿＿＿＿ ＿＿＿＿＿ ＿＿＿＿＿ me than she began to cry.

[10-12] 우리말과 뜻이 같도록 주어진 말을 사용하여 문장을 완성하시오.

10   우기가 끝날 때까지 날씨는 개지 않을 것이다. (the rainy season, over)
The weather won't clear up ＿＿＿＿＿ ＿＿＿＿＿ ＿＿＿＿＿ ＿＿＿＿＿.

11   Brian은 그가 Rachel과 헤어진 이래로 우울하다. (break up with)
Brian feels depressed ＿＿＿＿＿ ＿＿＿＿＿ ＿＿＿＿＿ ＿＿＿＿＿ ＿＿＿＿＿.

12   한국 팀이 경기에서 이길 때마다 사람들은 흥분한다. (the Korean team, win)
＿＿＿＿＿ ＿＿＿＿＿ ＿＿＿＿＿ ＿＿＿＿＿ ＿＿＿＿＿ a game, people get excited.

UNIT 2 조건·양보·결과를 나타내는 접속사

[1-3] 우리말과 뜻이 같도록 문장을 완성하시오.

1 수영 모자를 쓰지 않으면 너는 수영장 안으로 들어갈 수 없다.

You can't go in the pool _____ you wear a bathing cap.

2 나는 내일 비가 올지 안 올지 모른다.

I don't know _____ it will rain tomorrow or not.

3 그는 매우 똑똑했지만 직업을 찾을 수 없었다.

_____ he was very smart, he couldn't find a job.

[4-6] 두 문장의 뜻이 같도록 문장을 완성하시오.

4 He tried everything to repair his car, but he failed.

→ _____ _____ _____ _____ to repair his car, he failed.

5 If you don't make a reservation, you'll have to wait.

→ _____ _____ _____ _____ _____, you'll have to wait.

6 Apologize to her, and she will forgive you.

→ _____ _____ _____ _____ _____, she will forgive you.

[7-11] 우리말과 뜻이 같도록 주어진 말을 사용하여 문장을 완성하시오.

7 그녀는 종일 쉬었지만 기분이 전혀 나아지지 않았다. (rest)

_____ _____ _____ all day, she didn't feel any better.

8 만약 그가 사람들에게 친절하지 않으면 아무도 그를 도와주지 않을 것이다. (nice)

_____ _____ _____ _____ _____ to people, no one will help him.

9 설령 그가 우리를 도와주더라도 우리는 그것을 제시간에 끝낼 수 없다. (help)

_____ _____ _____ _____ _____, we can't finish it in time.

10 비가 매우 많이 내려서 우리는 외출할 수 없었다. (heavily, go out)

It rained _____ _____ _____ _____ _____ _____.

11 그녀는 아이가 잘 수 있도록 불을 껐다. (the child, sleep)

She turned off the light _____ _____ _____ _____.

UNIT **3** 짝으로 이루어진 접속사

[1-4] 우리말과 뜻이 같도록 문장을 완성하시오.

1   James는 정직할 뿐만 아니라 부지런하다.
    James is _____ _____ honest _____ _____ diligent.

2   내 아버지와 나는 둘 다 피부가 까맣다.
    _____ my father _____ I have dark skin.

3   우리는 가을이 너무 춥지도 너무 덥지도 않기에 좋아한다.
    We like autumn because it is _____ too cold _____ too hot.

4   그녀는 영어를 가르칠 뿐만 아니라 소설도 쓴다.
    She writes novels _____ _____ _____ teaches English.

[5-9] 주어진 말을 어법에 맞게 바꿔 쓰시오. (단, 현재시제로 쓸 것)

5   Both Kate and Peter _____ famous. (be)

6   Either you or he _____ to go there now. (have)

7   Neither Sam nor I _____ to watch sports. (like)

8   Not only she but also her sons _____ been satisfied. (have)

9   Mick, as well as you, _____ going to attend the meeting. (be)

[10-14] 우리말과 뜻이 같도록 주어진 말을 사용하여 문장을 완성하시오.

10 나는 런던도 파리도 가 본 적이 없다. (London, Paris)
    I've been to _____ _____ _____ _____.

11 나는 뱀과 이구아나 중 하나를 사고 싶다. (a snake, an iguana)
    I want to buy _____ _____ _____ _____ _____ _____.

12 너뿐만 아니라 나도 요리하는 것을 좋아한다. (love, cook)
    _____ _____ _____ _____ _____ _____ _____ _____ _____.

13 이 청바지는 싸지도 않고 입기에 편하지도 않다. (cheap, comfortable)
    These jeans are _____ _____ _____ _____ to wear.

14 요가는 몸과 마음 둘 다에 좋다. (the body, the mind)
    Yoga is good for _____ _____ _____ _____ _____ _____.

UNIT **1** 수의 일치

[1-4] 주어진 말을 어법에 맞게 바꿔 쓰시오. (단, 현재시제로 쓸 것)

1 Someone _____ to help the sick dog. (need)

2 100 dollars _____ like a lot of money to me. (sound)

3 The white rabbit and the brown rabbit _____ mine. (be)

4 Physics _____ one of the most popular subjects in my class. (be)

[5-10] be동사를 어법에 맞게 바꿔 쓰시오. (단, 현재시제로 쓸 것)

5 A number of horses _____ racing on the track.

6 The number of babies being born _____ decreasing.

7 Most of the homework _____ simple.

8 Most of her clothes _____ black and white.

9 The rest of us _____ getting tired and bored.

10 Some of the employees _____ against the new policy.

[11-15] 우리말과 뜻이 같도록 주어진 말을 사용하여 문장을 완성하시오.

11 우리들 각자 할 일을 가지고 있다. (each, have a job)

_____ _____ _____ _____ _____ _____ to do.

12 시각 장애인들은 특별한 개들의 도움을 받는다. (blind, help)

_____ _____ _____ _____ by special dogs.

13 그 사고에서 아무도 다치지 않았다. (nobody, injure)

_____ _____ _____ in the accident.

14 그 쿠키들 중 일부는 너무 딱딱했다. (some, the cookies, be)

_____ _____ _____ _____ _____ too hard.

15 젊은이들은 정치에 관심이 없다. (young, have)

_____ _____ _____ no interest in politics.

UNIT 2 시제의 일치

[1-4] 주어진 말을 어법에 맞게 바꿔 쓰시오.

1 He said that he _____ the movie before. (see)

2 The teacher said that Napoleon _____ Egypt in 1798. (invade)

3 He believed that his son _____ a great golfer. (become)

4 I found out that Coca-Cola _____ in 1886. (invent)

[5-9] 다음 문장을 주절이 과거인 문장으로 바꿀 때 빈칸에 알맞은 말을 쓰시오.

5 Chris thinks that his friend has a problem.
→ Chris _____ that his friend _____ a problem.

6 This book explains that Halloween is on October 31st.
→ This book _____ that Halloween _____ on October 31st.

7 I know that it is much colder on Mars than on Earth.
→ I _____ that it _____ much colder on Mars than on Earth.

8 Emily says that she will run in a marathon.
→ Emily _____ that she _____ run in a marathon.

9 My uncle says a little knowledge is a dangerous thing.
→ My uncle _____ a little knowledge _____ a dangerous thing.

[10-14] 우리말과 뜻이 같도록 주어진 말을 사용하여 문장을 완성하시오.

10 나는 내가 그 오디션에 합격할 수 있다고 믿었다. (pass)
I believed that _____ _____ _____ the audition.

11 그녀는 매일 아침 8시에 출근한다고 말했다. (go to work)
She said that _____ _____ _____ _____ at eight every morning.

12 사람들은 지구가 태양 주위를 돈다는 것을 몰랐다. (the Earth, go around, the Sun)
People didn't know that _____ _____ _____ _____ _____.

13 우리 어머니께서는 나에게 정직이 최선의 방책이라고 말씀하셨다. (honesty, the best policy)
My mother told me that _____ _____ _____ _____ _____.

14 그들은 그녀가 그들의 충고를 따라야 한다고 생각했다. (follow, advice)
They thought that _____ _____ _____ _____ _____ _____.

UNIT **3** 화법

[1-9] 두 문장의 뜻이 같도록 문장을 완성하시오.

1 She says to me, "You are a handsome boy."

→ She _____ me _____ _____ a handsome boy.

2 The teacher said to us, "Take out your textbooks."

→ The teacher _____ us _____ _____ _____ _____ textbooks.

3 He asked her, "Where is your house?"

→ He _____ her _____ _____ _____ _____.

4 Linda asked me, "Will you come to my birthday party?"

→ Linda _____ me _____ _____ _____ _____ _____ _____ birthday party.

5 He said to her, "Bring your camera tomorrow."

→ He told her _____ _____ _____ _____ _____ _____.

6 My mother asked me, "Has the movie finished already?"

→ My mother asked me _____ _____ _____ _____ _____ already.

7 The policeman told him not to move.

→ The policeman said to him, "_____ _____."

8 Jane told him that he looked nice that day.

→ Jane said to him, "_____ _____ _____ _____."

9 I asked her what made her happy.

→ I asked her, "_____ _____ _____ _____?"

[10-13] 우리말과 뜻이 같도록 주어진 말을 사용하여 문장을 완성하시오.

10 그는 나에게 당장 나가라고 말했다. (get out)

_____ _____ _____ _____ _____ _____ at once.

11 나는 그에게 그가 불어를 말할 수 있는지 물었다. (speak, French)

_____ _____ _____ _____ _____ _____ _____ _____.

12 그 학생들은 나에게 그들이 언제 점심을 먹을 수 있는지 물었다. (eat lunch)

_____ _____ _____ _____ _____ _____ _____.

13 그녀는 내게 정크 푸드를 먹지 말라고 충고했다. (advise, eat, junk food)

_____ _____ _____ _____ _____ _____ _____.

UNIT **1** 강조, 부정 구문, 병렬

[1-4] 두 문장의 뜻이 같도록 주어진 말을 사용하여 문장을 완성하시오.

1 Some boys in the class are smart, but others are not. (every)

→ _____ _____ _____ in the class is smart.

2 My answer isn't right. John's answer isn't right either. (neither, our)

→ _____ _____ _____ _____ is right.

3 My brother sometimes walks to school. (always)

→ My brother does _____ _____ _____ to school.

4 Some of my friends are from America, and some of them are from other countries. (all)

→ _____ _____ _____ _____ _____ are from America.

[5-7] 다음 밑줄 친 부분을 강조하는 it is / was … that 강조 구문을 완성하시오.

5 I enjoy <u>swimming</u> every weekend.

→ _____

6 My mother threw away <u>my old dolls</u>.

→ _____

7 <u>The movie star</u> visited the city.

→ _____

[8-12] 우리말과 뜻이 같도록 주어진 말을 사용하여 문장을 완성하시오.

8 나는 그 시험을 위해 정말 열심히 공부했다. (study)

I _____ _____ hard for the exam.

9 저 네 명의 학생들 중 아무도 그 책을 읽지 않았다. (those four)

_____ _____ _____ _____ _____ read the book.

10 Green 씨는 어린이와 동물을 정말 사랑한다. (love)

Ms. Green _____ _____ children and animals.

11 Mike는 영화 보는 것과 책 읽는 것 둘 다 즐긴다. (watch movies, read books)

Mike enjoys _____ _____ _____ _____ _____ _____.

12 모든 사람들이 많은 돈을 가지기를 원하는 것은 아니다. (every, person, have)

_____ _____ _____ _____ _____ _____ a lot of money.

UNIT **2** 도치

[1-4] 우리말과 뜻이 같도록 so나 neither[nor]를 사용하여 문장을 완성하시오.

1 A: I can't speak Japanese.   B: _____ _____ _____ . (나도 못해.)

2 A: I want to have a nice car.   B: _____ _____ _____ . (나도 원해.)

3 A: I don't like watching TV.   B: _____ _____ _____ . (나도 안 좋아해.)

4 A: I'm so tired.   B: _____ _____ _____ . (나도 그래.)

[5-9] 밑줄 친 부분을 강조하는 문장으로 바꿔 쓰시오.

5 He lay under the big tree.

   → _____ _____ _____ _____ _____ .

6 Errors are rarely found in this book.

   → _____ _____ _____ _____ in this book.

7 They never thought that he was her father.

   → _____ _____ _____ _____ that he was her father.

8 We went to the movies only on weekends.

   → _____ _____ _____ _____ _____ _____ to the movies.

9 A boy sat on the tall chair.

   → _____ _____ _____ _____ _____ _____ .

[10-13] 우리말과 뜻이 같도록 주어진 말을 사용하여 문장을 완성하시오.

10 나는 우리 팀이 또 다시 지리라고는 전혀 상상하지 않았다. (imagine)

   Little _____ _____ _____ that our team would lose again.

11 우리 아버지께서는 올해 퇴직하셨고 우리 어머니께서도 그랬다. (so)

   My father retired this year, and _____ _____ _____ _____ .

12 나는 그가 그의 약속을 어기리라고는 좀처럼 생각하지 않았다. (think)

   Hardly _____ _____ _____ that he would break his promise.

13 Jimmy는 금요일이 되어서야 그의 보고서를 마쳤다. (finish, essay)

   Not until _____ _____ _____ _____ _____ _____ .

WORKBOOK ANSWER

CHAPTER 01 부정사

UNIT 1 to부정사의 명사적 용법

1 It, to wear   2 what to do   3 It, to make
4 It, to have a pet   5 wants to go
6 to make coffee   7 how to use money
8 it difficult to finish   9 not to waste
10 It is good to have a true friend.
11 She couldn't decide which to choose.
12 They made it a rule to take a walk every night.

UNIT 2 to부정사의 형용사적 용법, 부사적 용법

1 to believe   2 to miss   3 to know that
4 to find   5 to talk to
6 You are to visit
7 to listen to this song
8 to buy a new bicycle
9 나는 입을 따뜻한 옷이 좀 필요하다.
10 그 배우는 깨어나 보니 자신이 슈퍼스타라는 것을 알게 되었다.
11 네가 건강을 유지하려고 한다면, 너는 정크 푸드를 먹어서는 안 된다.
12 그들은 일등상을 타서 매우 행복했다.

UNIT 3 to부정사의 의미상 주어, 시제, 수동태

1 have left   2 It   3 of
4 for   5 of
6 that they were   7 to have been
8 to be   9 seemed to enjoy yourself
10 nice of her to find
11 natural for her to be loved
12 wise of you to make a reservation
13 seemed to have been cooked

UNIT 4 목적격 보어로 쓰이는 to부정사와 원형부정사

1 bring   2 talk[talking]   3 to play
4 to go   5 to sing   6 to take
7 to go   8 do

9 stand[standing]
10 had my brother prepare
11 helps us make
12 felt the cat lie[lying]
13 expected me to buy
14 heard someone scream[screaming]

UNIT 5 to부정사를 이용한 주요 구문, 독립부정사

1 to find   2 to say   3 couldn't
4 cold enough   5 too, to
6 clever enough to speak
7 take you 20 minutes to get
8 To tell the truth
9 To make matters worse
10 It took me two hours to cook the spaghetti.
11 To be frank with you
12 too glad to sit still
13 old enough to ride the roller coaster

CHAPTER 02 동명사

UNIT 1 동명사의 역할

1 having   2 ○   3 ○
4 watching   5 hiding   6 her missing
7 your[you] catching   8 your[you] having won
9 not remembering   10 my[me] opening
11 He kept complaining about his job.
12 Having a balanced diet is important.
13 I'm sorry for not being with you.
14 I am tired of eating sandwiches for lunch.
15 riding a bicycle along the riverside

UNIT 2 목적어로 쓰이는 동명사와 to부정사

1 to lend   2 learning   3 commiting
4 to go   5 turning   6 to make
7 to invite   8 wearing   9 following

10 meeting   **11** forgot to see a doctor

12 kept calling Veronica

13 refused to show his ID

14 avoided mentioning his first love

UNIT 3   동명사를 이용한 주요 구문

1 handling   **2** trusting   **3** joining

4 drinking   **5** training

6 looking forward to   **7** go skating

8 is busy writing   **9** On[Upon] entering

10 cannot[can't] help saying 또는 cannot[can't] but say

11 prevents[keeps] me from going out

12 is worth visiting

13 spent two hours shopping for

14 It's no use regretting

CHAPTER
03 분사

UNIT 1   분사의 역할

1 smiling   **2** disappointing

3 painted   **4** broken   **5** running

6 shouting   **7** written by Harry

8 made in Switzerland

9 stolen from Scott

10 growing in the garden

11 singing on the stage

12 had my picture taken

13 watched a child making[make]

14 The child playing the violin

UNIT 2   분사구문

1 Because[As/Since] I had nothing to do

2 Because[As/Since] he was very busy

3 Though I have a car

4 If/When you break your promise

5 When/As/While I took a walk with my family

6 Taking bus number 33

7 Taking off his coat

8 Seeing his mother

9 Knowing how to do it

10 getting poor grades

11 Leaving early, we arrived on time.

12 Being in a hurry, I made many mistakes.

13 Drinking a cup of coffee, I read the magazine.

14 Buying this shirt, you'll get one free.

UNIT 3   분사구문의 부정, 시제, 수동태

1 Reading   **2** Not liking

3 Although seeing me   **4** Having injured his leg

5 Not knowing where to go

6 Having been born into a poor family

7 Having worked as a barista

8 Not watching   **9** Built 50 years ago

10 Having been   **11** Compared to

UNIT 4   주의해야 할 분사구문

1 folded   **2** Roughly speaking

3 Judging from   **4** being

5 그 아기가 잠이 들어서[들었을 때/든 후에/들자마자] 나는 TV를 껐다.

6 엄밀히 말해서 그녀는 수학을 잘하지 못한다.

7 알람이 크게 울렸을 때[울린 후에/울리자마자/울려서] 그는 잠이 깼다.

8 The day being sunny

9 with his legs crossed

10 with his dog following him

11 It getting dark

CHAPTER
04 시제

UNIT 1   현재완료

1 has gone   **2** have taken

3 has been ringing   **4** have forgotten

5 have already bought   **6** has been singing

7 haven't decided   **8** have never seen

9 나는 방금 집 청소를 마쳤다.

10 그녀는 지난 일요일 이래로 계속 몸이 좋지 않다.

11 Tim은 아직 역에 도착하지 않았다.

12 우리는 한 시간 동안 너를 기다려오고 있다.

1 hadn't[had not]　　2 begun
3 had　　　　　　　4 had
5 had　　　　　　　6 had been
7 had had　　　　　8 had already finished
9 had been raining　10 will have been waiting
11 We hadn't cleaned the house
12 She had gained weight
13 will have decided on
14 had already gone to bed

7 can't[cannot] have gone
8 must have broken
9 may[might] have failed
10 그들이 어젯밤에 함께 외출했을 리 없다.
11 그는 그 계약서에 서명하지 말았어야 했다.
12 우리는 서로 도울 수도 있었다.
13 그들은 서로 싸웠음이 틀림없다.
14 그녀는 오래전에 기자였는지도 모른다.

CHAPTER
06 수동태

CHAPTER
05 조동사

1 have to　　2 can　　　3 May
4 be able to　5 had to
6 don't have[need] to
7 can't[cannot] be
8 must[should] not
9 It may be true
10 We ought to[have to] prepare for the future
11 Do I have to go there
12 You should[must] obey your parents

1 had　　　2 rather　　3 used to
4 play　　　5 rather not
6 would rather walk, than
7 better not　8 used to　9 better wear
10 had better take care of
11 would watch TV
12 would rather dance than sing a song
13 would rather not see

1 have called　　2 have written
3 have washed　　4 have visited
5 have won　　　6 should have taken

1 has been invited　2 Was
3 belongs to　　　4 was held
5 is being made
6 I will be found by them.
7 The dog is being washed by my father.
8 Money must not be wasted (by us).
9 By whom was this delicious pasta made?
10 New clothes have been displayed since last week (by them).
11 will be taught　　12 was wounded
13 must not be washed　14 was developed

1 to wash　　2 to stop　　3 to cook
4 to become　5 entering　6 was called
7 was elected president (by the people)
8 were seen swimming[to swim] in the river by her
9 was made for me by my mother
10 was named Amy by us
11 He was heard speaking Chinese
12 The information was given to the police
13 She was given a present by her boyfriend
14 A basket of flowers was sent to me

1 with　　2 in　　　3 with
4 of　　　5 to

6　am depended on　　**7**　will be carried out

8　to have been successful

9　should be looked after

10　was turned off

11　was taken off

12　were filled with

13　is crowded with

14　am worried about

15　is said to be friendly

CHAPTER
07 가정법

UNIT 1 가정법 과거, 가정법 과거완료, 혼합 가정법

1　were　　　**2**　had had　　**3**　were

4　had stopped　　　**5**　would have

6　If they had done their homework, the teacher wouldn't[would not] have been disappointed.

7　If she knew his phone number, she could call him.

8　If the concert tickets hadn't[had not] been sold out, I could have gone to the show.

9　If he had known me well, he would have lent me his books.

10　If I weren't[were not] allergic to dogs, I could have one.

11　she would have solved

12　If my grandfather were alive

13　I could use it

14　if you were not busy

UNIT 2 I wish, as if, without[but for], it's time

1 could　　　　**2**　had had　　**3**　had watched

4　didn't[did not] live

5　hadn't[had not] been　　**6**　faced

7　Were it not[If it weren't] for

8　wish, had taken　　**9**　had won

10　had not been for　　**11**　wish, knew

12　we had left

13　as if[though] she had met

14　But for the key, we could not have opened

15　I wish it were

CHAPTER
08 관계사

UNIT 1 관계대명사

1　who[that]　　**2**　that　　　**3**　What

4　whose

5　This is the cat which[that] I found in the park.

6　The boy who[that] is playing the drums on the stage is my brother.

7　I moved to a house whose roof is blue.

8　I interviewed the actor who(m)[that] I've liked for a long time.

9　the oldest book that I have

10　the woman whose child is a genius

11　the monkeys which[that]

12　What he needs is

UNIT 2 관계부사

1　when　　　**2**　why　　　**3**　how

4　where　　　**5**　when　　　**6**　how

7　where　　　**8**　when　　　**9**　why

10　the way　　**11**　the season when

12　why he was absent from

13　the city where we spent our vacation

14　the way he makes candles

UNIT 3 복합 관계사

1　wherever　　**2**　However　　**3**　whenever

4　Whoever　　**5**　Whoever　　**6**　Wherever

7　whenever　　**8**　No matter how

9　whatever they buy　　**10**　wherever you go

11　No matter how long it takes

UNIT 4 주의해야 할 관계사의 용법

1　the watch (which[that]) she

2　the student (who(m)[that]) I

3　the man (who[that] is) selling

4　The skirt (which[that]) I'm

5　the new novel (which[that] was) written

6　at which　　**7**　with which　　**8**　on which

9　about whom　**10**　with whom　**11**　where

12　which　　　**13**　when　　　**14**　who

42

7 is	8 are	9 are		

10 are   11 Each of us has a job

12 The blind are helped

13 Nobody was injured

14 Some of the cookies were

15 The young have

UNIT 2 시제의 일치

1 had seen		2 invaded	
3 would become		4 was invented	
5 thought, had		6 explained, is	
7 knew, is		8 said, would	
9 said, is		10 I could pass	

11 she goes to work

12 the Earth goes around the Sun

13 honesty is the best policy

14 she had to follow their advice

UNIT 3 화법

1 tells, I am

2 told, to take out our

3 asked, where her house was

4 asked, if[whether] I would come to her

5 to bring her camera the next[following] day

6 if[whether] the movie had finished

7 Don't move

8 You look nice today

9 What makes you happy

10 He told me to get out

11 I asked him if[whether] he could speak French

12 The students asked me when they could eat lunch

13 She advised me not to eat junk food

---

4 Not all of my friends

5 It is swimming that I enjoy every weekend.

6 It was my old dolls that my mother threw away.

7 It was the movie star that[who] visited the city.

8 did study

9 None of those four students

10 does love

11 both watching movies and reading books

12 Not every person wants to have

UNIT 2 도치

1 Neither[Nor] can I

2 So do I

3 Neither[Nor] do I

4 So am I

5 Under the big tree he lay

6 Rarely are errors found

7 Never did they think

8 Only on weekends did we go

9 On the tall chair sat a boy

10 did I imagine

11 so did my mother

12 did I think

13 Friday did Jimmy finish his essay

CHAPTER

12 특수 구문

UNIT 1 강조, 부정 구문, 병렬

1 Not every boy

2 Neither of our answers

3 not always walk

MEMO

MEMO

MEMO

NE능률 교재 MAP

아래 교재 MAP을 참고하여 본인의 현재 혹은 목표 수준에 따라 교재를 선택하세요.
NE능률 교재들과 함께 영어실력을 쑥쑥~ 올려보세요!
MP3 등 교재 부가 학습 서비스 및 자세한 교재 정보는 www.nebooks.co.kr 에서 확인하세요.

초1-2	초3	초3-4	초4-5	초5-6
	그래머버디 1	그래머버디 2	그래머버디 3	Grammar Bean 3
	초등영어 문법이 된다 Starter 1	초등영어 문법이 된다 Starter 2	Grammar Bean 1	Grammar Bean 4
		초등 Grammar Inside 1	Grammar Bean 2	초등영어 문법이 된다 2
		초등 Grammar Inside 2	초등영어 문법이 된다 1	초등 Grammar Inside 5
			초등 Grammar Inside 3	초등 Grammar Inside 6
			초등 Grammar Inside 4	

초6-예비중	중1	중1-2	중2-3	중3
능률중학영어 예비중	능률중학영어 중1	능률중학영어 중2	Grammar Zone 기초편	능률중학영어 중3
Grammar Inside Starter	Grammar Zone 입문편	1316 Grammar 2	Grammar Zone 워크북 기초편	문제로 마스터하는 중학영문법 3
원리를 더한 영문법 STARTER	Grammar Zone 워크북 입문편	문제로 마스터하는 중학영문법 2	1316 Grammar 3	Grammar Inside 3
	1316 Grammar 1	Grammar Inside 2	원리를 더한 영문법 2	열중 16강 문법 3
	문제로 마스터하는 중학영문법 1	열중 16강 문법 2	중학영문법 총정리 모의고사 2	중학영문법 총정리 모의고사 3
	Grammar Inside 1	원리를 더한 영문법 1	쓰기로 마스터하는 중학서술형 2학년	쓰기로 마스터하는 중학서술형 3학년
	열중 16강 문법 1	중학영문법 총정리 모의고사 1	중학 천문장 3	
	쓰기로 마스터하는 중학서술형 1학년	중학 천문장 2		
	중학 천문장 1			

예비고-고1	고1	고1-2	고2-3	고3
문제로 마스터하는 고등영문법	Grammar Zone 기본편 1	필히 통하는 고등 영문법 실력편	Grammar Zone 종합편	
올클 수능 어법 start	Grammar Zone 워크북 기본편 1	필히 통하는 고등 서술형 실전편	Grammar Zone 워크북 종합편	
천문장 입문	Grammar Zone 기본편 2	TEPS BY STEP G+R Basic	올클 수능 어법 완성	
	Grammar Zone 워크북 기본편 2		천문장 완성	
	필히 통하는 고등 영문법 기본편			
	필히 통하는 고등 서술형 기본편			
	천문장 기본			

수능 이상/ 토플 80-89 · 텝스 600-699점	수능 이상/ 토플 90-99 · 텝스 700-799점	수능 이상/ 토플 100 · 텝스 800점 이상		
TEPS BY STEP G+R 1	TEPS BY STEP G+R 2	TEPS BY STEP G+R 3		

기초부터 내신까지 중학 영문법 완성

1316 GRAMMAR

정답 및 해설

LEVEL
3

NE 능률

기초부터 내신까지 중학 영문법 완성

1316

1316 GRAMMAR

정답 및 해설

LEVEL
3

01 부정사

UNIT 1 to부정사의 명사적 용법

pp.8 - 9

B

1 좋은 친구를 사귀는 것은 중요하다.
그녀는 신문 동아리에 가입하고 싶어 했다.
나의 꿈은 언젠가 달을 탐사하는 것이다.

2 운동하지 않고 건강을 유지하는 것은 어렵다.
Jason은 프로 미식축구 선수가 되는 것이 힘들다고 생각했다.

3 그는 나에게 응급 상황에서 무엇을 해야 할지 말해 주었다.
Ava는 앵무새 기르는 방법을 몰랐다.

Tip 주의! Jessie는 그녀의 딸에게 시험에서 절대 부정행위를 하지 말라고 조언했다.

SPEED CHECK

1 ② 2 ③ 3 ⑤

1 It은 가주어, to부정사구가 진주어
2 it은 가목적어, to부정사구가 진목적어
3 when to-v: '언제 …할지' (=『when+주어+should+동사원형』)
어휘 research report 연구 보고서 hand in …을 제출하다

PRACTICE TEST

A 1 to meet 2 to climb 3 to leave for
  4 to pronounce
B 1 It , to feel 2 who(m) to call
  3 where we should have
C 1 to improve 2 how to make 3 It, to take
  4 it, to write in 5 what to buy 6 not to enter

A

1 목적어로 쓰인 명사적 용법
2 보어로 쓰인 명사적 용법
3 when to-v: '언제 …할지'
4 it은 가목적어, to부정사구가 진목적어

B

1 It은 가주어, to부정사구가 진주어
2-3 『의문사+to-v』는 대개 『의문사+주어+should+동사원형』으로 바꿔 쓸 수 있음

C

1 목적어로 쓰인 명사적 용법
2 how to-v: '어떻게 …할지', '…하는 방법'
3 가주어 It과 진주어 to부정사구
4 가목적어 it과 진목적어 to부정사구
5 what to-v: '무엇을 …할지'
6 to부정사의 부정: not / never to-v

UNIT 2 to부정사의 형용사적 용법, 부사적 용법

pp.10 - 11

A

1 너는 그곳에 가는 가장 좋은 방법을 아니?

Tip 주의! 너는 쓸 연필이 필요하니?

2 너는 그 일을 8시까지 끝마쳐야 한다.
부통령은 다음 달에 중국을 방문할 예정이다.
우리가 그곳에 정각에 도착하려고 한다면 서둘러야 한다.
그들은 언젠가 다시 만날 운명이었다.
어둠 속에서 아무것도 보이지 않았다.

B

많은 사람들이 경기장에 입장하기 위해 기다리고 있다.
Tom은 그의 가족을 다시 보아서 매우 기뻤다.
그런 바보 같은 것을 믿다니 그는 어리석은 게 틀림없다.
Ann은 자라서 유명한 피겨 스케이팅 선수가 되었다.
그녀는 그 상자를 열고 결국 그것이 비어 있다는 것을 발견하고 말았다.
그가 말하는 것을 듣는다면 너는 그가 외국인이라고 생각할 것이다.
이 질문은 답하기에 쉬웠다.

Grammar UP

그녀는 소음을 차단하기 위해 창문을 닫았다.

SPEED CHECK

1 ③ 2 ②

1 to부정사구가 수식하는 명사(person)가 전치사 with의 의미상 목적어이므로 전치사를 반드시 씀
2 목적을 나타내는 부사적 용법
어휘 turn down (소리를) 낮추다

PRACTICE TEST

A 1 tell → to tell 2 in order → (in order / so as) to
  3 to play → to play with 4 have → to have

5 to write → to write on
B 1 to visit 2 shocked to see 3 are to wear
4 are to pass
C 1 나는 집에 일찍 와서 행복했다.
2 교장 선생님은 오늘 오후에 연설할 예정이다.
3 그렇게 많은 사람들 앞에서 소리를 지르다니 Olivia가 경솔했다.
4 Gavin는 구매할 집을 찾고 있었다.
5 우리는 따뜻한 날씨를 즐기기 위해 공원에 갈 것이다.
6 이 셔츠는 입기에 매우 편하다.

A

1 명사(news)를 수식하는 형용사적 용법
2 목적을 나타내는 부사적 용법. in order to-v나 so as to-v를 써서 목적의 의미를 강조할 수 있음.
3, 5 to부정사구가 수식하는 명사(toys/paper)가 전치사(with/on)의 의미상 목적어이므로 전치사를 반드시 같이 씀
4 감정의 원인을 나타내는 부사적 용법

B

1 목적을 나타내는 부사적 용법
2 감정의 원인을 나타내는 부사적 용법
3 의무를 나타내는 be to-v
4 의도를 나타내는 be to-v

C

1 감정의 원인을 나타내는 부사적 용법
2 예정을 나타내는 be to-v
3 판단의 근거·이유를 나타내는 부사적 용법
4 명사(house)를 수식하는 형용사적 용법
5 목적을 나타내는 부사적 용법
6 형용사(comfortable)를 수식하는 부사적 용법

UNIT 3 to부정사의 의미상 주어, 시제, 수동태

pp.12 - 13

A

1 그녀는 친구들을 만나는 것을 무척 좋아한다.
나의 부모님은 내가 의사가 되기를 기대하신다.
(우리는) 매일 운동하는 것이 좋다.
2 1) 여기 네가 풀어야 할 문제들이 있다.
우리가 최선을 다하는 것은 중요하다.
2) 그가 나를 집까지 바래다준 것은 친절했다.

B

1 그는 너를 사랑하는 것 같다.
2 그는 너를 사랑했던 것 같다.

C

1 우리는 다른 사람들을 존중하고 우리도 또한 존중받기를 바란다.
2 Mark는 학생회장으로 선출되어 행복했다.

SPEED CHECK

1 ④ 2 ③ 3 ③

1 사람의 성품·성격을 나타내는 형용사(wise)가 보어로 쓰이면 의미상 주어로 『of+목적격』을 씀
[어휘] apologize [동] 사과하다
2 to부정사의 시제가 문장의 시제보다 앞서므로 완료부정사(to have v-ed)를 씀
3 수동의 뜻을 가지며 to부정사의 시제가 문장의 시제와 같거나 그 이후를 나타낼 때 단순수동태(to be v-ed)를 씀
[어휘] payment [명] 지불

PRACTICE TEST

A 1 for them 2 me 3 of you 4 to have been
5 to have been repaired
B 1 to get worse 2 to have fought
3 to have broken 4 to be invited
C 1 seems to have been 2 to be protected
3 foolish of her to believe
4 impossible for them to finish
5 seems to know

A

1 to부정사의 의미상 주어는 대부분의 경우 『for+목적격』을 씀
2 to부정사의 의미상 주어가 문장의 목적어와 같으므로 의미상 주어를 따로 표시하지 않음
3 사람의 성품·성격을 나타내는 형용사(clever)가 보어이므로 의미상 주어로 『of+목적격』을 씀
4 to부정사의 시제가 문장의 시제보다 앞서므로 완료부정사(to have v-ed)를 씀
5 수동의 뜻을 가지며 to부정사의 시제가 문장의 시제보다 앞서므로 완료수동태(to have been v-ed)를 씀

B

1 to부정사의 시제와 문장의 시제가 같으므로 단순부정사(to-v)를 씀
2-3 to부정사의 시제가 문장의 시제보다 앞서므로 완료부정사(to have v-ed)를 씀
4 수동의 뜻을 가지며 to부정사의 시제가 문장의 시제와 같으므로 단순수동태(to be v-ed)를 씀

UNIT 4 목적격 보어로 쓰이는 to부정사와 원형부정사

pp.14 - 15

A

나는 그가 나에게 춤추는 법을 가르쳐 주기를 기대했다.
나는 Martha에게 그를 용서해달라고 부탁했다.

[Tip 주의!] 나는 엄마가 저녁을 준비하는 것을 도왔다.

B

1 나는 무언가 번쩍이는 것이 하늘에서 움직이는 것을 보았다.
그는 누군가가 그의 어깨를 만지는 것을 느꼈다.
2 그는 아들이 법학 전문 대학원에 가게 했다.
아빠는 내가 여동생의 생일 파티를 계획하게 했다.
나는 나의 개가 마당에서 자유로이 뛰어다니게 해 주었다.

[Tip 비교!] Jenny는 남자친구가 그녀의 배낭을 들게 했다.

Grammar UP

1 나는 그가 길을 건너고 있는 것을 보았다.
나는 내 이름이 불리는 것을 들었다.
2 Lily는 그녀의 차가 수리되도록 했다.

SPEED CHECK

1 ③ 2 ① 3 ④

1 「advise+목적어+to-v」
2 「사역동사(make)+목적어+원형부정사(능동)」
[어휘] wait in line 줄을 서서 기다리다
3 「지각동사(feel)+목적어+원형부정사(능동)/현재분사(능동·진행)」
[어휘] stare at …을 응시하다

PRACTICE TEST

A 1 take 2 to listen 3 get 4 to come 5 study
B 1 study 2 to turn up 3 play[playing] 4 cry
5 painted
C 1 had me prepare 2 watched the car washed
3 expect him to be 4 got me to think about
5 heard the man talk[talking]

A
1 「지각동사(see)+목적어+원형부정사(능동)」
2 「want+목적어+to-v」
3 「사역동사(let)+목적어+원형부정사(능동)」
4 「order+목적어+to-v」
5 「help+목적어+원형부정사[to-v]」

B
1 「사역동사(have)+목적어+원형부정사(능동)」
2 「tell+목적어+to-v」
3 「지각동사(listen to)+목적어+원형부정사(능동)/현재분사(능동·진행)」
4 「사역동사(make)+목적어+원형부정사(능동)」
5 「사역동사(have)+목적어+과거분사(수동)」

C
1 「사역동사(have)+목적어+원형부정사(능동)」
2 「지각동사(watch)+목적어+과거분사(수동)」
3 「expect+목적어+to-v」
4 「사역의 뜻을 갖는 get+목적어+to-v」
5 「지각동사(hear)+목적어+원형부정사(능동)/현재분사(능동·진행)」

UNIT 5 to부정사를 이용한 주요 구문, 독립부정사

pp.16 - 17

A

1 그는 너무 어려서 직장을 구할 수 없었다.
이 코트는 내가 입기에 너무 크다.
2 Kevin은 이 벽돌들을 나를 만큼 충분히 힘이 세다.
그 방은 내가 안에 더블 침대를 놓을 만큼 충분히 크다.
3 내가 학교까지 걸어가는 데 10분이 걸린다.
그가 내게 사과하는 데 2년이 걸렸다.

B

이상한 이야기지만, 나는 매일 밤 같은 꿈을 꾼다.
설상가상으로, 우리 팀의 최고의 선수가 그의 발목을 삐었다.
사실대로 말하면, 나는 놀랐고 당황스러웠다.

SPEED CHECK

1 ② 2 ⑤ 3 ②

1 「too+형용사/부사+to-v」: '너무 …해서 ~할 수 없다', '~하기에 너무 …하다'
2 「형용사/부사+enough to-v」: '…할 만큼 충분히 ~하다'
3 「it takes+목적격+시간+to-v」: '…가 ~하는 데 (시간)이 걸리다'
[어휘] pack [동] (짐을) 싸다

PRACTICE TEST

A 1 tall enough 2 too 3 him 4 To be frank
5 To make

B 1 so sleepy that I can't finish
2 so smart that she can solve
3 is big enough to carry 4 was too busy to go
C 1 healthy enough to leave 2 too far to walk to
3 To begin with 4 It took me, to set up
5 too sweet for her to drink

A

1 「형용사/부사+enough to-v」: '…할 만큼 충분히 ～하다'
2 「too+형용사/부사+to-v」: '너무 …해서 ～할 수 없다', '～하기에 너무 …하다'
3 「it takes+목적격+시간+to-v」: '…가 ～하는 데 (시간)이 걸리다'
4 to be frank (with you): '솔직히 말하면'
5 to make matters worse: '설상가상으로'

B

1, 4 「too+형용사/부사+to-v」와 「so+형용사/부사+that+주어 +can't」는 서로 바꿔 쓸 수 있음
2-3 「형용사/부사+enough to-v」와 「so+형용사/부사+that+ 주어+can」은 서로 바꿔 쓸 수 있음

C

1 「형용사/부사+enough to-v」
2 「too+형용사/부사+to-v」
3 to begin with: '우선', '먼저'
4 「it takes+목적격+시간+to-v」
5 「too+형용사/부사+의미상 주어+to-v」

REVIEW TEST pp.18 - 20

01 ② 02 ⑤ 03 ④ 04 ④ 05 ⑤ 06 ④ 07 how to get to 08 tall enough to hang 09 ⑤ 10 ③ 11 It was careless of me to leave the door unlocked. 12 not to eat 13 to play with 14 ⑤ 15 1) 너를 다 시 보아서 나는 행복하다. 2) 그는 그 대회에서 우승하기 위해 많이 연습했다. 3) 시험에서 만점을 받다니 그녀는 똑똑한 게 틀림 없다. 4) 그가 노래하는 것을 들으면, 너는 그가 단지 어린아이라 는 것을 믿지 못할 것이다. 16 ③ 17 seems to have been 18 ③ 19 ① to sit → to sit on, ⑤ for him → of him 20 took him three days to write 21 happy to be rewarded 22 too violent for teenagers to watch 23 only to hear

01 when to-v: '언제 …할지'
02 「사역동사(make)+목적어+원형부정사(능동)」

03 ⓐ 「사역의 뜻을 갖는 get+목적어+to-v」
ⓑ 「help+목적어+원형부정사(to-v)」
어휘 repairman 명 수리공 businessman 명 사업가, 경영자
04 ⓐ 「지각동사(hear)+목적어+원형부정사(능동)/현재분사(능동·진행)」
ⓑ 「advise+목적어+to-v」
어휘 fitness 명 건강 (상태) trainer 명 트레이너, 훈련시키는 사람
05 「지각동사(watch)+목적어+원형부정사(능동)/현재분사(능동·진행)」
어휘 encourage 동 격려하다; *권장하다
06 「expect+목적어+to-v」
어휘 book a flight 항공권을 예약하다
07 how to-v: '…하는 방법'
08 「형용사/부사+enough to-v」: '…할 만큼 충분히 ～하다'
어휘 hang 동 걸다
09 ⑤ 「so+형용사/부사+that+주어+can」은 「형용사/부사+ enough to-v」로 바꿔 쓸 수 있다.
too rich to buy → rich enough to buy
10 ③ 「지각동사(hear)+목적어+원형부정사(능동)/현재분사(능동·진행)」의 형태가 되어야 하므로 I heard him shouting for help.로 쓸 수 있다.
① → I made him do some chores. ② → Mr. Jones seems to have been tired last week. ④ → We asked the teacher what to do next. ⑤ → He will help you (to) choose healthy food.
어휘 chore 명 (일상의) 집안일 shout 동 외치다, 소리치다
11 be made of는 '…로 만들어지다'라는 뜻이다. 빈칸에 들어갈 of 와 보기에 제시된 단어로 보아, it 가주어, to부정사(구) 진주어 형태의 문장을 완성하면 된다. 사람의 성품·성격을 나타내는 형용사(careless)가 보이므로 의미상 주어로 「of+목적격」을 쓴다.
어휘 awesome 형 굉장한, 아주 멋진 careless 형 부주의한
12 문맥상 '먹지 않으려고'라는 의미가 되어야 자연스러우므로 to부정사의 부정인 not to eat을 쓴다.
어휘 be on a diet 다이어트[식이 요법] 중이다
heavy meal 양이 많은 식사
13 대명사(something)가 「to-v+전치사」의 의미상 목적어이므로 전치사 with를 쓴다.
14 보기와 ⑤는 to부정사의 형용사적 용법이고, ①은 목적을 나타내는 부사적 용법, ②-④는 명사적 용법이다.
어휘 stay up 안 자다, 깨어 있다 fog 명 안개
15 1)은 감정의 원인, 2)는 목적, 3)은 판단의 근거·이유, 4)는 조건을 나타내는 to부정사의 부사적 용법이다.
어휘 get a perfect score 만점을 받다
16 ③ 가능 또는 운명을 나타내는 be to-v: '～할 수 있다' 또는 '～할 운명이다'
어휘 passenger 명 승객 safety rule 안전 수칙
release 동 풀어 주다; *공개[발표]하다
creatively 부 창의적으로 desert 명 사막

17 to부정사의 시제가 문장의 시제보다 앞서므로 완료부정사 (to have v-ed)를 쓴다.
[어휘] be in trouble with …와 말썽이 있다 teammate [명] 팀 동료

18 ⓑ when to-v: '언제 …할지'
when calling → when to call
ⓓ 가목적어로 that이 아닌 it을 쓴다.
that → it
[어휘] master [동] 완전히 익히다, 터득하다 scold [동] 꾸짖다, 혼내다

19 ① 대명사(something)가 『to-v+전치사』의 의미상 목적어이므로 전치사 on을 쓴다.
⑤ 사람의 성품·성격을 나타내는 형용사(generous)가 보어이므로 의미상 주어로 『of+목적격』을 쓴다.
[어휘] take out …을 내놓다 garbage [명] 쓰레기
painful [형] 아픈, 고통스러운 donate [동] 기부하다
charity [명] 자선 단체

20 『it takes+목적격+시간+to-v』: '…가 ~하는 데 (시간)이 걸리다'
[어휘] article [명] (신문·잡지의) 글, 기사

21 수동의 뜻을 가지며 to부정사의 시제가 문장의 시제와 같으므로 단순수동태(to be v-ed)를 쓴다.
[어휘] reward [동] 보상하다 act [명] 행동

22 『too+형용사/부사+to-v』: '너무 …해서 ~할 수 없다', '~하기에 너무 …하다'
[어휘] violent [형] 폭력적인

23 부정적 결과를 나타내는 only to-v: '결국 …하고 말다'
[어휘] recorded [형] 녹음된

CHAPTER 02 동명사

UNIT 1 동명사의 역할

pp.22 - 23

B

1 마라톤에서 뛰는 것은 쉽지 않다.
온라인 쇼핑이 크게 대중화되었다.
2 나의 하루의 가장 좋은 부분은 가족과 함께 저녁 식사를 하는 것이다.
3 1) 그는 십 대 때 작곡을 시작했다.
2) 실수하는 것을 두려워하지 마라.
4 나는 그가 늦게까지 깨어 있는 것을 좋아하지 않는다.
Smith 씨는 그녀가 학교에 늦는 것에 대해 걱정한다.

[Tip 주의!] 그는 사실을 말하지 않은 것에 대해 사과했다.

C

1 그녀는 낯선 사람들을 친구로 사귀는 것을 잘한다.
2 나는 수업 중에 울었던 것이 부끄럽다.

D

1 그녀는 아이처럼 취급받는 것을 싫어한다.
2 그는 무시당했던 것에 대해 화가 나 있다.

SPEED CHECK

1 ③ 2 ②

1 전치사(of)의 목적어로 쓰인 동명사로, 능동의 뜻을 나타내며 동명사의 시제가 문장의 시제와 같으므로 단순동명사를 씀
[어휘] instead of … 대신에
2 동명사의 주어와 문장의 주어가 다를 때 의미상 주어를 동명사 앞에 소유격이나 목적격으로 나타냄

PRACTICE TEST

A 1 not being 2 him 3 developing
4 having eaten
B 1 she → her 2 being not → not being
3 visit → visiting 4 are → is
C 1 having wasted 2 his[him] being
D 1 protecting the environment
2 his[him] not quitting 3 being laughed at
4 having met her 5 her having been treated

A

1 동명사의 부정: not/never v-ing
2 동명사의 의미상 주어는 동명사 앞에 소유격이나 목적격으로 나타냄
3 문맥상 '개발하는 것'이라는 능동의 뜻을 나타내므로 단순동명사(v-ing)를 씀
4 yesterday로 보아 과거의 일로, 문장의 시제(현재)보다 앞서므로 완료동명사(having v-ed)를 씀

B

1 동명사의 의미상 주어는 동명사 앞에 소유격이나 목적격으로 나타냄
2 동명사의 부정: not/never v-ing
3 전치사(about)의 목적어로 쓰인 동명사
4 주어로 쓰인 동명사는 단수 취급함

C

1 '네 시간을 뺏은 것'은 과거의 일로, 동명사의 시제가 문장의 시제(현재)보다 앞서므로 완료동명사(having v-ed)를 씀
2 동명사의 의미상 주어는 동명사 앞에 소유격이나 목적격으로 나타냄

D

1 주격 보어로 쓰인 동명사
2 전치사(about)의 목적어로 쓰인 동명사로, 『소유격/목적격+not v-ing』의 어순으로 씀
3 수동의 뜻을 가지며 동명사의 시제가 문장의 시제(과거)와 같으므로 단순수동태(being v-ed)를 씀
4 동명사의 시제가 문장의 시제(과거)보다 앞서므로 완료동명사(having v-ed)를 씀
5 수동의 뜻을 가지며 동명사의 시제가 문장의 시제(현재)보다 앞서므로 완료수동태(having been v-ed)를 씀

UNIT 2 목적어로 쓰이는 동명사와 to부정사

pp.24 - 25

1 Robin은 매일 스케이트보드 타는 것을 즐긴다.
그녀는 한 달간 패스트푸드 먹는 것을 피했다.
2 저는 당신을 곧 다시 만나길 바랍니다.
그의 아들은 유치원에 가기를 거부했다.
3 1) 나는 풀밭 위를 걷는 것을 좋아한다.
그녀는 그녀의 친구들과 캠핑하러 가는 것을 무척 좋아한다.
2) 그는 지난해에 알프스 산을 본 것을 기억한다.
그녀는 항상 문을 잠글 것을 기억한다.
나는 그에게 전화한 것을 잊어버려서 또 전화했다.
우리의 파티 계획에 대해 그에게 전화할 것을 잊지 마라.
네 컴퓨터가 작동하지 않는다면 그걸 재부팅해 봐라.
나는 더 많은 채소를 먹으려고 노력했다.

[Tip 비교!] 그는 나에게 말하는 것을 멈췄다.
그는 나에게 말하기 위해 멈췄다.

SPEED CHECK

1 ③ 2 ②

1 consider v-ing: '…하기를 고려하다'
[어휘] lane [명] 길, (좁은) 도로
2 try to-v: '…하려고 노력하다'

PRACTICE TEST

A 1 to go 2 eating 3 to buy 4 writing 5 to do
6 to turn off 7 watching
B 1 moving 2 meeting 3 to become 4 to take
5 working
C 1 stopped to read
2 decided to break up with
3 refuses to listen to
4 continued to write
5 remember to attend

A

1 wish to-v: '…하기를 소망하다'
2 give up v-ing: '…하기를 포기하다'
3 promise to-v: '…하기로 약속하다'
4 finish v-ing: '…하기를 끝내다'
5 '최선을 다하려고 노력하다'라는 뜻이므로 try to-v
6 '다리미를 끌 것을 잊어버리다'라는 뜻이므로 forget to-v
7 '영화를 본 것을 기억하다'라는 뜻이므로 remember v-ing

B

1 consider v-ing: '…하기를 고려하다'
2 '그녀를 만난 것을 잊어버리다'라는 뜻이므로 forget v-ing
3 hope to-v: '…하기를 바라다'
4 want to-v: '…하기를 원하다'
5 '일하는 것을 멈추다'라는 뜻이므로 stop v-ing

C

1 stop to-v: '…하기 위해 멈추다'
2 decide to-v: '…하기로 결정하다'
3 refuse to-v: '…하기를 거부하다'
4 continue to-v[v-ing]: '계속 …하다'
5 remember to-v: '(미래에) …할 것을 기억하다'

UNIT 3 동명사를 이용한 주요 구문

pp.26 - 27

1 그녀는 일주일에 3일을 수영하러 간다.
나는 지난 토요일에 처음으로 낚시하러 갔다.
2 Jenny는 그 뮤지컬을 본 후 울고 싶었다.
나는 아무것도 하고 싶지 않다.
3 나는 여행하기를 고대하고 있다.
Owen은 그의 조카를 만나기를 손꼽아 고대하고 있다.
4 이 영화는 다시 볼 가치가 있다.
인생은 즐길 가치가 있다.
5 나는 내 블로그에 남긴 그의 댓글에 대해 걱정하지 않을 수 없다.

SPEED CHECK

1 ① 2 ⑤

1 go v-ing: '…하러 가다'
2 look forward to v-ing: '…하기를 고대하다'
[어휘] theater [명] 극장

PRACTICE TEST

A 1 surf → surfing 2 hike → hiking 3 in → from
4 listen → listening 5 can't help but forgiving → can't (help) but forgive 또는 can't help forgiving

B 1 buying 2 to eating 3 watching 4 making
5 reading 6 entering

C 1 kept on raining
2 has trouble[difficulty] parking
3 It's no use worrying about
4 look forward to working
5 There is no swimming
6 couldn't help telling a lie 또는 couldn't (help) but tell a lie

A

1 「spend+시간+(on) v-ing」: '…하는 데 시간을 쓰다'
2 go v-ing: '…하러 가다'
3 「keep+목적어+from v-ing」: '…가 ~하는 것을 막다'
4 look forward to v-ing: '…하기를 고대하다'
5 「cannot (help) but+동사원형」: '…하지 않을 수 없다' (= cannot help v-ing)

B

1 How about v-ing?: '…하는 게 어때?'
2 be used to v-ing: '…하는 것에 익숙하다'
3 feel like v-ing: '…하고 싶다'
4 be busy v-ing: '…하느라 바쁘다'
5 be worth v-ing: '…할 가치가 있다'
6 on[upon] v-ing: '…하자마자'

C

1 keep (on) v-ing: '계속 …하다'
2 have trouble[difficulty] (in) v-ing: '…하는 데 어려움을 겪다'
3 it's no use v-ing: '…해 봐야 소용없다'
4 look forward to v-ing: '…하기를 고대하다'
5 there is no v-ing: '…할 수 없다', '…하는 것은 불가능하다'
6 cannot help v-ing: '…하지 않을 수 없다' (= 「cannot (help) but+동사원형」)

REVIEW TEST pp.28 - 30

01 ③ 02 ③ 03 ① 04 pack, packing 05 comparing, being compared 06 ③ 07 ② 08 ④ 09 1) is looking forward to going to her new home 2) am not afraid of saying "No" 3) wants to be alone without being disturbed 10 ③ drinking not → not drinking, ④ are → is 11 ① being → to be, ④ to smoke → smoking 12 ④ 13 my[me] turning off the radio 14 On[Upon] arriving at the hotel 15 We could not help agreeing with his opinion. / We could not help but agree with his opinion. 16 ⑤ 17 ⑤ 18 denies having stolen 19 my[me] not bringing my textbook 20 having been overworked 21 ① 22 ②

01 go v-ing: '…하러 가다'
[어휘] bowl [동] 볼링을 하다

02 quit v-ing: '…하기를 그만두다'

03 동사 plan은 목적어로 to부정사를 쓰므로 ①의 빈칸에는 to ride가 와야 한다. enjoy, avoid는 목적어로 동명사를, like, love는 목적어로 동명사와 to부정사를 모두 쓸 수 있으므로 ②-⑤의 빈칸에는 riding이 올 수 있다.
[어휘] zip line 집라인 motorcycle [명] 오토바이

04 be busy v-ing: '…하느라 바쁘다'
[어휘] business trip 출장

05 문맥상 '비교당하는 것'이라는 수동의 뜻을 가지며 동명사의 시제가 문장의 시제와 같으므로 단순수동태(being v-ed)를 쓴다.
[어휘] compare to …와 비교하다

06 give up v-ing: '…하기를 포기하다'

07 promise to-v: '…하기로 약속하다'

08 전치사(about)의 목적어로 동명사(being)를 쓰고, 동명사의 의미상 주어는 동명사 앞에 소유격이나 목적격으로 나타낸다.

09 1) look forward to v-ing: '…하기를 고대하다'
2) 전치사(of)의 목적어로 동명사를 쓴다.
3) 전치사(without)의 목적어로 동명사를 쓰고, 동명사의 시제가 문장의 시제와 같으므로 단순수동태를 쓴다.
[어휘] disturb [동] 방해하다

10 ③ 동명사의 부정: not/never v-ing
④ 주어로 쓰인 동명사구는 단수 취급한다.
[어휘] bark [동] 짖다 tap [동] (가볍게) 두드리다 elect [동] 선출하다

11 ① wish to-v: '…하기를 소망하다'
④ stop to-v: '…하기 위해 멈추다' / stop v-ing: '…하는 것을 멈추다'
[어휘] cook [명] 요리사

12 ④ 동명사의 시제가 문장의 시제보다 앞서므로 완료동명사(having v-ed)를 쓴다.

13 동사 mind는 목적어로 동명사를 쓰며, 동명사의 의미상 주어는 동명사 앞에 소유격 또는 목적격으로 나타낸다.

14 「as soon as+주어+동사」: '…하자마자' (→ on[upon] v-ing)

15 cannot help v-ing: '…하지 않을 수 없다' (= 「cannot (help) but+동사원형」)

[어휘] agree with …에 동의하다 opinion [명] 의견, 견해

16 ⑤ be used to v-ing: '…하는 것에 익숙하다'

17 ⑤ 의미상 주어는 동명사 앞에 소유격이나 목적격으로 나타내고, 수동의 뜻을 가지며 동명사의 시제가 문장의 시제보다 앞서므로 완료수동태(having been v-ed)를 쓴다.

[어휘] criticize [동] 비판하다

18 동명사의 시제가 문장의 시제보다 앞서므로 완료동명사(having v-ed)를 쓴다.

19 전치사(with)의 목적어로 동명사를 쓰며, 동명사의 의미상 주어는 동명사 앞에 소유격이나 목적격으로 나타낸다. 동명사의 부정은 동명사 앞에 not이나 never를 쓴다.

20 수동의 뜻을 가지며 동명사의 시제가 문장의 시제보다 앞서므로 완료수동태(having been v-ed)를 쓴다.

[어휘] overwork [동] 과로하다, 혹사하다

21 ①은 주격 보어로 쓰인 동명사, 나머지는 목적어로 쓰인 동명사이다.

22 ⓐ 문맥상 '초대장을 보낼 것을 잊어버리다'라는 의미가 되어야 자연스러우므로 forget to-v를 쓴다. sending → to send
ⓒ 주어로 쓰인 동명사구는 단수 취급한다. are → is
ⓔ 동사 avoid는 목적어로 동명사를 쓴다.
to meet → meeting

CHAPTER 03 분사

UNIT 1 분사의 역할

pp.32 - 33

[A]

1 이 새로운 소설은 흥미진진하다.
Sam은 누군가가 창문을 똑똑 두드리고 있는 소리를 들었다.

2 Green 씨는 2주 전에 그 지붕이 수리되게 했다.
그녀는 그 탈출한 뱀을 찾고 있다.

[B]

1 우는 아기/상처 입은 마음
저기에 앉아 있는 남자가 Kelly의 남자친구이다.

2 어린이들이 앉아서 로봇을 가지고 놀고 있었다.
나는 그녀가 수업 중에 졸고 있는 것을 보았다.

Grammar UP

나의 과학 시험 점수는 실망스러웠다.
나는 나의 과학 시험 점수에 실망했다.

SPEED CHECK

1 ③ 2 ②

1 뒤에서 명사(books)를 수식하고 '쓰인'이라는 수동의 뜻을 나타내므로 과거분사

2 주어(The food)가 감정을 일으키므로 현재분사

PRACTICE TEST

A 1 hidden 2 waving 3 smiling 4 called
5 moved

B 1 surprised, surprising
2 interesting, interested
3 exciting, excited

C 1 made 2 standing 3 sent 4 tested
5 bored

A

1 보물이 '숨겨진' 것이므로 과거분사(수동)

2 남자가 '손을 흔들고 있는' 것이므로 현재분사(능동·진행)

3 아기가 '미소 짓고 있는' 것이므로 현재분사(능동·진행)

4 그의 이름이 '불리는' 것이므로 과거분사(수동)

5 주어 Mary가 감정을 느끼므로 과거분사(수동)

B

1 주어(I)가 감정을 느끼므로 과거분사
주어(The results)가 감정을 일으키므로 현재분사

2 진주어(to learn 이하)가 감정을 일으키므로 현재분사
주어(She)가 감정을 느끼므로 과거분사

3 목적어(the film)가 감정을 일으키므로 현재분사
주어(I)가 감정을 느끼므로 과거분사

C

1 모니터가 '만들어진' 것이므로 과거분사(수동)

2 소녀가 '서 있는' 것이므로 현재분사(능동·진행)

3 편지가 '보내진' 것이므로 과거분사(수동)

4 눈이 '검사되는' 것이므로 과거분사(수동)

5 주어(They)가 감정을 느끼므로 과거분사

UNIT 2 분사구문

pp.34 - 35

[A]

일등상을 탔을 때 그는 행복했다.

B

1 집에 들어갔을 때 우리는 아이들이 위층에서 뛰어다니는 소리를 들었다.

2 Ken은 그의 손을 흔들면서 걸어갔다.
   그 기차는 6시에 서울을 떠났고 9시에 부산에 도착했다.

3 소년이었기 때문에 그는 그 소녀의 감정을 이해할 수 없었다.

4 할리우드에 가면 너는 많은 유명한 사람들을 볼 수 있을 것이다.

5 한 영화배우의 집 근처에 살고 있음에도 불구하고 나는 그녀를 한 번도 보지 못했다.

Grammar UP

그 가수는 춤을 추면서 청중을 향해 돌아섰다.
→ 춤을 추면서 그 가수는 청중을 향해 돌아섰다.

SPEED CHECK

1 ④ 2 ②

1 이유를 나타내는 분사구문

2 동시동작을 나타내는 분사구문

PRACTICE TEST

A 1 Sitting 2 Being 3 Jogging 4 Joining
B 1 Forgetting the password
  2 Although looking weak
  3 taking a memo
C 1 Seeing Juliet
  2 Arriving at the store[shop]
  3 Searching the Internet 4 Being
  5 Though[Although] explaining

A

1 When/As/While/After/As soon as I sat on the sofa, ...

2 Because[As/Since] it is slow, ...

3 When/As/While/After/As soon as he jogged along the street, ...

4 If you join this club, ...

B

1 이유를 나타내는 분사구문

2 양보를 나타내는 분사구문은 일반적으로 접속사를 남겨 둠

3 동시동작을 나타내는 분사구문

C

1-2 때를 나타내는 분사구문

3 조건을 나타내는 분사구문

4 이유를 나타내는 분사구문

5 양보를 나타내는 분사구문

UNIT 3 분사구문의 부정, 시제, 수동태

pp.36 - 37

A

잠잘 시간이 충분하지 않아서 그는 수업 시간에 졸았다.

B

1 그녀의 눈을 들여다볼 때 나는 그녀가 나를 사랑한다는 것을 알 수 있다.

2 많이 먹었기 때문에 그녀는 더 이상 먹고 싶지 않다.
   내 일을 끝냈기 때문에 나는 언제든지 너를 도울 수 있다.

C

1 질문에 답하도록 요청받았을 때 그는 무엇을 해야 할지 몰랐다.

2 캐나다에서 자랐기 때문에 그는 영어를 잘 말한다.

Grammar UP

배가 고프기 때문에 나는 뭔가 먹고 싶다.

SPEED CHECK

1 ⑤ 2 ②

1 부사절의 시제가 주절의 시제보다 앞설 때 완료 분사구문(having v-ed)을 씀

2 분사구문의 수동태(being / having been v-ed)에서 being이나 having been은 생략할 수 있어서 과거분사만 남음
   (← Being interested in history, ...)
   어휘 historical 휑 역사의

PRACTICE TEST

A 1 Written 2 Not having 3 Excited
  4 Having seen 5 Fired
B 1 (Being) Used well, the new technique can be very useful.
  2 Having lived in a big city, she knows little about country life.
  3 (Having been) Robbed before, I always lock the door.
  4 Having lost my cell phone, I can't call her now.
C 1 Surprised at 2 Not paying attention
  3 Having read 4 having been invited

A

1 부사절의 생략된 주어 the book이 영어로 '쓰인' 것이므로 분사구문의 수동태(being/having been v-ed)를 씀. being이나 having been은 생략 가능

2 분사구문의 부정은 분사 앞에 not이나 never를 씀

3 부사절의 생략된 주어 Mark가 '신난' 것이므로 분사구문의 수동태(being v-ed)를 씀. being은 생략 가능

4 부사절의 시제가 주절의 시제보다 앞설 때 완료 분사구문(having v-ed)을 씀

5 부사절의 생략된 주어 he가 '해고된' 것이고, 부사절의 시제가 주절의 시제보다 앞서므로 분사구문의 완료수동태(having been v-ed)를 씀. having been은 생략 가능

B

1 분사구문의 단순수동태: (being) v-ed

2, 4 완료 분사구문: having v-ed

3 분사구문의 완료수동태: (having been) v-ed

UNIT 4 주의해야 할 분사구문

pp.38 - 39

1 그 보고서를 읽은 후에 팀장은 회의를 소집했다.

2 비가 오기 시작했기 때문에 우리는 집에 서둘러 돌아갔다.

3 1) 나는 네가 내 앞에 서 있는 채로는 일에 집중할 수가 없다.
　2) Jessica는 그녀의 다리를 꼰 채 앉아 있었다.

Grammar UP

네 입에 음식을 가득 넣은 채 말하지 마라.
그 여배우는 아름다운 드레스를 입은 채 무대에 올랐다.
그녀는 그녀의 아기를 품에 안은 채 남편을 기다렸다.

4 엄밀히 말해서 네 답은 틀리다.
일반적으로 말해서 한국어는 배우기 쉽지 않다.

SPEED CHECK

1 ③　2 ②

1 부사절의 주어(비인칭 주어 it)가 주절의 주어(we)와 다르므로 부사절의 주어를 분사구문의 주어로 남겨 둠

2 명사(her music)와 분사의 관계가 능동이므로 『with+(대)명사+현재분사』: '…이 ~한 채'

PRACTICE TEST

A **1** Considering　**2** closed　**3** The lesson being
　　4 dancing　**5** While

B

1 The sun setting　**2** The traffic light turning green
3 It having rained heavily
4 There being a strong wind

C

1 with the cat sleeping　**2** with the sun hidden
3 with his head buried

A

1 문맥상 '그의 나이를 고려하면'이 자연스러우므로 Considering

2 명사(his eyes)와 분사의 관계가 수동이므로 『with+(대)명사+과거분사』

3 부사절의 주어(The lesson)가 주절의 주어(we)와 다르므로 부사절의 주어를 분사구문의 주어로 남겨 둠

4 명사(my friends)와 분사의 관계가 능동이므로 『with+(대)명사+현재분사』

5 뜻을 명확히 하기 위해 접속사(While)를 생략하지 않은 분사구문

B

부사절의 주어가 주절의 주어와 다를 때 부사절의 주어를 분사구문의 주어로 남겨 둠

3 부사절의 시제가 주절의 시제보다 앞서므로 완료 분사구문(having v-ed)을 씀

C

『with+(대)명사+분사』 구문은 동시동작을 나타낼 때 사용되며, (대)명사와 분사의 관계가 능동이면 현재분사를, 수동이면 과거분사를 씀

REVIEW TEST

pp.40 - 42

01 ③　**02** ③　**03** ⑤　**04** ④　**05** satisfying
06 We felt excited when the player hit a home run.
07 Having read the same book several times　**08** Not having heard anything about the new teacher
09 The elevator's doors being nearly closed　**10** ⑤
11 ④　**12** with birds flying　**13** with the TV turned on　**14** ⑤　**15** ①　**16** As he read the last page of the book　**17** If you open the box　**18** and served her some tea　**19** Because[As / Since] I had been inspired by Picasso　**20** ③　**21** Not having taken a break
22 when talking to　**23** The dog barking

01 뒤에서 명사(vegetables)를 수식하고 '길러진'이라는 수동의 뜻이므로 과거분사를 쓴다.
어휘 local ⑱ 지역의

02 때를 나타내는 분사구문 ← When / As / After / As soon as / While she entered the room, ...

03 부사절의 시제가 주절의 시제보다 앞서므로 완료 분사구문
   (having v-ed)을 쓴다.
   어휘 stuck 휑 갇힌, 움직일 수 없는

04 Not knowing what to do로 쓸 수 있다. 분사구문의 부정은
   분사 앞에 not이나 never를 쓴다.
   ← Because[As/Since] he didn't know what to do, ...
   어휘 bite 동 물어뜯다

05 목적어(her new job)가 감정을 일으키므로 현재분사

06 주어(We)가 감정을 느끼므로 현재분사(exciting)가 아니라
   과거분사(excited)가 되어야 한다.
   어휘 excite 동 신이 나게 하다 hit a home run 홈런을 치다

07 부사절의 시제가 주절의 시제보다 앞서므로 완료 분사구문
   (having v-ed)을 쓴다.

08 완료 분사구문의 부정: not/never having v-ed
   어휘 curious 휑 궁금한, 호기심이 많은

09 부사절의 주어(the elevator's doors)가 주절의 주어(a man)
   와 다르므로 부사절의 주어를 분사구문의 주어로 남겨 둔다.
   어휘 nearly 부 거의

10 ⑤ Roughly speaking ('대강 말하자면') → Frankly
   speaking
   어휘 reject 동 거절하다 personality 명 성격
        promote 동 승진시키다

11 ④ 단순 분사구문이 쓰인 것으로 보아, 부사절과 주절의 시제
   (can't afford)가 같으므로 현재시제를 쓴다.
   didn't → don't
   어휘 afford 동 (…을 살) 여유[형편]가 되다

12 명사(birds)와 분사의 관계가 능동이므로 『with+(대)명사+현재
   분사』: '…이 ~한 채'

13 명사(the TV)와 분사의 관계가 수동이므로 『with+(대)명사+과거
   분사』: '…이 ~된 채'

14 ⑤ 문맥상 '야기된 사고'라는 수동의 뜻이므로 과거분사를 쓴다.
   causing → caused
   어휘 increase 동 증가하다

15 ① 부사절 Because[As/Since] she was angry를 분사구
   문으로 바꾼 것으로, Being이 적절하다.
   Be → Being
   어휘 comb 명 빗 scenery 명 경치, 풍경

16 동시동작을 나타내는 분사구문

17 조건을 나타내는 분사구문

18 연속상황을 나타내는 분사구문
   어휘 serve 동 (음식을) 제공하다, 내다

19 이유를 나타내는 분사구문의 완료수동태
   어휘 inspire 동 영감을 주다

20 ⓐ 사무실이 '칠해지는' 것이므로 과거분사(수동)를 쓴다.
   painting → painted
   ⓓ 분사구문의 부정
   Hearing not → Not hearing
   어휘 delivery 명 배달(물) nervously 부 초조하게

21 완료 분사구문의 부정: not/never having v-ed
   ← Because[As/Since] she hadn't taken a break, ...

22 분사구문의 뜻을 명확히 하기 위해 접속사 when을 그대로 둘 수
   있다.
   ← ... when you talk to elderly people.

23 주절의 주어(I)와 부사절의 주어(The dog)가 다르므로 부사절의
   주어를 분사구문의 주어로 남겨 둔다.
   ← Because[As/Since] the dog barked at me, ...

CHAPTER 04 시제

UNIT 1 현재완료

pp.44 - 45

A

1 나는 그렇게 놀라운 광경을 한 번도 본 적이 없다.

2 그들은 50년이 넘도록 결혼한 상태이다.
   Tip 비교! 우리는 2006년부터 친구였다.
          우리는 8년 동안 친구였다.

3 그는 막 휴가에서 돌아왔다.

4 나는 이 장갑의 한쪽을 잃어버렸다. (나는 지금 그것을 가지고 있지
   않다.)

Tip 주의! 그 미용실은 어제 폐업했다.

✓ Grammar UP

나는 미국에 두 번 가 본 적이 있다.
그는 미국에 가버렸다. (그는 지금 여기에 없다.)

B

나는 3주째 운전 교습을 받고 있다.
(→ 나는 3주 전에 운전 교습을 받기 시작했다. 나는 여전히 운전 교습
을 받고 있다.)

SPEED CHECK

1 ④ 2 ④

1 계속을 나타내는 현재완료

2 have gone to: '…에 가고 (지금 여기에) 없다'

PRACTICE **TEST**

A **1** went **2** for **3** visited **4** has been doing
5 has been
B **1** has been to
2 has forgotten
3 have been watching
C **1** 너는 얼마나 오랫동안 James를 알아 왔니?
(= 너는 James를 안 지 얼마나 됐니?)
2 그 회사는 이미 다양한 상품들을 출시했다.
3 나는 살면서 멕시코 음식을 한 번도 먹어 본 적이 없다.
4 그는 다리가 부러져서 스키를 타러 갈 수 없다.
5 Emma는 수 시간 동안 Kevin을 기다려 오고 있다.

A

1, 3 명백하게 과거를 나타내는 말(a week ago/last weekend)
이 있으므로 과거시제
2 『for+기간』: '… 동안'
4 과거(두 시간 전)에 숙제를 시작해서 현재에도 진행 중이므로 현재
완료 진행형: '…해 오고 있다'
5 계속을 나타내는 현재완료: '(지금까지 계속) …해 왔다'

B

1 have been to: '…에 가 본 적이 있다'
2 결과를 나타내는 현재완료: '…해버렸다 (그래서 지금은 ~이다)'
3 과거(한 시간 전)에 영화를 보기 시작해서 현재에도 진행 중이므로
현재완료 진행형

C

1 계속을 나타내는 현재완료
2 완료를 나타내는 현재완료
3 경험을 나타내는 현재완료
4 결과를 나타내는 현재완료
5 현재완료 진행형

UNIT **2**   **과거완료, 미래완료**

pp.46 - 47

그는 토론토로 오기 전에 큰 도시에 와 본 적이 한 번도 없었다.
Noah는 코치가 되기 전에 골프 선수였다.
내가 학교에 도착했을 때 시험이 이미 시작됐었다.
그는 팔을 다친 상태여서 농구를 할 수 없었다.

✔ Grammar UP

나는 어머니가 나에게 사 주셨던 그 지갑을 잃어버렸다.

그 전화가 울렸을 때 나는 두 시간 동안 공부하고 있었다.
경찰은 그 도둑을 잡기 전에 3년 동안 그를 찾고 있었다.

내일이면 우리는 여기에 일주일째 있게 될 것이다.
나는 미국으로 떠나기 전에 영어를 숙달하게 될 것이다.

D

Ava가 부산에 도착할 때 그녀는 6시간 이상 운전하고 있는 게 될 것이다.
네가 집에 올 때쯤 나는 2시간 동안 요리하고 있는 게 될 것이다.

SPEED CHECK

1 ④   **2** ③

1 경험을 나타내는 과거완료
2 미래의 특정 시점에 완료될 일을 나타내는 미래완료

PRACTICE **TEST**

A **1** will have gotten **2** had taken
3 had been sleeping **4** had met
5 will have been
B **1** had gone **2** Had
3 had posted 또는 had been posting
4 will have finished **5** had slept
C **1** had been watching **2** will have lived
3 had left **4** will have been crying **5** had lost

A

1 미래의 특정 시점(졸업할 때쯤)에 완료될 일을 나타내므로 미래완료
2 Ben이 괜찮아졌던 과거 시점보다 휴식을 취했던 것이 더 이전의
일이므로 대과거
3 과거(큰 소리를 들었을 때)에도 계속 자고 있었으므로 과거완료 진행형
4 Lisa가 기억했던 과거 시점보다 그녀의 고객을 만났던 것이 더 이
전의 일이므로 대과거
5 미래의 특정 시점(내일)에도 진행 중일 일이므로 미래완료 진행형

B

1 결과를 나타내는 과거완료
2 경험을 나타내는 과거완료
3 완료를 나타내는 과거완료 또는 과거 이전에 시작된 일(메시지를 게
시하는 것)이 과거(내가 집에 돌아왔을 때)에도 진행 중이었음을 나
타내는 과거완료 진행형
4 미래의 특정 시점(다음 주)에 완료될 일을 나타내므로 미래완료
5 계속을 나타내는 과거완료

C

1 과거완료 진행형
2 미래완료
3 대과거
4 미래완료 진행형
5 결과를 나타내는 과거완료

REVIEW TEST pp.48 - 50

01 ④ 02 ⑤ 03 ④ 04 have known 05 had never played 06 ③, ④ 07 ⑤ 08 ⑤ 09 ⑤ 10 ④ 11 has ended, ended 12 has taken, will have taken 13 had played 14 has been painting 15 ① 16 My coworker has gone to Rome. 17 ③ 18 ③ 19 ④ 20 I will have been traveling around Europe 21 The magic show had already finished

01 since('… 이래로')가 있고 과거에 일어난 일이 현재까지 영향을 미치므로 현재완료(계속)를 쓴다.
[어휘] motion picture 영화 (필름)
02 미래의 특정 시점(이번 주말)에 완료될 일이므로 미래완료를 쓴다.
03 완료를 나타내는 과거완료
[어휘] travel [동] 여행하다; *이동하다
04 계속을 나타내는 현재완료
05 경험을 나타내는 과거완료
06 각각 계속을 나타내는 현재완료, 현재완료 진행형 문장으로, for, since 등의 어구와 함께 주로 쓴다. yesterday, last, ago 등과 같이 명백하게 과거를 나타내는 말과 함께 쓰지 않는다.
[어휘] pour [동] (비가) 마구 쏟아지다
07 과거에 시작된 일이 현재에도 진행 중일 때 현재완료 진행형을 쓴다.
08 죽은 과거 시점보다 시를 썼던 것이 더 이전의 일이므로 대과거를 쓴다.
[어휘] poem [명] (한 편의) 시
09 경험을 나타내는 과거완료
[어휘] abroad [부] 해외로[에]
10 과거부터 현재까지 계속되는 일이므로 현재완료(계속)를 쓴다.
11 명백하게 과거를 나타내는 말(last week)이 있으므로 과거시제를 쓴다.
[어휘] annual [형] 매년의, 연례의
12 미래의 특정 시점에 완료될 일을 나타내므로 미래완료를 쓴다.
13 샤워를 한 과거 시점보다 농구를 했던 것이 더 이전의 일이므로 대과거를 쓴다.
14 과거에 시작해서 현재에도 진행 중인 일이므로 현재완료 진행형을 쓴다.
15 보기와 ①은 경험, ②는 완료, ③과 ⑤는 계속, ④는 결과를 나타내는 현재완료이다.
[어휘] microwave oven 전자레인지
16 have gone to: '…에 가고 (지금 여기에) 없다'
[어휘] coworker [명] 함께 일하는 사람, 동료
17 ③ 계속을 나타내는 과거완료
has been → had been
[어휘] take off (비행기가) 이륙하다
18 ⓐ 미래의 특정 시점(next Saturday)에 완료될 일이므로 미래완료를 쓴다.
ⓑ since는 기준 시점과 함께 쓴다.
ⓒ 계속을 나타내는 과거완료
[어휘] retire [동] 은퇴하다
19 ⓒ 미래의 특정 시점(next year)까지 계속될 일이므로 미래완료를 쓴다.
has been → will have been
ⓔ 과거 이전에 시작된 일이 과거까지 계속되었으므로 과거완료(계속) 또는 과거완료 진행형을 쓴다.
has been standing → had stood/had been standing
[어휘] admit [동] 인정하다 stand in line 줄을 서다
20 미래의 특정 시점(next Monday)에도 진행 중일 일이므로 미래완료 진행형을 쓴다.
21 완료를 나타내는 과거완료
[어휘] magic show 마술 쇼 student hall 학생 회관

CHAPTER 05 조동사

UNIT 1 can, must, should / ought to, may, need

pp.52 - 53

1 우리는 프랑스어를 한국어로 번역할 수 있다.
지금 제가 주문을 받아도 될까요?
저 사람은 Tom일 리가 없다. 그는 캐나다에 가고 없다.
[Tip 주의!] 그녀는 내년에 운전할 수 있을 것이다.

2 군인은 제복을 입어야 한다.
그는 병원에서의 봉사 활동 후에 피곤한 것이 틀림없다.
[Tip 주의!] 너는 연극 중에 전화를 사용해서는 안 된다.
너는 이 로션을 살 필요가 없다.

3 너는 균형 잡힌 식사를 해야 한다.
너는 이 기회를 놓쳐서는 안 된다.

4 너는 7시 이후에는 아무 때나 여기에 와도 좋다.
그것은 사실일지도, 사실이 아닐지도 모른다.

5 그가 토요일에 일할 필요가 있니?
그녀는 매일 산책할 필요가 있다.
Tip 비교! 너는 나에게 사과할 필요가 없다.

SPEED CHECK

①

「can't[cannot]+동사원형」: '…할 수 없다' (능력·가능)

PRACTICE TEST

A 1 be able to 2 ought not to 3 don't have to
4 may 5 must
B 1 has to 2 May
C 1 can't[cannot] be 2 may not come
3 must/should be careful
4 must/should not judge
5 don't have[need] to turn down
6 must be 7 need not hurry

A

1 두 개의 조동사를 함께 쓸 수 없으므로 can 대신 be able to를 씀
2 ought to의 부정: ought not to
3 불필요를 나타내는 don't have to
4 약한 추측을 나타내는 may
5 강한 추측을 나타내는 must

B

1 의무를 나타내는 must는 have to[has to]로 바꿔 쓸 수 있음
2 허가를 나타내는 can과 may

C

1 can't[cannot]: '…일 리가 없다' (부정 추측)
2 may: '…일지도 모른다' (약한 추측)
3 must/should: '…해야 한다' (의무)
4 must not(강한 금지)/should not: '…해서는 안 된다'
5 don't have[need] to: '…할 필요가 없다' (불필요)
6 must: '…임이 틀림없다' (강한 추측)
7 need not: '…할 필요가 없다' (불필요) (= don't have[need] to)

UNIT 2 had better, would rather, would, used to

pp.54 - 55

1 너는 수업 시간에 주의 깊게 듣고 필기를 하는 게 좋겠다.
어두워지기 전에 집에 도착하고 싶다면 너는 서두르는 게 좋겠다.
우리는 직장에 다시는 늦지 않는 게 좋겠다.

2 비가 오기 시작한다. 나는 집에 머무르는 편이 낫겠다.
나는 김 선생님의 수업을 듣지 않는 편이 낫겠다.
Tip 비교! 나는 게임을 하느니 차라리 운동을 하겠다.
나는 옷에 나의 돈을 쓰느니 차라리 음식에 쓰겠다.

3 나는 가끔 Jacob과 자전거를 타러 가곤 했다.
우리 가족은 주말마다 야구를 하곤 했다.

4 나는 주말마다 등산을 가곤 했다.
Bella는 그녀가 아이였을 때 산타클로스를 믿었다.
나는 규칙적으로 운동하지 않았었다.
Tip 주의! 나는 나의 친구들과 나의 꿈에 관해 이야기하곤 했다.
우리 집 옆에는 카페가 하나 있었다.

SPEED CHECK

1 ① 2 ③

1 「had better+동사원형」: '…하는 게 좋겠다' (강한 충고나 권고)
[어휘] decision [명] 결정, 결심
2 used to: '…하곤 했다' (과거의 습관)

PRACTICE TEST

A 1 had better 2 rather 3 used to 4 than
5 had better not
B 1 had better 2 used to 3 would rather 4 would
C 1 used to like
2 rather not go
3 would play board games
4 would rather quit than
5 had better not tell

A

1 had better: '…하는 게 좋겠다' (강한 충고나 권고)
2 would rather: '(차라리) …하는 편이 낫다' (선호)
3 used to: '…이었다' (과거의 상태)
4 would rather A than B: 'B하느니 차라리 A하겠다'
5 had better의 부정: had better not

B

1 had better not: '…하지 않는 게 좋겠다'
2 used to: '…이었다' (과거의 상태)
3 would rather A than B: 'B하느니 차라리 A하겠다'
4 would: '…하곤 했다' (과거의 습관)

C

2 would rather의 부정: would rather not

UNIT 3 조동사+have v-ed

pp.56 - 57

1 Marie는 그녀의 비행기를 놓쳤다. 그녀는 속상했음이 틀림없다.
그는 내게 거짓말을 했음이 틀림없다. 그는 내 눈을 계속 피했다.
2 내 남동생이 그런 어려운 책을 읽었을 리 없다.
David가 나를 알아봤을 리 없다. 나는 가면을 쓰고 있었다.
3 그 콘서트는 훌륭했다. 너는 왔어야 했는데.
나는 그런 어리석은 실수는 하지 말았어야 했는데.
4 Eric은 찬 음식을 먹고 복통을 겪었을지도 모른다.
나는 내 열쇠를 찾을 수 없다. 나는 그것들을 내 차에 두고 왔을지도 모른다.
5 나는 더 오래 잘 수 있었지만 일찍 일어났다.
너는 더 조심할 필요가 있다. 그 사고에서 너는 누군가를 다치게 할 수도 있었다.

SPEED CHECK

1 ④ 2 ⑤

1 should have v-ed: '…했어야 했는데 (하지 않았다)'
2 may[might] have v-ed: '…했을지도 모른다'

PRACTICE TEST

A 1 should 2 may 3 can't 4 must
B 1 must → should
2 could → may[might]
3 should → can't
4 may → must
C 1 should have taken
2 shouldn't have asked
3 can't have forgotten
4 may[might] have broken
5 must have taken
6 could have answered

A

1 should have v-ed: '…했어야 했는데 (하지 않았다)'
2 may[might] have v-ed: '…했을지도 모른다'
3 can't have v-ed: '…했을 리 없다'
4 must have v-ed: '…했음이 틀림없다'

C

2 should not have v-ed: '…하지 말았어야 했는데 (했다)'
6 could have v-ed: '…할 수도 있었다'

REVIEW TEST

pp.58 - 60

01 ② 02 ① 03 ④ 04 don't have[need] to 05 ④ 06 ⑤ 07 can't[cannot] be 08 should have checked 09 used to 10 ③ 11 ② 12 ② 13 ⑤ 14 1) had better go to bed earlier 2) may get cold in the evening 3) can't prepare dinner for myself 15 ③ 16 ⑤ 17 ①, ④ 18 You had better not go there alone. 19 should, must 20 have to, must 21 may, should 22 ④ 23 would rather drink water than 24 may[might] have watched 25 should have helped 26 could have been

01 '…할 수 없었다'가 자연스러우므로 couldn't를 쓴다.
[어휘] break down 고장 나다
02 '…일지도 모른다'가 자연스러우므로 약한 추측을 나타내는 조동사 may를 쓴다.
[어휘] weird [형] 이상한
03 ④ She must have passed it.으로 쓸 수 있다.
must have v-ed: '…했음이 틀림없다' (과거의 일에 대한 강한 추측)
[어휘] driving test 운전면허 시험 recently [부] 최근에
04 문맥상 '…을 살 필요가 없다'라는 뜻이므로 don't have[need] to를 쓴다.
05 should는 의무, 충고를 나타내는 조동사로, ought to로 바꿔 쓸 수 있다.
06 can이 '…할 수 있다'라는 뜻의 능력·가능을 나타낼 때 be able to로 바꿔 쓸 수 있다.
[어휘] communicate with …와 의사소통하다
07 '…일 리가 없다'라는 뜻의 부정 추측을 나타낼 때는 can't[cannot]를 쓴다.
[어휘] be satisfied with …에 만족하다 current [형] 현재의, 지금의
08 should have v-ed: '…했어야 했는데 (하지 않았다)' (과거의 일에 대한 후회나 유감)
[어휘] ruin [동] 엉망으로 만들다
09 과거의 습관을 나타낼 때는 used to나 would를 쓴다.
10 ③ 과거의 상태를 나타낼 때는 used to를 쓴다.
would → used to
[어휘] dive [동] 물속으로 뛰어들다 temple [명] 사원, 절
suspect [명] 용의자
11 ② 명백하게 과거를 나타내는 말(yesterday)이 있으므로 조동사 must의 과거형인 had to를 쓰거나 과거의 일에 대한 강한 추측을 나타내는 must have v-ed를 쓴다.
must → had to 또는 must have left
[어휘] respect [동] 존경하다; *존중하다
12 must: '…임이 틀림없다' (강한 추측); '…해야 한다' (의무)
[어휘] cancel [동] 취소하다 stranger [명] 낯선 사람
13 used to: '…하곤 했다' (과거의 습관); '…이었다' (과거의 상태)

14 1) had better: '…하는 게 좋겠다' (강한 충고나 권고)
2) may: '…일지도 모른다' (약한 추측)
3) can't[cannot]: '…할 수 없다' (능력·가능)

15 must have v-ed: '…했음이 틀림없다' (과거의 일에 대한 강한 추측)
[어휘] staff [명] 직원 exhausted [형] 지친

16 두 개의 조동사를 함께 쓸 수 없으므로 must 대신 have to를 쓴다.
[어휘] meet [동] 만나다; *마중 가다

17 ① can't have v-ed: '…했을 리 없다' (과거의 일에 대한 강한 의심) → David는 그 돈을 훔쳤을 리 없다.
④ don't have[need] to: '…할 필요가 없다' (불필요) → 너는 저 모자를 살 필요가 없다.

18 had better not: '…하지 않는 게 좋겠다'

19 must have v-ed: '…했음이 틀림없다' (과거의 일에 대한 강한 추측)

20 must: '…임이 틀림없다' (강한 추측)
[어휘] sold out (물건이) 다 팔린, 매진된

21 should have v-ed: '…했어야 했는데 (하지 않았다)' (과거의 일에 대한 후회나 유감)
[어휘] concentrate [동] 집중하다

22 ⓐ ought to의 부정은 ought not to이다.
ought to not → ought not to
ⓒ 두 개의 조동사를 함께 쓸 수 없으므로 can 대신 be able to를 쓴다. will can → will be able to
[어휘] challenge [명] 도전

23 would rather A than B: 'B하느니 차라리 A하겠다'

24 may[might] have v-ed: '…했을지도 모른다' (과거의 일에 대한 약한 추측)

25 should have v-ed: '…했어야 했는데 (하지 않았다)' (과거의 일에 대한 후회나 유감)

26 could have v-ed: '…할 수도 있었다' (과거의 일에 대한 가능성이나 후회)
[어휘] troublemaker [명] 말썽꾸러기, 문제아

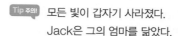

CHAPTER 06 수동태

UNIT 1 수동태의 의미와 형태

pp.62 - 63

A

그 물고기는 한 어린 소년에 의해 잡혔다.
한 어린 소년이 그 물고기를 잡았다.

[Tip 주의!] 모든 빛이 갑자기 사라졌다.
Jack은 그의 엄마를 닮았다.

B

피자는 전 세계적으로 사랑받는다.
그 다리는 20년 전에 지어졌다.

C

1 너는 너의 일에 대해 30달러를 지급받을 것이다.
2 그 아기는 그녀의 부모님으로부터 많은 사랑을 받아 왔다.
3 그 에스컬레이터는 수리되고 있다.
4 이 기계는 누구에 의해서도 쉽게 작동될 수 있다.

Grammar UP

누구에 의해 이 아름다운 그림이 그려졌니?
(← 누가 이 아름다운 그림을 그렸니?)

SPEED CHECK

1 ⑤ 2 ③

1 전통 의상이 '불리는' 것이므로 수동태: 『be동사+v-ed(+by+행위자)』
[어휘] traditional [형] 전통적인

2 아름다운 해변이 '보일 수 있는' 것이므로 조동사의 수동태: 『조동사+be v-ed』

PRACTICE TEST

A 1 was written 2 happened 3 be fixed
4 has been 5 being 6 be achieved

B 1 The problem is being discussed by the managers.
2 I have not been told about the business trip by my boss.
3 The errors must be corrected by the programmers.
4 The main dish will be prepared by the chef.

C 1 had to be canceled 2 is being washed
3 will be held 4 has been broken
5 should be returned 6 was bitten by

A

1 단편 소설이 '쓰인' 것이므로 수동태
2 목적어가 필요 없는 동사 happen은 수동태로 쓰지 않음
3 조동사의 수동태: 『조동사+be v-ed』
4 새로운 아이디어가 '제안된' 것이므로 완료형 수동태: have / had been v-ed

5 진행형 수동태: 『be동사+being v-ed』
6 그녀의 목표가 '달성될' 것이므로 미래시제 수동태: will be v-ed

UNIT 2 4형식 · 5형식 문장의 수동태

pp.64 - 65

1 그 농부는 그에게 빵 한 덩이를 주었다.
→ 그는 그 농부에 의해 빵 한 덩이가 주어졌다.
→ 빵 한 덩이가 그 농부에 의해 그에게 주어졌다.

Tip 주의! 나의 아버지는 나에게 새 자전거를 한 대 사 주셨다.
→ 새 자전거 한 대가 나를 위해 나의 아버지에 의해 구입되었다.

2 1) 그의 미소는 나를 행복하게 만들었다.
→ 나는 그의 미소에 의해 행복해졌다.
나의 선생님은 내게 수업 시간에 조용히 하라고 말했다.
→ 나는 나의 선생님에 의해 수업 시간에 조용히 하라는 말을 들었다.
사람들은 셰익스피어를 역대 가장 위대한 작가들 중 한 명으로 여긴다.
→ 셰익스피어는 역대 가장 위대한 작가들 중 한 명이라고 여겨진다.
2) Sue는 그가 창가에 서 있는 것을 보았다.
→ 그가 창가에 서 있는 것이 Sue에 의해 보였다.
3) 그들은 내가 그 규칙을 따르게 했다.
→ 나는 그들에 의해 그 규칙을 따르게 되었다.

SPEED CHECK

1 ⑤ 2 ⑤

1 4형식 문장의 간접목적어를 주어로 한 수동태
[어휘] sleeping bag 침낭
2 make가 사역동사일 때 목적격 보어로 쓰인 동사원형은 수동태 문장에서 to부정사로 바꿈
[어휘] memorize [동] 외우다, 기억하다

PRACTICE TEST

A 1 surfing 2 given 3 to 4 popular 5 to go
B 1 was brought a thick coat, was brought to me
2 was found sleeping on the couch
3 were allowed to come an hour later
4 was bought for the princess
C 1 was asked to donate 2 was heard speaking
3 was not shown to 4 were made to wear
5 was made for

A
1 지각동사의 목적격 보어로 쓰인 동사원형은 수동태 문장에서 현재분사나 to부정사로 바꿈
2 4형식 문장의 간접목적어를 주어로 하는 수동태 문장에서는 직접목적어 앞에 전치사를 쓰지 않음
3 4형식 문장의 직접목적어를 주어로 하는 대부분의 수동태 문장에서 간접목적어 앞에 전치사 to를 씀
4 대부분 5형식 문장의 목적격 보어는 수동태 문장에서 그대로 둠
5 make가 사역동사일 때 목적격 보어로 쓰인 동사원형은 수동태 문장에서 to부정사로 바꿈

B
1 동사 bring이 쓰인 4형식 문장은 간접목적어와 직접목적어 각각을 주어로 하는 두 가지 형태의 수동태가 가능
2-3 대부분 5형식 문장의 목적격 보어는 수동태 문장에서 그대로 둠
4 동사 buy가 쓰인 4형식 문장은 직접목적어만 수동태 문장의 주어로 하며, 간접목적어 앞에 전치사 for를 씀

C
5 동사 make가 쓰인 4형식 문장은 직접목적어만 수동태 문장의 주어로 하며, 간접목적어 앞에 전치사 for를 씀

UNIT 3 주의해야 할 수동태

pp.66 - 67

1 그녀는 내 시험 결과에 기뻐했다.
너는 음악 동아리에 가입하는 데 관심이 있니?

Tip 주의! 이 목걸이는 순금으로 만들어졌다.
빵은 밀가루로 만들어진다.

2 그는 트럭에 의해 치였지만 다치지 않았다.
그 환자는 그의 손녀에 의해 보살펴졌다.
3 그들은 그 병원이 문을 닫아야 한다고 결정했다.
→ 그 병원이 문을 닫아야 한다고 (그들에 의해) 결정되었다.

Tip 주의! 그들은 이 만화 영화가 아이들에게 인기 있다고 말한다.
→ 이 만화 영화는 아이들에게 인기 있다고 (그들에 의해) 일컬어진다.

SPEED CHECK

1 ① 2 ③ 3 ④

1 be covered with[in]: '…로 덮여 있다'
[어휘] sidewalk [명] 보도, 인도
2 동사구의 수동태는 동사구 전체를 하나의 동사로 묶어 취급
3 목적어가 that절인 동사 think는 that절의 주어를 수동태 문장의

주어로 할 때 that절의 동사를 to부정사로 바꿈

어휘 benefit 명 이득, 혜택

PRACTICE **TEST**

A **1** with **2** is looked up to **3** to be **4** was put off
5 to

B **1** The tortoise was laughed at by
2 is thought that Sophie is a brilliant pianist (by them), is thought to be a brilliant pianist (by them)
3 is believed that stress causes many health problems (by people), is believed to cause many health problems (by people)

C **1** was satisfied with **2** was surprised at
3 is interested in
4 are expected to participate in
5 were taken care of

A

1 be crowded with: '…로 붐비다'
2, 4 동사구의 수동태는 동사구 전체를 하나의 동사로 묶어 취급
3 목적어가 that절인 동사 say는 that절의 주어를 수동태의 주어로 할 때 that절의 동사를 to부정사로 바꿈
5 be known to: '…에게 알려지다'

B

1 동사구의 수동태는 동사구 전체를 하나의 동사로 묶어 취급
2-3 목적어가 that절인 문장은 가주어 it을 사용하여 『it+be동사+v-ed that .....』의 형태로 수동태를 만듦. think와 believe는 that절의 주어를 수동태 문장의 주어로 할 수 있으며, 이때 that절의 동사는 to부정사로 바꿈

C

1 be satisfied with: '…에 만족하다'
2 be surprised at: '…에 놀라다'
3 be interested in: '…에 관심이 있다'
4 목적어가 that절인 문장의 수동태
5 동사구의 수동태

REVIEW TEST
pp.68 - 70

01 ④   02 ④   03 ③   04 have posted, have been posted   05 is resembled by, resembles   06 ⑤   07 ⑤
08 ⑤   09 ③   10 ②   11 ③   12 were sold   13 to be

14 The subway was filled with passengers.   15 ③, ⑤
16 ②, ④   17 is covered with[in / by] snow   18 is made of wood   19 ③   20 ③   21 was made to pay   22 is being printed

01 궁전의 대문이 '잠긴' 것이므로 수동태(『be동사+v-ed』)를 쓴다.
어휘 gate 명 대문   lock 동 잠그다

02 완료형 수동태: have / had been v-ed
어휘 site 명 위치, 장소; *(인터넷) 사이트   server 명 (컴퓨터의) 서버

03 make가 사역동사일 때 목적격 보어로 쓰인 동사원형은 수동태 문장에서 to부정사로 바꾼다.
어휘 academy 명 학원

04 사진들이 '게시되어 온' 것이므로 현재완료형 수동태를 쓴다.

05 상태를 나타내는 동사 resemble은 수동태로 쓰지 않는다.

06 진행형 수동태: 『be동사+being v-ed』
어휘 redecorate 동 다시 장식하다, 다시 꾸미다

07 대부분 5형식 문장의 목적격 보어는 수동태 문장에서 그대로 둔다.
어휘 review 동 (재)검토하다; *복습하다   previous 형 이전의

08 조동사의 수동태: 『조동사+be v-ed』
어휘 obey 동 따르다, 복종하다

09 4형식 문장의 직접목적어를 주어로 하는 수동태 문장에서 ⓐ 동사가 send일 때 간접목적어 앞에 전치사 to를 쓰고, ⓑ 동사가 make일 때 전치사 for를 쓴다.

10 ⓐ be surprised at: '…에 놀라다'
ⓑ be crowded with: '…로 붐비다'

11 보기와 ①, ②, ④, ⑤는 모두 빈칸에 to가 와야 한다.
③ 동사 buy가 쓰인 4형식 문장은 직접목적어만 수동태 문장의 주어로 하며, 간접목적어 앞에 전치사 for를 쓴다.
보기: 대부분 5형식 문장의 목적격 보어는 수동태 문장에서 그대로 둔다.
① 목적어가 that절인 동사 say는 that절의 주어를 수동태의 주어로 할 때 that절의 동사를 to부정사로 바꿈
② make가 사역동사일 때 목적격 보어로 쓰인 동사원형은 수동태 문장에서 to부정사로 바꿈
④ 4형식 문장의 직접목적어를 주어로 하는 수동태 문장에서 동사가 give일 때 간접목적어 앞에 전치사 to를 씀
⑤ be known to: '…에게 알려지다'
어휘 remain 동 계속 …이다   patient 형 참을성 있는
delay 명 지연   summit 명 (산의) 정상

12 책이 '팔린' 것으로 수동의 뜻이고, last week로 보아 시제가 과거이므로 『be동사의 과거형+v-ed』를 쓴다.
어휘 for half price 반값에

13 목적어가 that절인 동사 say는 that절의 주어를 수동태 문장의 주어로 할 때 that절의 동사를 to부정사로 바꾼다.

14 be satisfied with: '…에 만족하다' / be filled with: '…로 가득 차다'
어휘 passenger 명 승객

15 ③ 목적어가 that절인 문장은 가주어 it을 사용하여 『it+be동사+v-ed that ....』의 형태로 수동태를 만들며, 동사가 believe일 때 that절의 주어를 수동태 문장의 주어로 하고 동사를 to부정사로 바꿀 수 있다.
He → It 또는 that he is → to be
⑤ 4형식 문장의 간접목적어를 주어로 하는 수동태에서는 직접목적어 앞에 전치사를 쓰지 않는다.
to many → many
[어휘] suggestion [명] 제안 witness [명] 목격자 murder [명] 살인 aquarium [명] 수족관 farewell [명] 작별

16 ② 동사구의 수동태는 동사구 전체를 하나의 동사로 묶어 취급한다.
was taken care → was taken care of
④ 보안 카메라가 '설치된' 것이므로 수동태를 쓴다.
installed → were installed
[어휘] kitten [명] 새끼 고양이 security camera 보안 카메라 install [동] 설치하다 bracelet [명] 팔찌

17 be covered with[in / by]: '…로 덮여 있다'

18 be made of: '…로 만들어지다' (원형이 남음)

19 ⓐ 지각동사의 목적격 보어로 쓰인 동사원형은 수동태 문장에서 현재분사나 to부정사로 바꾼다.
break → breaking[to break]
ⓓ 미래시제 수동태: will be v-ed
will release → will be released
[어휘] due to … 때문에 release [동] 풀어 주다; *출시하다

20 ③ 동사 make가 쓰인 4형식 문장은 수동태로 바꿀 때 간접목적어 앞에 전치사 for를 쓴다. to → for
[어휘] model [형] 모형의

21 make가 사역동사일 때 목적격 보어로 쓰인 동사원형은 수동태 문장에서 to부정사로 바꾼다.
[어휘] speeding [명] 과속

22 진행형 수동태: 『be동사+being v-ed』

CHAPTER 07 가정법

UNIT 1 가정법 과거, 가정법 과거완료, 혼합 가정법

pp.72 - 73

1 만약 Eric이 약하지 않다면 그는 무거운 가구를 들어올릴 수 있을 텐데.
(→ Eric이 약하기 때문에 그는 무거운 가구를 들어올릴 수 없다.)

2 만약 내가 알람 소리를 들었더라면 나는 그 약속에 늦지 않았을 텐데.
(→ 내가 알람 소리를 듣지 못했기 때문에 나는 그 약속에 늦었다.)

3 만약 어젯밤에 눈이 많이 오지 않았더라면 오늘 도로가 얼어붙지 않을 텐데.
(→ 어젯밤에 눈이 많이 왔기 때문에 오늘 도로가 얼어붙어 있다.)

Grammar UP

만약 미나가 내일 내 파티에 오면 나는 매우 행복할 것이다.
만약 미나가 내일 내 파티에 온다면 나는 매우 행복할 텐데.

SPEED CHECK

1 ③ 2 ④ 3 ③

1 가정법 과거: 『If+주어+were / 동사의 과거형, 주어+would[could / might]+동사원형』

2 가정법 과거완료: 『If+주어+had v-ed, 주어+would[could / might] have v-ed』

3 혼합 가정법: 『If+주어+had v-ed, 주어+would[could / might]+동사원형』

PRACTICE TEST

A 1 were, could join 2 had not left, could wear 3 had not remembered, could not have come
B 1 were 2 had practiced 3 have succeeded 4 had eaten 5 wouldn't need 6 had followed
C 1 took, would save 2 had fixed, could use 3 had had, would have baked 4 were, could go

A

1 가정법 과거: 『If+주어+were / 동사의 과거형, 주어+would[could / might]+동사원형』

2 혼합 가정법: 『If+주어+had v-ed, 주어+would[could / might]+동사원형』

3 가정법 과거완료: 『If+주어+had v-ed, 주어+would[could / might] have v-ed』

B

1, 5 현재 사실의 반대를 가정하는 가정법 과거
2-3 과거 사실의 반대를 가정하는 가정법 과거완료
4, 6 과거에 실현되지 못한 일이 현재까지 영향을 미치는 상황을 가정할 때 쓰는 혼합 가정법

C

1, 4 가정법 과거 2 혼합 가정법 3 가정법 과거완료

UNIT 2 I wish, as if, without [but for], it's time

pp.74 - 75

1 1) 내가 과학 시험의 모든 답을 안다면 좋을 텐데.
(→ 내가 과학 시험의 모든 답을 알지 못해서 유감이다.)
2) 네가 그에게 저 사진을 보여 주지 않았더라면 좋을 텐데.
(→ 네가 그에게 저 사진을 보여 줬다니 유감이다.)

2 1) Diana는 마치 그에 대해 모든 것을 아는 것처럼 말한다.
(→ 사실, Diana는 그에 대해 모든 것을 알지는 못한다.)
2) Harry는 마치 어젯밤에 잠을 자지 않았던 것처럼 보인다.
(→ 사실, Harry는 어젯밤에 잠을 잤다.)

3 만약 태양이 없다면 지구상의 어떤 것도 생존할 수 없을 텐데.
만약 이 지도가 없었더라면 우리는 길을 잃었을 텐데.

4 우리가 새로운 접근법을 취해야 할 때이다.

Grammar UP

만약 내가 너라면 나는 너의 이웃들을 돕는 것을 주저하지 않을 텐데.
만약 그녀의 지원이 없었더라면 나는 대학을 마치지 못했을 텐데.

SPEED CHECK

1 ② 2 ⑤

1 now가 있으므로 현재의 소망을 나타내는 「I wish+가정법 과거」
2 before가 있으므로 과거 사실의 반대를 가정하는 「as if[though]+가정법 과거완료」
[어휘] behave [동] 행동하다

PRACTICE TEST

A 1 were 2 hadn't been[had not been]
3 had not been[hadn't been]
4 hadn't gone[had not gone]
5 had watched
6 took
B 1 I wish I had 2 If it had not been for
3 as if[though] she had had 4 Had I realized
C 1 as if[though] he were
2 as if[though] he had seen
3 Without his laptop
4 I wish I had made a reservation
5 It's time you went

A

1 현재 사실의 반대를 가정하는 「as if+가정법 과거」
2, 4 과거 사실과 반대되는 소망을 나타내는 「I wish+가정법 과거완료」
3 「if it had not been for ...,+가정법 과거완료」: '(만약) …가 없었다면, ~했을 텐데'
5 과거 사실의 반대를 가정하는 「as if+가정법 과거완료」
6 「it's time+가정법 과거」: '(이제) …해야 할 때이다'

B

1 현재의 소망을 나타내는 「I wish+가정법 과거」
2 가정법 과거완료에 쓰인 without[but for]는 if it had not been for로 바꿀 수 있음
3 과거 사실의 반대를 가정하는 「as if[though]+가정법 과거완료」
4 가정법 문장에서 if절의 동사가 had일 때 if는 생략할 수 있으며, if절의 주어와 동사를 도치함

C

1 「as if[though]+가정법 과거」
2 「as if[though]+가정법 과거완료」
3 「without ...,+가정법 과거」
4 「I wish+가정법 과거완료」
5 「it's time+가정법 과거」

REVIEW TEST pp.76 - 78

01 ④ 02 ④ 03 1) But for 2) Had it not been for [If it hadn't been for] 04 as if[though] he were an American 05 had taken 06 ③ 07 ② 08 ④ 09 bought, had bought 10 It had, Had it 또는 If it had 11 만약 내가 이 챕터를 복습했더라면 나는 네 질문들에 답할 수 있을 텐데. 12 만약 그 여행 안내서가 없었다면 우리는 그 모든 관광 명소를 방문하지 못했을 텐데. 13 I wish they had not painted the wall green. 14 ③ 15 would not have missed 16 could buy 17 ③ 18 ⑤ 19 ③ 20 It's time he won 21 Were it not for the soldiers[If it weren't for the soldiers] 22 If I had been close with

01 과거 사실의 반대를 가정하므로 가정법 과거완료: 「If+주어+had v-ed, 주어+would[could/might] have v-ed」
02 과거에 실현되지 못한 일이 현재까지 영향을 미치는 상황을 가정할 때 쓰는 혼합 가정법: 「If+주어+had v-ed, 주어+would[could/might]+동사원형」
[어휘] refrigerator [명] 냉장고
03 「without[but for] ...,+가정법 과거완료」 구문에서 without[but for]는 if it had not been for로 바꿔 쓸 수 있다. 접속사 if를 생략할 경우 if절의 주어와 동사를 도치해 had it not been for를 쓴다.
[어휘] flashlight [명] 손전등 entrance [명] 출입구
04 「as if[though]+가정법 과거」는 현재 사실의 반대를 가정한다.

05 과거에 실현되지 못한 일이 현재까지 영향을 미치는 상황을 가정할 때 혼합 가정법을 쓴다.

06 과거를 나타내는 last Sunday가 있으므로 과거 사실의 반대를 가정하는 『as if[though]+가정법 과거완료』를 쓴다.

07 과거 사실과 반대되는 소망을 나타내므로 『I wish+가정법 과거완료』를 쓴다.

08 가정법 과거: 『if+주어+were/동사의 과거형, 주어+would[could/might]+동사원형』

[어휘] lost-and-found center 분실물 취급소
cost [동] (값·비용이) …이다[들다]

09 과거에 실현되지 못한 일이 현재까지 영향을 미치는 상황을 가정하므로 혼합 가정법을 쓴다.

10 과거 사실의 반대를 가정하는 『if it had not been for ...,+가정법 과거완료』에서 접속사 if를 생략할 경우 if절의 주어와 동사를 도치한다.

11 혼합 가정법: '(과거에) 만약 …했더라면 (지금) ~할 텐데'

[어휘] review [동] 복습하다

12 『had it not been for ...,+가정법 과거완료』: '(만약) …가 없었다면 ~했을 텐데'

[어휘] tourist attraction 관광 명소

13 『I wish+가정법 과거완료』: '…했더라면 좋을 텐데'

14 ③ 혼합 가정법: 『If+주어+had v-ed, 주어+would[could/might]+동사원형』

[어휘] fever [명] (병으로 인한) 발열, 열

15 과거 사실의 반대를 가정하는 가정법 과거완료

16 현재 사실의 반대를 가정하는 가정법 과거

17 ③ last year로 보아, 과거 사실의 반대를 가정하므로 『as if+가정법 과거완료』를 쓴다.
lived → had lived

[어휘] assistance [명] 도움 complete [동] 완료하다, 끝마치다
essay [명] 과제물, 리포트

18 ⑤ 과거에 실현되지 못한 일이 현재까지 영향을 미치는 상황을 가정하므로 혼합 가정법을 쓴다.
wouldn't have been → wouldn't be

[어휘] go out with …와 데이트하다

19 ⓒ 과거 사실의 반대를 가정하므로 가정법 과거완료를 쓴다.
hurried → had hurried
ⓓ 과거 사실과 반대되는 소망을 나타내므로 『I wish+가정법 과거완료』를 쓴다.
have enjoyed → had enjoyed

20 『it's time+가정법 과거』: '(이제) …해야 할 때이다'

[어휘] award [명] 상, 상품

21 『were it not for[If it weren't for] ...,+가정법 과거』: '(만약) …가 없다면 ~할 텐데'

[어휘] soldier [명] 군인

22 가정법 과거완료: 『If+주어+had v-ed, 주어+would[could/might] have v-ed』 ('만약 …했더라면 ~했을 텐데')

CHAPTER 08 관계사

UNIT 1 관계대명사

pp.80 - 81

Emily는 작가이다. + 그녀는 영어 교육에 관한 열 권의 책을 썼다.
→ Emily는 영어 교육에 관한 열 권의 책을 쓴 작가이다.

[Tip 주의!] Bianca는 그녀의 정원을 지나가고 있던 소년과 개에게 소리를 질렀다.

1 나는 스페인어를 아주 잘 말할 수 있는 한 소녀를 안다.
탁자 위에 있는 그 소포는 Kelly의 것이다.

2 나는 항상 짖는 개를 가진 이웃이 한 명 있다.
나는 직업이 대중음악을 작곡하는 것인 한 남자를 만난 적이 있다.

3 네가 어제 만난 그 여자는 카페를 하나 소유하고 있다.
내가 쇼핑몰에서 산 그 핸드백은 비싸다.

4 나를 놀라게 했던 것은 그녀의 나쁜 태도였다.
네가 크리스마스에 원하는 것을 나에게 말해 줄 수 있니?
이것이 우리가 먹고 싶었던 것이다.

SPEED CHECK

1 ④ 2 ⑤

1 관계사절 내에서 목적어 역할을 하고, 선행사가 사물(The magic show)이므로 목적격 관계대명사 which를 씀

2 선행사를 포함하며 명사절(목적어)을 이끄는 관계대명사 what

PRACTICE TEST

A 1 that 2 what 3 whose 4 which 5 who

B 1 who[that] wants to be an astronaut
2 which[that] was planted
3 that the director made
4 whose name I can't remember

C 1 people who[that] are
2 which[that] I borrowed
3 a friend whose hobby
4 What my daughter wants is
5 that didn't agree with

A

1 선행사가 『사람+사물』일 때 주로 관계대명사 that을 씀

2 선행사를 포함하며 명사절(보어)을 이끄는 관계대명사 what

3 관계사절 내에서 수식하는 명사(screen)의 소유격 역할을 하는 소유격 관계대명사 whose

4 선행사가 사물(the wine)인 목적격 관계대명사 which

5 선행사가 사람(The man)인 주격 관계대명사 who

B

1 선행사가 사람(a friend)인 주격 관계대명사 who[that]

2 선행사가 사물(the pear tree)인 주격 관계대명사 which[that]

3 서수(first)가 선행사를 수식할 때 주로 관계대명사 that을 씀

4 관계사절 내에서 수식하는 명사(name)의 소유격 역할을 하는 소유격 관계대명사 whose

C

1 선행사가 사람(people)인 주격 관계대명사 who[that]

2 선행사가 사물(The novel)인 목적격 관계대명사 which[that]

3 관계사절 내에서 수식하는 명사(hobby)의 소유격 역할을 하는 소유격 관계대명사 whose

4 선행사를 포함하며 명사절(주어)을 이끄는 관계대명사 what. what이 이끄는 명사절은 단수 취급

5 the only가 선행사를 수식할 때 주로 관계대명사 that을 씀

UNIT 2 관계부사

pp.82 - 83

나는 그해를 안다. + 첫 번째 월드컵이 그때 열렸다.
→ 나는 첫 번째 월드컵이 열렸던 그해를 안다.

Tip 주의! 내가 일하는 그 건물에는 엘리베이터가 세 대 있다.

1 여름은 복숭아가 가장 맛있는 시기이다.

2 이곳은 내 친구들과 내가 숨바꼭질하곤 했던 장소이다.

3 너는 James와 그의 가족이 고향을 떠난 이유를 알고 있니?

4 나에게 이 복사기가 작동하는 방법을 보여 줄 수 있니?

Grammar UP

Kevin은 그가 그의 가장 친한 친구를 처음 만난 때를 상기한다.
이곳은 내가 지난 일요일에 Mike를 기다렸던 곳이다.
네가 왜 학교에 결석했는지 나에게 말해 줘.

SPEED CHECK

1 ② **2** ③

1 장소를 나타내는 명사(The town)가 선행사이므로 관계부사 where

2 이유를 나타내는 명사(reason)가 선행사이므로 관계부사 why

PRACTICE TEST

A **1** when **2** where **3** why **4** how **5** in which
B **1** where **2** how **3** when **4** why
C **1** how he completed **2** the day when
    3 the reason why **4** the place where

A

1 때를 나타내는 명사(the season)를 선행사로 하는 관계부사 when

2 장소를 나타내는 명사(a place)를 선행사로 하는 관계부사 where

3 문맥상 'Jake가 처벌받은 이유'가 자연스러우므로 관계부사 why를 씀. 관계부사의 선행사가 일반적인 명사(the reason)일 때 관계부사나 선행사 중 하나를 생략하는 경우가 많음

4 선행사 the way와 관계부사 how는 함께 쓰지 않음

5 장소를 나타내는 명사(The town)가 선행사이므로 관계부사 where를 대신할 수 있는 in which를 씀

B

1 선행사(the middle school)가 장소를 나타내므로 at which는 관계부사 where로 바꿀 수 있음

2 방법을 나타내는 명사를 선행사로 하는 관계부사 how[the way]

3 선행사(the year)가 때를 나타내므로 in which는 관계부사 when으로 바꿀 수 있음

4 선행사(the reason)가 이유를 나타내므로 for which는 관계부사 why로 바꿀 수 있음

C

1 방법을 나타내는 명사를 선행사로 하는 관계부사 how[the way]

2 때를 나타내는 명사(the day)를 선행사로 하는 관계부사 when

3 이유를 나타내는 명사(the reason)를 선행사로 하는 관계부사 why

4 장소를 나타내는 명사(the place)를 선행사로 하는 관계부사 where

UNIT 3 복합 관계사

pp.84 - 85

Jane은 그녀의 엄마가 그녀를 위해 요리해 주는 것은 무엇이든지 무척 좋아한다.
무슨 일이 일어나더라도 나는 나의 목표를 성취할 것이다.

Grammar UP

너는 네가 좋아하는 무슨 책이든지 읽어도 된다.
어느 길로 가더라도 너는 우체국에 도착할 수 있다.

B

네가 원할 때는 언제나 우리 집에 와라.

언제 당신이 오더라도 당신은 환영받을 것입니다.

그 가수는 그가 가는 곳은 어디든지 사람들을 끌어 모은다.

내가 아무리 열심히 노력했더라도 나는 내 셔츠에서 얼룩을 지울 수 없었다.

SPEED CHECK

1 ① 2 ⑤

1 '…하는 사람은 누구든지'의 뜻으로 명사절(주어)을 이끄는 복합 관계대명사 whoever

2 '아무리 …하더라도'의 뜻으로 부사절을 이끄는 복합 관계부사 however

PRACTICE TEST

A 1 Whoever 2 wherever 3 Whichever
  4 Whatever 5 Whenever 6 However
B 1 Wherever 2 Whoever 3 However
  4 Whatever
C 1 Whatever you do
  2 Whoever comes
  3 Whenever I feel stressed
  4 However high the car's price is
  5 Whatever decisions

A

1 명사절(주어)을 이끄는 복합 관계대명사 whoever: '…하는 사람은 누구든지'

2 부사절을 이끄는 복합 관계부사 wherever: '어디서 …하더라도'

3 부사절을 이끄는 복합 관계형용사 whichever: '어느 …라도'

4 부사절을 이끄는 복합 관계대명사 whatever: '무엇이[을] …하더라도'

5 부사절을 이끄는 복합 관계부사 whenever: '언제 …하더라도'

6 부사절을 이끄는 복합 관계부사 however: '아무리 …하더라도'

B

1 no matter where = wherever '어디서 …하더라도'

2 anyone who = whoever '…하는 사람은 누구든지'

3 no matter how = however '아무리 …하더라도'

4 no matter what = whatever '무엇이[을] …하더라도'

C

1 부사절을 이끄는 복합 관계대명사 whatever

2 명사절(주어)을 이끄는 복합 관계대명사 whoever

---

3 부사절을 이끄는 복합 관계부사 whenever

4 부사절을 이끄는 복합 관계부사 however

5 부사절을 이끄는 복합 관계형용사 whatever: '무슨 …라도'

UNIT 4 주의해야 할 관계사의 용법

pp.86 - 87

A

1 나는 Anna에게 전화했지만 그녀는 전화를 받지 않았다.

  그는 많은 노래를 썼고, 그것들은 많은 사람들에 의해 사랑 받는다.

> Grammar UP
>
> 우리는 그 문을 열려고 노력했으나, 그것은 불가능했다.
>
> 나는 병원에서 나의 상사를 봤는데, 그것을 나는 예상하지 못했다.

2 학교 축제는 다음 주에 열릴 것인데, 그때 기말고사가 끝난다.

  나는 샌프란시스코에 갔는데, 그곳에서 Brown 씨를 만났다.

B

1 나는 네가 언급했던 그 서점을 기억할 수 없다.

  Tip 주의! 그 이어폰은, 내가 사고 싶었던 것인데 이미 다 팔렸다.

2 저기서 커피를 마시고 있는 그 여자는 나의 사촌이다.

C

이것이 그 스포츠 스타가 사는 집이다.

> Grammar UP
>
> 이것은 내가 가장 자랑스러워하는 금메달이다.

SPEED CHECK

②

선행사가 사물(the things)이고 전치사(about)의 목적어로 쓰인 목적격 관계대명사 which

PRACTICE TEST

A 1 climbing 2 whom 3 which 4 where
B 1 that 2 X 3 whom 4 X 5 who are
  6 that were
C 1 who 2 which 3 where 4 whom

A

1 『주격 관계대명사+be동사』가 생략되어 분사구(climbing the tree)가 남음

2 사람(the man)을 선행사로 하고 전치사 with의 목적어로 쓰인 목적격 관계대명사 whom. 전치사 뒤에는 관계대명사 that을 쓸 수 없음

3 앞 절 전체를 선행사로 하는 계속적 용법의 관계대명사 which

4 장소를 나타내는 선행사(the zoo)를 부가적으로 설명하는 계속적 용법의 관계부사 where

B

1, 3 동사 및 전치사의 목적어로 쓰인 목적격 관계대명사는 생략할 수 있음

2 전치사 뒤에 있는 목적격 관계대명사는 생략할 수 없음

4 계속적 용법으로 쓰인 목적격 관계대명사는 생략할 수 없음

5-6 『주격 관계대명사+be동사』는 뒤에 형용사구나 분사구가 올 때 생략할 수 있음

C

계속적 용법으로 쓰인 관계대명사는 『접속사+대명사』로, 관계부사는 『접속사+부사』로 바꿔 쓸 수 있다.

1 사람(Adam)을 선행사로 하고 계속적 용법으로 쓰인 관계대명사 who

2 앞 절 전체를 선행사로 하고 계속적 용법으로 쓰인 관계대명사 which

3 장소를 나타내는 명사(Busan)를 선행사로 하고 계속적 용법으로 쓰인 관계부사 where

4 사람(The girl)을 선행사로 하고 전치사 to의 목적어로 쓰인 목적격 관계대명사 whom

REVIEW TEST pp.88 - 90

01 ③ 02 ③ 03 ④ 04 However 05 where 06 ① 07 ⑤ 08 ④ 09 ③ 10 Here are the plates which [that] we bought today. 11 where, in which, which [that] 12 ④ 13 1) the day[date] when 2) where 3) how 14 ⑤ 15 ⑤ 16 ② the way how → how[the way], ③ Wherever → Whenever 17 ② which → that, ⑤ which → where 18 ③ 19 Whoever enjoys dancing 20 a coat whose buttons 21 why I decided to sell

01 said의 목적절을 선행사로 하는 계속적 용법의 관계대명사 which를 쓴다.

02 선행사(winter)가 때를 나타내는 명사이므로 관계부사 when을 쓴다.

03 Whatever she says, it always makes everybody smile.로 쓸 수 있다. '무엇이[을] …하더라도'라는 뜻의 부사절을 이끄는 복합 관계대명사 whatever가 쓰인 문장이 되어야 한다.

04 '아무리 …하더라도'라는 뜻의 no matter how는 복합 관계부사 however로 바꿔 쓸 수 있다.

[어휘] brilliant [형] 우수한, 뛰어난 universe [명] 우주

05 장소를 나타내는 명사(Guam)가 선행사이므로 관계부사 where를 쓴다. 계속적 용법으로 쓰인 관계부사 where는 『접속사+부사』인 and there와 바꿔 쓸 수 있다.

06 ① 선행사가 사물(the pool)이고 관계사절에서 목적어 역할을 하므로 목적격 관계대명사 which[that]를 쓴다. ②-⑤는 선행사가 때를 나타내는 명사이고 뒤에 완전한 절이 이어지므로 관계부사 when을 쓴다.

[어휘] celebrity [명] 유명 인사 pass away 사망하다, 돌아가시다
season [명] 계절; *(특정 활동이 행해지는) 시기

07 ⑤ 동사나 전치사의 목적어로 쓰인 목적격 관계대명사나 『주격 관계대명사+be동사』는 생략할 수 있지만 주격 관계대명사는 생략할 수 없다.

[어휘] walk past …을 지나치다

08 선행사를 포함하며 명사절(목적어, 보어)을 이끄는 관계대명사 what을 쓴다.

[어휘] put off 미루다, 연기하다 till [전] …까지 order [동] 주문하다

09 '…하는 사람은 누구든지'라는 뜻의 명사절(목적어)을 이끄는 복합 관계대명사 whoever를 쓴다.

[어휘] feel free to-v 마음대로 …하다 polite [형] 예의 바른

10 선행사가 사물(the plates)이고, 관계사절에서 목적어 역할을 하므로 목적격 관계대명사 which[that]를 쓴다.

[어휘] plate [명] 접시, 그릇

11 장소를 나타내는 명사(the log cabin)를 선행사로 하는 관계부사 where를 쓴다. 관계부사 where는 『전치사+관계대명사』인 in which로 바꿔 쓸 수 있다. 이때 전치사를 관계사절 끝에 쓰면 목적격 관계대명사 which[that]를 생략할 수 있다.

[어휘] log cabin [명] 통나무 오두막집

12 ④의 that은 접속사이고 나머지는 모두 관계대명사이다.

[어휘] be full of …로 가득 차 있다
be responsible for …에 책임이 있다

13 1) March 3는 날짜를 나타내므로 선행사 the day[date], 관계부사 when을 쓴다.
2) Lake Louise는 장소를 나타내므로 관계부사 where를 쓴다. 선행사로 일반적인 명사(the place)가 쓰여 생략되었다.
3) 문맥상 '낚시하는 방법을 배울 것'이므로 방법을 나타내는 관계부사 how를 쓴다.

[어휘] fish [동] 낚시하다

14 ⓐ 명사절(주어)을 이끄는 복합 관계대명사 whoever: '…하는 사람은 누구든지'
ⓑ 부사절을 이끄는 복합 관계형용사 whichever: '어느 …라도'
ⓒ 복합 관계부사 wherever: '어디서 …하더라도'

[어휘] attend [동] 참석하다 sample [명] 견본품
local customs 지역적 풍습

15 ⑤ 전치사 뒤에는 관계대명사 that을 쓸 수 없다.

16 ② 선행사 the way와 관계부사 how는 함께 쓰지 않는다.

③ 문맥상 'Jenny가 쉬는 시간을 가질 때는 언제나'라는 뜻이 자연스러우므로 복합 관계부사 whenever를 쓴다.

어휘 technician 몡 기사, 기술자　challenging 혱 힘든

17 ② 선행사가 『사람+동물』일 때는 주로 관계대명사 that을 쓴다.

⑤ 장소를 나타내는 명사(the aquarium)가 선행사이고, 뒤에 주어와 목적어가 있는 완전한 절이 이어지므로 관계부사 where를 쓴다.

어휘 tag 몡 (어떤 표시를 하기 위해 붙인) 꼬리표

aquarium 몡 수족관

18 ⓑ 문맥상 '개의 꼬리'이므로 수식하는 명사(tail)의 소유격 역할을 하는 소유격 관계대명사 whose를 쓴다. which → whose

ⓓ 관계대명사 that은 계속적 용법으로 쓸 수 없다. that → who

어휘 adopt 동 입양하다　tail 몡 (동물의) 꼬리　table tennis 탁구

19 명사절(주어)을 이끄는 복합 관계대명사 whoever를 쓴다.

20 수식하는 명사(buttons)의 소유격 역할을 하는 소유격 관계대 명사 whose를 쓴다.

21 이유를 나타내는 관계부사 why를 쓴다. 관계부사 why의 선행 사가 이유를 나타내는 일반적인 명사(the reason)이므로 생략 할 수 있다.

CHAPTER
09 비교 구문

UNIT 1 비교 구문

pp.92 - 93

1 Kelly는 Jenny만큼 수영을 잘한다.

나쁜 습관은 스트레스만큼 위험할 수 있다.

이 안락의자는 저것만큼 편안하지는 않다.

2 나의 집은 그의 것보다 더 크다.

Sam은 Joe보다 더 유머 감각이 있다.

Tip 비교! 버스를 타는 것은 택시를 타는 것보다 덜 비싸다.

✓ Grammar UP

1 우리의 군대는 적의 것보다 우수했다.

2 나는 이런 비 오는 날에는 나가는 것보다 집에 있는 것을 더 좋아한다.

3 Ted는 우리 반에서 가장 재능 있다. (Ted는 우리 반에서 가장 재능있는 학생이다.)

Diana는 모든 학교 치어리더들 중 가장 나이가 어리다. (Diana는 모든 학교 치어리더들 중 가장 나이가 어린 치어리더이다.)

Liz는 물속에서 가장 오래 숨을 참을 수 있다.

SPEED CHECK

1 ①　**2** ④　**3** ⑤

1 『not as[so]+원급+as』: '…만큼 ~하지는 않은/않게'

어휘 calm 혱 침착한, 차분한

2 『형용사/부사의 비교급+than』: '…보다 더 ~한/하게'

3 『the+형용사/부사의 최상급』: '가장 …한/하게'

PRACTICE **TEST**

A 1 heavy　2 earlier　3 most　4 most　5 to
6 strongest

B 1 not as[so] light　2 busier than
3 the cheapest of

C 1 is harder
2 not as[so] thoughtful as
3 the oldest building
4 as enjoyable as
5 less beautiful than

A

1 『as+형용사/부사의 원급+as』: '…만큼 ~한/하게'

2 『형용사/부사의 비교급+than』: '…보다 더 ~한/하게'

3 문맥상 '모든 것 중에서 화학을 가장 싫어하는 것'이므로 much의 최상급인 most를 씀. 부사의 최상급 앞에는 the를 붙이지 않기도 함

4 『the+최상급+in+장소·범위를 나타내는 단수명사』: '… (안)에서 가장 ~한/하게'

5 prefer A to B: 'B보다 A를 더 좋아하다'

6 『the+최상급+of+비교 대상이 되는 명사』: '… 중 가장 ~한/하게'

B

1 『not as[so]+원급+as』: '~만큼 …하지는 않은/않게'

2 『형용사/부사의 비교급+than』: '…보다 더 ~한/하게'

3 『the+최상급+of+비교 대상이 되는 명사』: '… 중 가장 ~한/하게'

C

5 『less+원급+than』: '…보다 덜 ~한/하게'

UNIT 2 여러 가지 최상급 표현

pp.94 - 95

1 Emma는 우리 학교에서 가장 재미있는 학생이다.

우리 학교의 어떤 학생도 Emma만큼 재미있지는 않다.

우리 학교의 어떤 학생도 Emma보다 더 재미있지 않다.

Emma는 우리 학교의 다른 어떤 학생보다 더 재미있다.
Emma는 우리 학교의 다른 모든 학생들보다 더 재미있다.

2 추수 감사절은 미국에서 가장 큰 휴일들 중 하나이다.
피카소는 세계에서 가장 훌륭한 예술가들 중 하나였다.
그 시장은 우리 도시에서 가장 존경 받는 사람들 중 하나이다.

3 그것은 우리가 지금까지 본 것 중 가장 긴 강이다.
Jill은 내가 지금까지 만난 사람 중 가장 정직한 소녀이다.
이것은 내가 지금까지 본 것 중 가장 끔찍한 영화이다.

SPEED CHECK

1 ② 2 ①

1 『비교급+than any other+단수명사』는 최상급의 뜻을 나타냄
2 『No (other)+명사+...+as[so]+원급+as』는 최상급의 뜻을 나타냄

PRACTICE TEST

A 1 good 2 the biggest 3 cities 4 more
5 athletes

B 1 as[so] delicious as,
more delicious than,
more delicious than any other dish,
more delicious than all the other dishes
2 as[so] boring as,
more boring than,
more boring than all the other books,
the most boring book

C 1 the highest mountain I have ever climbed
2 one of the most popular flowers

A

1 최상급을 나타내는 『No (other)+명사+...+as[so]+원급+as』
2 『the+최상급(+that)+주어+have ever v-ed』: '지금까지 …한 것[사람] 중 가장 ~한'
3 『one of the+최상급+복수명사』: '가장 …한 것[사람]들 중 하나'
4 최상급을 나타내는 『비교급+than any other+단수명사』
5 최상급을 나타내는 『비교급+than all the other+복수명사』

B

원급과 비교급을 사용한 최상급 표현
『the+최상급』
→ 『No (other)+명사+...+as[so]+원급+as』
→ 『No (other)+명사+...+비교급+than』
→ 『비교급+than any other+단수명사』
→ 『비교급+than all the other+복수명사』

UNIT 3 비교 구문을 이용한 표현

pp.96 - 97

1 행복은 돈보다 훨씬 더 중요하다.
Jack은 나보다 훨씬 더 적은 채소를 먹는다.

[Tip 주의!] 그 새로운 스마트폰은 예전 것보다 더 비싸다.

2 Paul은 버스 정류장으로 가능한 한 빠르게 달렸다.

3 세계는 점점 더 작아지고 있다.
시간이 흐르면서 나의 영어 실력은 점점 더 좋아졌다.

[Tip 주의!] 그 농구 경기는 점점 더 흥미진진해지고 있다.

4 네가 열심히 공부할수록 네 점수는 더 높아질 것이다.
날씨가 따뜻해질수록 내 기분은 더 좋아진다.

5 그의 정원은 네 것의 두 배로 크다.
네 머리카락은 내 머리카락보다 세 배로 길다.

SPEED CHECK

1 ② 2 ③ 3 ②

1 『much/even/far/a lot+비교급+than』: '…보다 훨씬 더 ~한/하게' (비교급 강조)
[어휘] politics [명] 정치

2 『the+비교급, the+비교급』: '…(하면) 할수록 더 ~하다'
[어휘] sweat [동] 땀을 흘리다

3 『배수사+as+원급+as』: '…의 몇 배로 ~한/하게' (= 『배수사+비교급+than』)
[어휘] luggage [명] (여행용) 짐, 수하물

PRACTICE TEST

A 1 far 2 possible 3 more 4 as expensive as
5 more and more

B 1 The better, the more 2 as quietly as he could
3 four times as big as

C 1 worse and worse 2 five times as thick as
3 The longer, the more tired
4 as quickly as possible
5 much[even/far] more serious

A

1 비교급 강조: 『much/even/far/a lot+비교급+than』
부사 very는 비교급을 강조할 수 없음
2 『as+원급+as possible』: '가능한 한 …한/하게'
3 『the+비교급, the+비교급』: '…(하면) 할수록 더 ~하다'
4 『배수사+as+원급+as』: '…의 몇 배로 ~한/하게'

5 비교급이 『more+원급』인 경우, '점점 더 …한/하게'는 『more and more+원급』으로 씀

B

1 『the+비교급, the+비교급』: '…(하면) 할수록 더 ~하다'
2 『as+원급+as possible』은 『as+원급+as+주어+can』으로 바꿔 쓸 수 있음
3 『배수사+비교급+than』은 『배수사+as+원급+as』로 바꿔 쓸 수 있음

C

1 『비교급+and+비교급』: '점점 더 …한/하게'

REVIEW TEST pp.98 - 100

01 ③ 02 ④ 03 ① 04 ② 05 loudest and loudest, louder and louder 06 more, the most 07 to 08 ⑤ 09 No, as[so] scary as 10 as attractive as they can 11 (A) It is three times heavier than a bowling ball. (B) It is three times as heavy as a bowling ball. 12 ⑤ 13 (1) the cheapest (2) twice as expensive as (3) cheaper than 14 ③ 15 Alex, David, James, Nate 16 1) as, as 2) No, more, than 3) four times as, as 17 ③ 18 ④ 19 ② 20 one of the most successful designers 21 less comfortable

01 『the+비교급, the+비교급』: '…(하면) 할수록 더 ~하다'
02 비교급이 『more+원급』인 경우, '점점 더 …한/하게'는 『more and more+원급』으로 쓴다.
[어휘] nervous [형] 초조한
03 The new medicine is much[even/far/a lot] more effective for a stomachache.로 쓸 수 있다. 『much[even/far/a lot]+비교급+than』은 '…보다 훨씬 더 …한/하게'의 뜻으로, 비교급을 강조하는 표현이다. 부사 very는 비교급을 강조할 수 없다.
[어휘] effective [형] 효과적인
04 『비교급+than any other+단수명사』는 최상급의 뜻을 나타낸다.
05 『비교급+and+비교급』: '점점 더 …한/하게'
06 『the+최상급(+that)+주어+have ever v-ed』: '지금까지 …한 것[사람] 중 가장 ~한'
[어휘] convenient [형] 편리한
07 superior(우수한)와 같이 -or로 끝나는 형용사는 비교 표현에 than이 아니라 to를 쓴다. / prefer A to B: 'B보다 A를 더 좋아하다'
[어휘] product [명] 제품, 상품 competitor [명] 경쟁자, 경쟁 상대 distance [명] 거리
08 ⑤ Harry의 음악 점수(90)는 Mia의 음악 점수(50)보다 더 높다. not higher → higher
09 『No (other)+명사+...+as[so]+원급+as』는 최상급의 뜻을 나타낸다.
[어휘] ride [명] 타기; *(놀이공원의) 놀이 기구 amusement park 놀이공원
10 『as+원급+as possible』은 『as+원급+as+주어+can』으로 바꿔 쓸 수 있다.
[어휘] attractive [형] 매력적인
11 『배수사+as+원급+as』는 '…의 몇 배로 ~한/하게'의 뜻으로, 『배수사+비교급+than』으로 바꿔 쓸 수 있다.
[어휘] bowling ball [명] 볼링공
12 ⑤ 『배수사+as+원급+as』이므로 그대로 둔다.
13 (1) cheese sandwich의 가격이 가장 싸므로 『the+최상급』을 쓴다.
(2) chicken burger는 cheese sandwich보다 두 배 더 비싸므로 『배수사+as+원급+as』를 쓴다.
(3) bacon sandwich는 chicken burger보다 싸므로 『비교급+than』을 쓴다.
14 ③은 '어떤 것도 건강보다 덜 중요하지는 않다.'라는 뜻이다. less → more
15 『No (other)+명사+...+비교급+than』은 최상급의 뜻을 나타낸다.
16 1) 『as+원급+as』: '…만큼 ~한/하게'
2) 『No (other)+명사+...+비교급+than』: '어떤 것도 …보다 ~하지 않은/않게'
3) 『배수사+as+원급+as』: '…의 몇 배로 ~한/하게'
17 ⓑ 『one of the+최상급+복수명사』: '가장 …한 것[사람]들 중 하나'
conductor → conductors
ⓔ 최상급의 뜻을 나타내는 표현은 『No (other)+명사+...+as[so]+원급+as』나 『No (other)+명사+...+비교급+than』이다.
more interesting as → as[so] interesting as 또는 more interesting than
[어휘] conductor [명] 지휘자 outgoing [형] 외향적인, 사교적인
18 ④ 『the+비교급, the+비교급』: '(…하면) 할수록 더 ~하다'
the safe → the safer
[어휘] impressive [형] 인상적인 call [동] …라고 부르다; *전화하다
19 ② 동사 speak를 수식하는 부사의 원급이 필요하다.
『as+원급+as possible』: '가능한 한 …한/하게'
slower → slowly
[어휘] weigh [동] 무게가 …이다 lecture [명] 강의 day [명] 하루; *낮
20 『one of the+최상급+복수명사』: '가장 …한 것[사람]들 중 하나'
[어휘] successful [형] 성공한
21 『less+원급+than』: '…보다 덜 ~한/하게'
[어휘] comfortable [형] 편안한

CHAPTER
⑩ 접속사

pp.102 - 103

1 내가 온라인으로 영어 강의를 듣고 있는 동안에 Sam은 그의 숙제를 했다.

Tip 비교! 첫 번째 음료는 공짜인 반면에, 두 번째 (음료)는 7달러이다. 나는 그에게 동의하지만, 여전히 내 의견이 좋은 것이라고 생각한다.

2 우리는 점심을 먹으면서 우리의 여름 계획에 관해 이야기했다.
Nicole은 나이가 들어감에 따라 더 책임감 있게 되었다.
교통이 매우 혼잡했기 때문에 우리는 그 회의에 늦었다.

3 나는 운동을 시작한 이래로 몸이 훨씬 더 나아졌다.
스파게티는 요리하기 쉽기 때문에 매우 인기 있다.

4 초콜릿을 넣고 그것이 완전히 녹을 때까지 기다려라.

5 Alex는 시카고를 방문할 때마다 같은 호텔에 묵는다.

6 Carrie는 실험실에 들어오자마자 넘어졌다.

Tip 주의! 나는 비가 그치면 떠날 것이다.

SPEED CHECK

1 ② 2 ②

1 while: '…하는 동안에'
2 since: '… 이래로'

PRACTICE TEST

A 1 while 2 since 3 As 4 As soon as 5 hear
B 1 As soon as 2 every[each] time
  3 As[Since / Because] 4 since
C 1 until[till] her daughter fell asleep
  2 while other students are studying
  3 Every[Each] time I see a shooting star
  4 As[Since / Because] he didn't apologize

A
1 while: '…하는 동안에'
2 since: '… 이래로'
3 as: '…함에 따라'
4 as soon as: '…하자마자'
5 시간을 나타내는 부사절에서는 미래를 나타내더라도 미래시제 대신

B
1 on v-ing: '…하자마자' (= as soon as)
2 whenever: '…할 때마다' (= every[each] time)
3 as[since / because]: '… 때문에'
4 since: '… 이래로'

C
1 until[till]: '…할 때까지'

pp.104 - 105

1 만약 내일 눈이 오면 나는 나의 아이들과 눈사람을 만들 것이다.

Grammar UP

나는 Jean이 우리 공부 모임에 참여할지 (안 할지) 모른다.

2 우리가 야생 동물을 보호하지 않으면 그들은 멸종할 것이다.

Tip 주의! 만약 내가 가장 좋아하는 소설가를 만나면 나는 사인을 받을 것이다.

3 비록 Lucas는 수학을 열심히 공부했지만, 시험에서 좋은 점수를 받을 수 없었다.
비록 그는 경험은 가장 적지만, 그 회사의 가장 훌륭한 기자이다.

4 설령 네가 택시를 타더라도 너는 네 비행편을 놓칠 것이다.

5 그 커피가 맛이 정말 좋아서 나는 한 잔을 더 마셨다.
안개가 너무 짙은 날이어서 나는 아주 조심해서 운전했다.

Tip 비교! 청중들이 당신(의 말)을 들을 수 있도록 더 크게 말해 주세요.

 Grammar UP

Annie가 회사를 떠날 거라는 것은 사실이다.
나는 그녀가 영국에서 최고의 가수라고 생각한다.
문제는 우리가 시간이 부족하다는 것이다.

SPEED CHECK

③

「although[though]+사실」: '비록 …지만'

PRACTICE TEST

A 1 unless 2 Though 3 If 4 that
B 1 will drive → drives
  2 If → Although[Though] / Even though

3 get → will get

4 so → such 또는 a beautiful place → beautiful

C **1** Even if I apologize **2** unless she takes notes

3 even though he doesn't express

4 so scary that **5** It is fortunate that

6 so that she could understand it

A

1 unless: '…하지 않으면'

2 though: '비록 …지만'

3 if: '만약 …라면'

4 『so＋형용사/부사＋that』: '매우 …해서 ~하다'

B

1 조건을 나타내는 부사절에서는 미래를 나타내더라도 미래시제 대신 현재시제를 씀

2 『although[though]/even though＋사실』: '비록 …지만'

3 if가 이끄는 절이 명사절이므로 미래를 나타낼 때 미래시제를 씀

4 『such(＋a[an])＋형용사＋명사＋that』/『so＋형용사/부사＋that』: '매우 …해서 ~하다'

C

1 『even if＋가상의 일』: '설령 …할지라도'

2 unless: '…하지 않으면'

3 『even though＋사실』: '비록 …지만'

4 『so＋형용사/부사＋that』: '매우 …해서 ~하다'

5 가주어 it의 진주어인 명사절을 이끄는 접속사 that

6 『so that＋주어＋동사』: '…가 ~하기 위하여', '…가 ~하도록' (＝『in order that＋주어＋동사』)

UNIT 3 짝으로 이루어진 접속사

pp.106 - 107

1 우리 부모님은 나를 신뢰하고 지지하신다.
Danny는 볶음밥과 볶음면 둘 다 매우 잘 요리한다.

2 Cathy는 바보 아니면 천재이다.
수프에 설탕이나 꿀을 넣어라.

3 Paul은 춤추는 것에도 노래하는 것에도 흥미가 없다.
내 남편도 나도 뉴질랜드에 가 본 적이 없다.

4 노숙자에게는 음식뿐만 아니라 보호소도 필요하다.
그 강의는 지루할 뿐만 아니라 어려웠다.

Grammar UP

너와 Jack 둘 다 사람들에게 친절하다.
Alex 아니면 내가 틀렸다.
Ben도 너도 그녀의 결혼식에 초대받지 못했다.

너뿐만 아니라 나도 고전 음악을 좋아한다.

SPEED CHECK

1 ② **2** ④ **3** ③

1 both A and B: 'A와 B 둘 다'
어휘 quality 명 (품)질

2 neither A nor B: 'A도 B도 아닌'
어휘 field 명 들판; *분야

3 not only A but also B: 'A뿐만 아니라 B도'
어휘 friendly 형 친절한; *친숙한 faithful 형 충직한

PRACTICE **TEST**

A **1** either **2** need **3** Both **4** am

B **1** either, or **2** Both, and **3** not only, but also

4 neither, nor

C **1** both history and biology

2 neither big nor crowded

3 either stay here or go

4 not only money but also fame

5 as well as in the 1990s

6 nor I get an allowance

A

1 either A or B: 'A와 B 중 하나'

2 both A and B는 복수 취급

3 both A and B: 'A와 B 둘 다'

4 not only A but also B는 B에 동사의 수를 일치시킴

B

1 either A or B: 'A와 B 중 하나'

2 both A and B: 'A와 B 둘 다'

3 B as well as A: 'A뿐만 아니라 B도' (≒ not only A but also B)

4 neither A nor B: 'A도 B도 아닌'

C

6 neither A nor B는 B에 동사의 수를 일치시킴

REVIEW TEST

pp.108 - 110

01 ① **02** ② **03** ④ **04** am, are **05** will get, get
06 It was so hot that I wanted to go for a swim. / 매우 더워서 나는 수영하러 가고 싶었다. **07** ④, ⑤ **08** ②, ⑤

09 Even if 10 1) Both, and 2) Neither, nor 3) Not only, but also 11 ④ 12 ⑤ 13 Unless he eats less and exercises more 14 blue jeans as well as a cap 15 ⑤ 16 ④ 17 ③ 18 ③ 19 ⑤ 20 ② has → have, ⑤ if → unless 또는 stop → don't stop 또는 will not meet → will meet 21 ① wasn't → was, ④ write → writes 22 if[whether] he will come back 23 so that I can travel

01 if: '만약 …라면'

02 as: '(동시에) …할 때', '…하면서'
   어휘 uniform 뎽 제복, 군복, 교복 look in …을 들여다보다

03 ④ either A or B는 'A와 B 중 하나'의 뜻으로, B에 동사의 수를 일치시키므로 are는 바르게 쓰였다.
   어휘 vet 뎽 수의사 animal trainer 조련사

04 both A and B는 복수 취급한다.
   어휘 go on a business trip 출장 가다

05 시간을 나타내는 부사절에서는 미래를 나타내더라도 미래시제 대신 현재시제를 쓴다.

06 「so+형용사/부사+that」: '매우 …해서 ∼하다'
   어휘 go for a swim 수영하러 가다

07 every time: '…할 때마다' (= each time / whenever)

08 as soon as: '…하자마자' (≒ the moment[minute/instant])

09 「even if+가상의 일」: '설령 …할지라도'

10 1) both A and B: 'A와 B 둘 다'
   2) neither A nor B: 'A도 B도 아닌'
   3) not only A but also B: 'A뿐만 아니라 B도'
   어휘 lawyer 뎽 변호사

11 ⓐ unless: '…하지 않으면' ⓑ as: '…함에 따라'
   어휘 urgent 뎽 긴급한 come up 나오다; *생기다, 발생하다
   approach 뎽 다가오다 mosquito 뎽 모기

12 ⓐ as soon as: '…하자마자' ⓑ since: '… 때문에'
   어휘 go off (알람이) 울리다 promote 뎽 승진시키다
   hard 뎽 열심히

13 unless: '…하지 않으면' (= if … not)
   어휘 gain weight 체중이 늘다

14 not only A but also B: 'A뿐만 아니라 B도'
   (≒ B as well as A)

15 if: '…인지' (명사절); '만약 …라면' (조건의 부사절)
   어휘 rumor 뎽 소문, 유언비어

16 since: '… 때문에'; '… 이래로'
   어휘 enter 뎽 …에 들어가다; *입학하다

17 while: '…하는 동안'; '…하는 반면에'
   어휘 burn 뎽 태우다; *데다

18 ③ 조건을 나타내는 부사절에서는 미래를 나타내더라도 미래시제 대신 현재시제를 쓴다. → if it rains tomorrow
   어휘 postpone 뎽 미루다, 연기하다 wood 뎽 나무, 목재; *((pl.)) 숲

reserve 뎽 예약하다

19 ⑤의 as는 '… 때문에'라는 뜻이고, 나머지는 '(동시에) …할 때', '…하면서'라는 뜻이다.
   어휘 stop by 잠시 들르다 cross 뎽 건너다
   bump into (우연히) 마주치다

20 ② either A or B는 B에 동사의 수를 일치시킨다.
   ⑤ 문맥상 '…하지 않으면'의 뜻인 if … not 또는 unless를 쓴다.
   어휘 tease 뎽 놀리다

21 ② neither A nor B('A도 B도 아닌')는 부정의 뜻을 포함한다.
   ④ not only A but also B는 B에 동사의 수를 일치시킨다.

22 if[whether]: '…인지' (명사절)
   명사절에서는 미래를 미래시제로 나타낸다.

23 「so (that)+주어+동사」: '…가 ∼하기 위하여', '…가 ∼하도록'
   어휘 save 뎽 구하다; *(돈을) 모으다

CHAPTER
⑪ 일치와 화법

UNIT 1 수의 일치

pp.112 - 113

1 1) 우리 반의 모든 학생이 수영하는 법을 배우고 있다.
   누구 나를 도와줄 수 있는 사람 있니?
   2) 경제학은 그가 가장 좋아하는 과목이다.
   필리핀은 수천 개의 섬으로 이루어져 있다.
   3) 7시간은 수면에 충분한 시간이다.
   50달러가 나에게 상금으로 주어졌다.
   4) 탄산음료를 마시는 것은 네 건강에 좋지 않다.
   세계가 원하는 것은 평화이다.

2 1) Caitlin과 나는 동갑이다.
   Tip 주의 카레라이스는 매우 맛있다.
   2) 부상을 입은 사람들은 즉시 병원으로 옮겨졌다.
   3) 많은 사람들이 버스 정류장에 줄을 서 있다.
   Tip 비교! 신생아의 수가 매년 감소하고 있다.

✓ Grammar UP

지구 표면의 4분의 3은 물이다.
일부 오렌지는 상했다.

SPEED CHECK

1 has 2 is 3 were 4 are

1 『each＋단수명사＋단수동사』
2 학문명은 복수형이라도 단수 취급
3 『a number of＋복수명사』는 복수 취급
4 (both) A and B는 복수 취급

PRACTICE TEST

A 1 runs 2 is 3 work 4 is 5 are 6 is 7 are
   8 has
B 1 is 2 ○ 3 is 4 has 5 pay 6 Is
C 1 Nobody knows   2 Chatting with my friends helps
   3 The young are   4 A number of students were

A
1 『each＋단수명사＋단수동사』
2 학문명은 복수형이라도 단수 취급
3 (both) A and B는 복수 취급
4 명사절은 단수 취급
5 『the＋형용사』가 '…한 사람들'이라는 뜻일 때 복수 취급
6 금액의 단위는 단수 취급
7 『부분 표현(most)＋of＋명사』는 명사에 동사의 수를 일치시킴
8 『the number of＋복수명사』는 '…의 수'라는 뜻으로, 단수 취급

B
1 『부분 표현(half)＋of＋명사』는 명사에 동사의 수를 일치시킴
2 『a number of＋복수명사』는 복수 취급
3 거리의 단위는 단수 취급
4 『every＋단수명사＋단수동사』
5 『the＋형용사』가 '…한 사람들'이라는 뜻일 때 복수 취급
6 -thing으로 끝나는 대명사는 단수 취급

C
1 -body로 끝나는 대명사는 단수 취급
2 명사구는 단수 취급
3 『the＋형용사』가 '…한 사람들'이라는 뜻일 때 복수 취급
4 『a number of＋복수명사』는 복수 취급

UNIT 2   시제의 일치

pp.114 - 115

1 1) 우리는 그가 지금 건강하다고 생각한다.
   그는 내가 새 아파트를 구하고 있어 왔다는 것을 안다.
   우리 엄마는 내가 그녀의 도움이 필요할 거라는 것을 안다.
   2) 나는 그가 나에 대해 걱정한다고 생각했다.
   그는 그녀가 스쿨버스를 놓쳤다는 것을 알았다.
   그녀는 내가 은행에서 일하고 있어 왔다는 것을 알았다.

2 1) Josh는 서울이 한국의 수도인 것을 배웠다.
   나의 부모님은 정직이 최선의 방책이라고 말씀하셨다.
   2) 나는 간디가 1869년에 태어났다고 배웠다.
   3) 나는 예전 우리 동네 그곳에 아직도 그 레몬 나무가 있다는 것을
   알게 되었다.
   Kate는 커피 한 잔으로 그녀의 하루를 시작한다고 말했다.

SPEED CHECK

1 ③ 2 ② 3 ②

1 주절의 시제가 과거이고 '노래를 작곡한 것'이 '노래를 부른 것'보다
   먼저 일어난 일이므로 과거완료를 씀
2 종속절이 변하지 않는 사실일 때 주절의 시제와 관계없이 현재시제
   를 씀
3 종속절이 역사적 사실일 때 주절의 시제와 관계없이 과거시제를 씀
   어휘 steam engine 증기 기관

PRACTICE TEST

A 1 flows 2 fought 3 has 4 have
B 1 Jack had planted the red roses
   2 Luke would break up with her
   3 Heo Gyun wrote
C 1 had quit   2 the early bird catches
   3 skips breakfast   4 dropped a bomb
   5 said that he was nervous

A
1 과학적 사실은 주절의 시제와 관계없이 현재시제를 씀
2 역사적 사실은 주절의 시제와 관계없이 과거시제를 씀
3 현재의 사실은 주절의 시제와 관계없이 현재시제를 쓸 수 있음
4 속담은 주절의 시제와 관계없이 현재시제를 씀
   어휘 Walls have ears. 벽에도 귀가 있다.
   (낮말은 새가 듣고 밤말은 쥐가 듣는다.)

B
1 주절의 시제가 과거가 되면 종속절의 과거시제는 과거완료로 바꿈
2 주절의 시제가 과거가 되면 조동사 will은 과거형인 would로 바꿈
3 역사적 사실은 주절의 시제와 관계없이 과거시제를 씀

C
1 주절의 시제가 과거이고, '일을 그만둔 것'이 '알게 된 것'보다 먼저
   일어난 일이므로 과거완료를 씀
2 속담은 주절의 시제와 관계없이 현재시제를 씀
3 현재의 습관은 주절의 시제와 관계없이 현재시제를 쓸 수 있음
4 역사적 사실은 주절의 시제와 관계없이 과거시제를 씀

5 주절의 시제가 과거이고, 종속절이 주절과 같은 시점이므로 종속절에 과거시제를 씀

UNIT 3 화법

pp.116 - 117

1 John은 나에게 "나는 바람을 쐬고 싶어."라고 말했다.
→ John은 나에게 그가 바람을 쐬고 싶다고 말했다.
2 1) 그 코치는 나에게 "너는 키가 몇이니?"라고 물었다.
→ 그 코치는 나에게 내가 키가 몇인지 물었다.

> **Tip 주의!** 모두가 나에게 "누가 너를 구해 줬니?"라고 물었다.
> → 모두가 나에게 누가 나를 구해 줬는지 물었다.

2) Hans는 나에게 "나랑 조깅하러 갈래?"라고 물었다.
→ Hans는 나에게 내가 그와 조깅하러 갈지 물었다.
3 Jill은 나에게 "즉시 나에게 다시 전화해."라고 말했다.
→ Jill은 나에게 즉시 그녀에게 다시 전화해 달라고 부탁했다.

> **Tip 주의!** 그녀는 그녀의 아이에게 "소리 지르지 마."라고 말했다.
> → 그녀는 그녀의 아이에게 소리 지르지 말라고 말했다.

1 너는 그녀가 어디에 가고 있는지 아니?
(← 너는 아니? + 그녀가 어디에 가고 있니?)
2 나는 그녀가 내 선물을 좋아할지 확신이 없다.
(← 나는 확신이 없다. + 그녀가 내 선물을 좋아할까?)

SPEED CHECK

(that) he would be back the next[following] day

평서문의 간접화법 전환: 『say[tell+목적어](+that)+주어+동사』
tomorrow는 간접화법에서 the next[following] day로 바뀜

PRACTICE TEST

A **1** told **2** if **3** not to drink **4** it was **5** what you
B **1** remember → to remember
2 would our table → our table would
3 was it → it was **4** if → what
C **1** my brother to take his umbrella
2 where he had bought that tablet
3 if[whether] she had ever been to Hawaii
4 (that) he didn't know how to play the guitar
5 (that) she would show him the pictures the next[following] day
6 if[whether] he had done something wrong

A

1 『tell+목적어』
2 의문사가 없는 의문문은 간접화법으로 전환 시 『ask(+목적어)+if[whether]+주어+동사』의 어순으로 씀
3 부정 명령문은 간접화법으로 전환 시 don't나 never를 없애고 동사원형을 not to-v로 바꿈
4 의문사가 있는 의문문은 간접화법으로 전환 시 『ask(+목적어)+의문사+주어+동사』의 어순으로 씀
5 의문사가 있는 간접의문문의 어순: 『의문사+주어+동사』

B

1 명령문의 간접화법 전환: 『tell[ask, order, advise 등]+목적어+to-v』
2 의문사가 있는 의문문은 간접화법으로 전환 시 『ask(+목적어)+의문사+주어+동사』의 어순으로 씀
3-4 의문사가 있는 간접의문문의 어순: 『의문사+주어+동사』
4 간접의문문에서 '무엇'을 뜻하는 의문사 what이 필요함

C

1 명령문의 간접화법 전환: 『tell[ask, order, advise 등]+목적어+to-v』
2 지시대명사 this는 간접화법에서 that으로 바뀜
3, 6 의문사가 없는 의문문은 간접화법으로 전환 시 『ask(+목적어)+if[whether]+주어+동사』의 어순으로 씀
4-5 평서문의 간접화법 전환: 『say[tell+목적어](+that)+주어+동사』

REVIEW TEST

pp.118 - 120

01 ① **02** ② **03** ①, ④ **04** ③ **05** ① **06** ① **07** were, was **08** that, if[whether] **09** had been, was **10** ③ **11** ④ **12** ② **13** not to make noise in the library **14** where she could wash her hands **15** (that) he wants to join the newspaper club **16** ② **17** ① **18** 1) if[whether] she lived with her grandparents 2) what her favorite song was 3) if[whether] she could play the piano **19** ④, ⑤ **20** ③ **21** her sister would go shopping **22** what I was looking for **23** (M)ost (o)f (t)he (s)tudents (w)ere (s)tudying (m)ath

01 과학적 사실은 주절의 시제와 관계없이 현재시제를 쓴다.
> **어휘** Jupiter 영 목성 planet 영 행성

02 과거시제이고, -body로 끝나는 대명사는 단수 취급한다.
03 ①, ④ 의문사가 없는 의문문은 간접화법으로 전환 시 접속사 if나 whether를 쓴다. 피전달문의 인칭 전환은 인칭대명사를 전달자에 맞춰 바꾼다.
04 ⓐ 『부분 표현(분수)+of+명사』는 명사에 동사의 수를 일치시킨다.

ⓑ 주절의 시제가 과거이고, 종속절이 주절과 같은 시점이므로 과거시제를 쓴다. 『every+단수명사+단수동사』

05 ⓐ 주절의 시제가 과거이고, 종속절이 주절과 같은 시점이므로 과거시제를 쓴다. 『the number of+복수명사』는 '…의 수'의 뜻으로, 단수 취급한다.
ⓑ 『a number of+복수명사』는 '많은 …'의 뜻으로, 복수 취급한다.
[어휘] lung cancer 폐암 gather [동] 모여들다

06 ⓐ 목적어(me)가 있고, 과거에 말한 것이므로 told를 쓴다.
ⓑ 현재에도 지속되는 습관은 주절의 시제와 관계없이 현재시제를 쓸 수 있다.
[어휘] the senior center 양로원

07 학문명은 복수형이라도 단수 취급한다.
[어휘] politics [명] 정치학

08 의문사가 없는 의문문의 간접화법: 『ask(+목적어)+if[whether]+주어+동사』
[어휘] battery charger 배터리 충전기

09 역사적 사실은 주절의 시제와 관계없이 항상 과거시제를 쓴다.
[어휘] dynasty [명] 왕조 found [동] 설립하다

10 ③ 명령문의 간접화법: 『tell[ask, order, advise 등]+목적어+to-v』 open → to open

11 ④ 전달되는 문장의 시제를 주절의 시제에 맞춰 과거로 바꾼다. can buy → could buy

12 ② 화법 전환 시 직접화법의 문장이 평서문일 경우 say는 say로, say to는 tell로 바꾼다. 또한, 장소가 다를 때 here는 there로 바꾼다. told → said, here → there
[어휘] hand in …을 제출하다 receive [동] 받다

13 부정 명령문은 간접화법으로 전환 시 don't나 never를 없애고 동사원형을 not to-v로 바꾼다.

14 의문사가 있는 의문문은 간접화법으로 전환 시 『ask(+목적어)+의문사+주어+동사』의 어순으로 쓰고, 전달자에 맞춰 인칭대명사를 바꾸며 시제 일치의 원칙에 따른다.

15 간접화법 전환 시 전달자에 맞춰 인칭대명사를 바꾸고 동사의 수와 시제를 일치시킨다.

16 역사적 사실은 주절의 시제와 관계없이 과거시제를 쓴다.
[어휘] compose [동] 작곡하다

17 현재에도 지속되는 사실은 주절의 시제와 관계없이 현재시제를 쓸 수 있다.

18 1), 3) 의문사가 없는 의문문의 간접화법: 『ask(+목적어)+if[whether]+주어+동사』
2) 의문사가 있는 의문문의 간접화법: 『ask(+목적어)+의문사+주어+동사』

19 ④ 『the+형용사』가 '…한 사람들'의 뜻일 때는 복수 취급한다. is → are
⑤ 격언은 주절의 시제와 관계없이 현재시제를 쓴다. made → makes
[어휘] cheerful [형] 발랄한 physics [명] 물리학
disabled [형] 장애를 가진 remind [동] 상기시키다

20 ⓐ 명사구는 단수 취급한다. are → is
ⓓ -thing으로 끝나는 대명사는 단수 취급한다. Are → Is
[어휘] cigarette [명] 담배 harmful [형] 해로운

21 주절의 시제가 과거이므로 조동사의 과거형 would를 쓴다.

22 의문사가 있는 의문문의 간접화법: 『ask(+목적어)+의문사+주어+동사』
[어휘] clerk [명] (가게의) 점원

23 『부분 표현(most)+of+명사』는 명사에 동사의 수를 일치시킨다.

CHAPTER 12 특수구문

UNIT 1 강조, 부정 구문, 병렬

pp.122 - 123

A

1 나는 Brian이 나에게 이야기한 것을 믿었다.
→ 나는 Brian이 나에게 이야기한 것을 정말 믿었다.
이 버섯 수프는 맛이 짜다.
→ 이 버섯 수프는 정말 맛이 짜다.

2 나는 어제 지하철에서 Joe를 봤다.
→ 어제 지하철에서 Joe를 본 사람은 바로 나였다.
→ 내가 어제 지하철에서 본 사람은 바로 Joe였다.
→ 내가 어제 Joe를 본 것은 바로 지하철에서였다.
→ 내가 지하철에서 Joe를 본 것은 바로 어제였다.

작은 파란 차 한 대를 산 사람은 바로 Anthony였다.

B

1 그 시험의 모든 문제가 쉬운 것은 아니었다.
Hugo가 항상 열심히 일하는 것은 아니다.

2 그 학생들 중 아무도 전에 이 테마파크를 방문한 적이 없었다.
그들 둘 다 유학 갈 계획을 가지고 있지 않다.

C

Erica는 영리하고 예쁘며 재미있다.
너는 라운지에서 컴퓨터를 사용하거나 잡지를 읽을 수 있다.

SPEED CHECK

1 ③ 2 ②

1 do를 이용한 동사 강조: 『do/does/did+동사원형』

last weekend로 보아 과거시제이므로 did로 동사 강조

2 부사구(in Pyeongchang)를 강조한 it is/was ... that 강조 구문

PRACTICE **TEST**

A 1 is David that[who] 2 was in March that
  3 did take pictures
B 1 Neither 2 Not all 3 not always 4 None
C 1 Not every American 2 It was the high price that
  3 None of us 4 do want 5 drawing, playing

A

1 주어(David)를 강조하는 it is/was ... that 강조 구문으로, 강조하고자 하는 말이 사람일 때 that 대신 who를 쓸 수 있음

2 부사구(in March)를 강조하는 it is/was ... that 강조 구문

3 과거시제 동사의 강조는 『did+동사원형』을 씀

B

1 neither: '둘 다 …하지 않다' (both의 전체부정)

2 not all: '모두 …인 것은 아니다' (부분부정)

3 not always: '항상 …인 것은 아니다' (부분부정)

4 none: '아무도 …하지 않다' (all의 전체부정)

C

1 not every: '모두 …인 것은 아니다' (부분부정)

2 주어(the high price)를 강조하는 it is/was ... that 강조 구문

3 none: all의 전체부정

4 현재시제 동사의 강조는 『do/does+동사원형』을 쓰는데, 주어가 복수형이므로 do를 씀

5 짝으로 이루어진 접속사(not only A but also B)에서 A와 B는 문법적으로 동일한 형태와 구조를 씀. 『전치사(at)+동명사』

UNIT 2 도치

pp.124 - 125

Ⓐ

1 비가 내렸다.
  문 옆에 큰 상자가 하나 있었다.

  Tip 비교! 그가 위로 올라갔다.

2 그녀는 결코 다른 사람들에게 도움을 청하지 않는다.
  Joe는 좀처럼 그의 감정을 얼굴에 드러내지 않는다.
  나는 내가 체중이 10kg 늘었다는 것을 전혀 깨닫지 못했다.
  그 콘서트는 신났을 뿐만 아니라 매우 싸기도 했다.
  나는 그의 약속을 좀처럼 믿을 수 없었다.

  Tip 비교! 최근에야 나는 진실을 알았다.

3 나는 지난주에 예술의 전당에 갔어. – 나도 갔어.
  나는 복권에 당첨된 적이 없어. – 나도 없어.

✓ Grammar **UP**

Alice는 자정이 되고 나서야 비로소 집에 왔다.

SPEED CHECK

1 ② 2 ③

1 부정어(구)를 강조하기 위한 도치(일반동사가 있는 문장): 『부정어 (rarely)+do/does/did+주어+동사원형』

2 『so+동사+주어』: '(앞서 한 말에 대해) …도 또한 그렇다'. 앞 문장의 동사(write)가 일반동사이고 현재시제이므로 do를 씀

PRACTICE **TEST**

A 1 came the sun 2 was hers 3 Neither
  4 will she 5 did Eva
B 1 sat a crow 2 does the department store close
  3 have I watched 4 passes the boat
C 1 Neither has my sister 2 was a white tiger
  3 Hardly could Stella believe 4 So do I
  5 Never did I dream

A

1 방향·장소의 부사(구)를 강조하기 위한 도치: 『부사(구)+동사+주어』

2 『so+동사+주어』: '(앞서 한 말에 대해) …도 또한 그렇다'

3 『neither[nor]+동사+주어』: '(앞서 한 말에 대해) …도 또한 그렇지 않다'

4 부정어(구)를 강조하기 위한 도치(조동사가 있는 문장): 『부정어 (never)+조동사+주어』

5 부정어(구)를 강조하기 위한 도치(일반동사가 있는 문장): 『부정어 (little)+do/does/did+주어+동사원형』

B

1, 4 방향·장소의 부사(구)를 강조하기 위한 도치: 『부사(구)+동사+주어』

2 부정에 가까운 의미를 갖는 only를 문장 맨 앞에 써도 주어와 동사를 도치함

3 부정어(구)를 강조하기 위한 도치(조동사가 있는 문장): 『부정어 (never)+조동사+주어』

C

1 『neither[nor]+동사+주어』: '(앞서 한 말에 대해) …도 또한 그렇지 않다'. 앞 문장의 동사에 조동사(have)가 있으므로 조동사(has)를 씀

2 방향·장소의 부사(구)를 강조하기 위한 도치: 『부사(구)+동사+주어』

3 부정어(구)를 강조하기 위한 도치(조동사가 있는 문장): 『부정어(hardly)+조동사+주어』

4 『so+동사+주어』: '(앞서 한 말에 대해) …도 또한 그렇다'. 앞 문장의 동사가 일반동사이고 현재시제이므로 do를 씀

5 부정어(구)를 강조하기 위한 도치(일반동사가 있는 문장): 『부정어(never)+do/does/did+주어+동사원형』

REVIEW TEST   pp.126 - 128

01 ⑤ 02 ② 03 ② 04 ③ 05 On the bookshelves lay a thick layer of dust. 06 Hardly did I expect that I would get stuck in traffic. 07 ③ 08 ④ 09 ② 10 have I thought of 11 Neither of 12 None of the boys 13 Not all of the girls 14 ③ 15 ② 16 ③ 17 ⑤ 18 ③ 19 ② did answered → did answer, ③ writing → to write 또는 to sing → singing 20 are three cups 21 are not always interesting 22 Little can I imagine living without electricity.

01 주어를 강조하는 it is/was ... that 강조 구문
어휘 run over (사람·동물을) 치다 statue 몡 상, 조각상

02 긍정문 뒤에서 '(앞서 한 말에 대해) …도 또한 그렇다'라는 뜻을 나타낼 때는 『so+do/does/did/be동사/조동사+주어』를 쓴다.
어휘 chew 동 씹다

03 ②의 did는 일반동사('…을 했다')이고 나머지는 동사를 강조한다.
어휘 respect 동 존경하다

04 ③의 It은 가주어이고 나머지는 it is/was ... that 강조 구문의 it이다.
어휘 flea market 벼룩시장

05 장소를 나타내는 부사(구)를 강조하기 위한 도치: 『부사(구)+동사+주어』를 쓴다.
어휘 thick 혱 두꺼운; *자욱한 layer 몡 막, 층, 겹 lie 동 (…의 상태에) 있다, 놓여 있다 (lay-lain) bookshelf 몡 책꽂이, 서가 (pl. bookshelves)

06 부정어(구)를 강조하기 위한 도치(일반동사가 있는 문장): 『부정어(hardly)+do/does/did+주어+동사원형』
어휘 stuck in traffic 교통이 막힌

07 부정문 뒤에서 '(앞서 한 말에 대해) …도 또한 그렇지 않다'라는 뜻을 나타낼 때는 『neither[nor]+do/does/did/be동사/조동사+주어』를 쓴다. 앞 문장의 동사가 일반동사이고 과거시제이므로 did를 쓴다.

08 '아무도 교실에 없는' 것이므로 all의 전체부정인 none('아무도 …하지 않다')을 쓴다.

09 Not every comic book is useless.로 쓸 수 있다. not

every는 '모두 …인 것은 아니다'라는 뜻의 부분부정이다. 따라서 none이 아니라 not이 와야 한다.
어휘 useless 혱 쓸모없는 comic book 만화책

10 부정어(구)를 강조하기 위한 도치(조동사가 있는 문장): 『부정어(never)+조동사+주어』
어휘 major 몡 (대학생의) 전공

11 'John과 나 둘 다 마라톤을 끝내지 못한' 것이므로 both의 전체부정인 neither('둘 다 …하지 않다')를 쓴다.

12 none: '아무도 …하지 않다' (all의 전체부정)
어휘 cap 몡 (테 없는) 모자

13 not all: '모두 …인 것은 아니다' (부분부정)

14 ⓐ 과거시제이므로 동사(come) 앞에 did를 써서 강조한다.
ⓑ 『so+동사+주어』: '(앞서 한 말에 대해) …도 또한 그렇다' 앞 문장의 동사(thought)가 일반동사이고 과거시제이므로 did를 쓴다.
어휘 rude 혱 무례한

15 부정어(구)를 강조하기 위한 도치(조동사가 있는 문장): 『부정어(never)+조동사+주어』

16 it is/was ... that 강조 구문은 강조하고자 하는 말을 it is/was와 that 사이에 둔다.

17 ⑤ 부정에 가까운 의미를 갖는 only를 문장 맨 앞에 써도 주어와 동사를 도치한다. 과거시제이고 일반동사가 있는 문장이므로 『only+did+주어+동사원형』의 어순이 된다.
I realized → did I realize
어휘 warning 몡 경고 pigeon 몡 비둘기 silly 혱 어리석은

18 ⓐ 짝으로 이루어진 접속사(neither A nor B)에서 A와 B는 문법적으로 동일한 형태와 구조를 쓴다.
my car → in my car
ⓓ 『neither[nor]+동사+주어』: '(앞서 한 말에 대해) …도 또한 그렇지 않다'
So → Neither[Nor]
어휘 run 동 뛰다; *운영하다 laundry shop 세탁소 missing 혱 없어진

19 ② 『do/does/did+동사원형』의 형태로 동사를 강조한다.
③ 짝으로 이루어진 접속사(B as well as A)에서 A와 B는 문법적으로 동일한 형태와 구조를 쓴다.
어휘 fountain 몡 분수

20 장소를 나타내는 부사(구)를 강조하기 위한 도치: 『부사(구)+동사+주어』

21 not always: '항상 …인 것은 아니다' (부분부정)

22 부정어(구)를 강조하기 위한 구문(조동사가 있는 문장): 『부정어(little)+조동사+주어』
어휘 imagine 동 상상하다 electricity 몡 전기

실전 모의고사 1회 pp.129 - 131

01 ② 02 ③ 03 ① 04 ⑤ 05 ⑤ 06 I wonder if he will release a new album. 07 who, who is 또는 who 생략 08 ⑤ 09 ② 10 ④ 11 had not been for 12 Whatever 13 ④ 14 ② 15 However 16 running 17 ⑤ 18 ③ 19 1) I had a girlfriend 2) I got better grades in science 3) I were a soccer team captain 20 ④ 21 ① 22 ③ 23 ⑤ 24 the funniest person that I have ever met 25 No other fruit is more popular than apples

01 사역동사로 쓰인 have의 목적어와 목적격 보어의 관계가 수동이므로 목적격 보어로 과거분사를 쓴다.
[어휘] washing machine 세탁기

02 문맥상 '알래스카 원주민들이 어떻게 살았는지'라는 의미가 되어야 자연스러우므로 방법을 나타내는 관계부사 how를 쓴다.
[어휘] native [명] 토착민, 현지인

03 사역동사 let의 목적어와 목적격 보어의 관계가 능동이므로 목적격 보어로 원형부정사를 쓴다.

04 『if it had not been for ...,+가정법 과거완료』로 주절에 『주어+would[could/might] have v-ed』를 쓴다.

05 결과를 나타내는 과거완료

06 문맥상 '만약 …라면'이라는 뜻의 조건을 나타내는 접속사 if가 대화의 빈칸에 와야 한다. 한편, 명사절을 이끄는 접속사 if는 '…인지'라는 뜻이다.
[어휘] release [동] 발매하다

07 명사(the man)를 뒤에서 수식하는 분사구 앞에는 『주격 관계대명사+be동사』가 생략되어 있다고 볼 수 있다.

08 계속을 나타내는 현재완료이고 기준 시점과 함께 쓰였으므로 since('… 이래로')를 쓴다.

09 가정법 과거: 『If+주어+were/동사의 과거형, 주어+would[could/might]+동사원형』

10 shouldn't have v-ed: '…하지 말았어야 했는데 (했다)' (과거의 일에 대한 후회나 유감)
[어휘] mad [형] 미친; *(미친 듯이) 화가 난

11 『without[but for] ...,+가정법 과거완료』 구문에서 without[but for]은 if it had not been for로 바꿔 쓸 수 있다.
[어휘] succeed [동] 성공하다

12 '무엇이[을] …하더라도'라는 뜻의 no matter what은 부사절을 이끄는 복합 관계대명사 whatever로 바꿔 쓸 수 있다.

13 feel like v-ing: '…하고 싶다'

14 plan은 목적어로 to부정사를 쓴다.

15 복합 관계부사 however: '아무리 …하더라도' (= no matter how)

16 분사가 수식어구와 함께 쓰여 길어질 때는 뒤에서 명사를 수식한다.
[어휘] hill [명] 언덕

17 ⑤ 부정어(구)를 강조하기 위한 도치(일반동사가 있는 문장): 『부정어(never)+do/does/did+주어+동사원형』
Never finished she → Never did she finish
[어휘] on time 정각에

18 ③ 분사구문의 부정은 분사 앞에 not을 쓴다.
→ Not knowing what to do
[어휘] still [형] 조용한; *움직이지 않는

19 『I wish+가정법 과거』: 현재 사실과 반대되는 일을 소망
[어휘] captain [명] 선장; *주장

20-21 간접화법 전환 시 전달자에 맞춰 인칭대명사를 바꾸고 동사는 시제 일치의 원칙에 맞춰 바꾼다.

20 의문사가 있는 의문문의 간접화법 전환: 『ask(+목적어)+의문사+주어+동사』

21 의문사가 없는 의문문의 간접화법 전환: 『ask(+목적어)+if[whether]+주어+동사』

22 He was brought up by an old man.으로 쓸 수 있다. 동사구의 수동태는 동사구 전체를 하나의 동사로 묶어 취급한다.
[어휘] bring up (아이를) 키우다

23 not every: '모두 …인 것은 아니다' (부분부정)

24 『the+최상급(+that)+주어+have ever v-ed』: '지금까지 …한 것[사람] 중 가장 ~한'

25 최상급의 뜻을 나타내는 『No (other)+명사+ ... +비교급+than』

실전 모의고사 2회 pp.132 - 134

01 ④ 02 ② 03 ② 04 ④ 05 ③ 06 ② 07 had, ended 08 don't, every 09 (K)orean (s)tudents (a)re (n)ot (a)lways (b)usy 10 ② 11 ① 12 Since[since] 13 as 14 ② 15 ④ 16 ③ 17 ⑤ 18 Being honest 19 Having finished 20 The man told them not to bring any food into the pool. 21 ④ had lost 22 ④ 23 were 24 had had 25 ② 26 ④ 27 1) more popular than 2) twice as common as 3) the least common

01 앞의 명사구 a famous clock을 수식하는 말로 '불리는'이라는 수동의 뜻이므로 과거분사 called를 쓴다.

02 문맥상 이유를 나타내는 관계부사 why를 쓴다.

03 『though+사실』: '비록 …지만'

04 명사절을 이끄는 복합 관계대명사 whichever: '…하는 어느 것이든지'

05 사람의 성품·성격을 나타내는 형용사가 보어로 쓰이면 to부정사(to help)의 의미상 주어로 『of+목적격』을 쓴다.

06 ② 과거의 습관('…하곤 했다')을 나타낼 때는 would와 used
　　 to를 둘 다 쓸 수 있지만, 과거의 상태('…이었다')를 나타낼 때는
　　 used to만 쓴다.

　　 어휘 pine tree 소나무　cut down (나무 등을) 베다

07 완료를 나타내는 과거완료

08 not every: '모두 …인 것은 아니다' (부분부정)

09 not always: '항상 …인 것은 아니다' (부분부정)

10 ② 관계대명사가 전치사의 목적어로 쓰일 때, 전치사가 관계대명
　　 사절 끝에 있을 경우 그 관계대명사는 생략할 수 있다.

11 사역동사로 쓰인 have는 목적격 보어로 원형부정사나 과거분사
　　 를 쓴다.

12 접속사 since: '… 때문에'; '… 이래로'

13 접속사 as: '(동시에) …할 때'; '… 때문에'

14 considering: '…을 고려하면', '…을 감안하면'

15 명사(her eyes)와 분사의 관계가 수동이므로 『with+(대)명사+
　　 과거분사』: '…이 ～된 채'

16 『it's time+가정법 과거』: '(이제) …해야 할 때이다'

17 ⑤ 계속을 나타내는 현재완료/과거완료 또는 현재완료 진행형/
　　 과거완료 진행형을 쓴다.
　　 was watching → has watched/had watched 또는
　　 has been watching/had been watching

18 분사구문은 접속사 및 주절과 동일한 부사절의 주어를 생략하고
　　 동사를 현재분사(v-ing)로 바꿔서 만든다.

19 부사절의 시제가 주절의 시제보다 앞서므로 완료 분사구문(having
　　 v-ed)을 쓴다.

20 부정 명령문을 간접화법으로 전환 시 don't를 없애고 동사원형
　　 을 not to-v로 바꾼다.

21 ④ 내가 목걸이를 '찾은' 것보다 '잃어버린' 것이 더 이전의 일이
　　 므로 대과거(had v-ed)를 쓴다.

22 보기와 ④의 if는 '…인지'의 뜻으로, 명사절을 이끄는 접속사이고
　　 나머지는 조건절을 이끄는 접속사로, '만약 …라면'의 뜻이다.

23 가정법 과거: 『If+주어+were/동사의 과거형, 주어+would
　　 [could/might]+동사원형』

24 가정법 과거완료: 『If+주어+had v-ed, 주어+would[could/
　　 might] have v-ed』

25 ⓐ 『the number of+복수명사』는 '…의 수'의 뜻으로, 단수 취
　　 급한다.
　　 ⓑ 『the+형용사』는 '…한 사람들'의 뜻으로, 복수 취급한다.

　　 어휘 rapidly 彤 급속하게　charity 몡 자선 단체

26 과거(세 시간 전)에 눈이 내리기 시작해서 현재에도 눈이 내리고
　　 있으므로 현재완료 진행형(have/has been v-ing)을 쓴다.

27 1) 『비교급+than any other+단수명사』는 최상급의 뜻을 나타낸다.
　　 2) 『배수사+as+원급+as』: '…의 몇 배로 ～한/하게'
　　 3) 『the+형용사/부사의 최상급』: '가장 …한/하게'

MEMO

MEMO

기초부터 내신까지 중학 영문법 완성

1316
GRAMMAR LEVEL 3